4

W9-BST-493

The Gospel of Rutba

THE
GOSPEL
OF RUTBA

WAR, PEACE, AND
THE GOOD SAMARITAN
STORY IN IRAQ

GREG BARRETT

ORBIS BOOKS

Maryknoll, New York 10545

Founded in 1970, Orbis Books endeavors to publish works that enlighten the mind, nourish the spirit, and challenge the conscience. The publishing arm of the Maryknoll Fathers and Brothers, Orbis seeks to explore the global dimensions of the Christian faith and mission, to invite dialogue with diverse cultures and religious traditions, and to serve the cause of reconciliation and peace. The books published reflect the views of their authors and do not represent the official position of the Maryknoll Society. To learn more about Maryknoll and Orbis Books, please visit our website at www.maryknollsociety.org.

Copyright © 2012 by Greg Barrett

No part of this publication may be reproduced or transmitted in any form or by any means, electronic or mechanical, including photocopying, recording, or any information storage or retrieval system, without prior permission in writing from the publisher.

Queries regarding rights and permissions should be addressed to: Orbis Books, P.O. Box 302, Maryknoll, NY 10545-0302.

Manufactured in the United States of America

Library of Congress Cataloging-in-Publication Data

Barrett, Greg, 1961-
     The gospel of Rutba : war, peace, and the Good Samaritan story in Iraq / Greg Barrett.
        p. cm.
     Includes bibliographical references (p.) and index.
     ISBN 978-1-57075-951-2 (cloth); eISBN 978-1-60833-113-0
     1. Missions—Iraq—Rutba. 2. Missions to Muslims. 3. Iraq War, 2003-2011. I. Title.
   BV3210.I7B37   2012
   261.8'7309567—dc23
                         2012010565

To the hands that rocked my cradle and those of my sons.

Good parents rule.

I'm crazy blessed to have been raised by two
and to call another my wife.

CONTENTS

WAR LESSON

Peace activist Shane Claiborne and the author at Jordan-Iraq border, January 2010.
Photo credit: Jamie Moffett

This book is the story of parallel events occurring in a desert outpost in Iraq in 2003 and 2010. The chapters are staggered between those years: odd numbered chapters based in 2003; even numbered in 2010. However, no chapter is an island. There are no clean separations of time—not in the book; not in life. Every yesterday influenced today. Every today, tomorrow. Every parent, every child, every war, every bomb, every bullet that finds its target leaves an impression that continues through time.

How well our history informs us, shapes perspectives and prejudices, is a matter separate and subjective. But its influence is immortal, from Holy Land clashes to stock market crashes, from the Ottoman Empire to an American Superpower . . . and so on.

Which brings us to Iraq. Literally. Twice. Some lessons are so revealing and counterintuitive that they bear repeating. Still, history repeats.

So, here you go.

Nine days into the 2003 war three American peacemakers figured they were as good as dead after their taxi was wrecked on a desolate stretch of an Iraqi highway. Injuries—serious and critical—were not considered to be the biggest threat. Survival hinged on the humanity of the "enemy." The nearest town, Rutba, was a hub of the Ba'athist despot; it was reputed to be hard, hostile, gritty. Civilian Americans didn't go there. Iraq's Fedayeen fighters were there, and three days earlier the town's only hospital had been bombed by U.S. forces.

Spoiler alert: Rutba saved the Americans. Never hesitated. Refused payment, even. Hugged them, bandaged them, stitched them, planted kisses on their cheeks, and sent them away from the war that they were stuck in. It asked only that the Americans use this lesson of shared humanity to seed more of it. Pay it forward.

Fifteen days into 2010 the three Americans returned to Rutba and were given more seeds for planting and sharing. This time they brought with them an Iraq war combat veteran and student peacemaker; a Christian Peacemaker Teams member who had been kidnapped in Iraqi Kurdistan; an Iraqi-Muslim who, after the invasion, moved from the United States to Iraq and founded a Muslim peace movement; a documentary filmmaker; and me.

As in 2003, the peacemakers returned in 2010 without guns or any conventional security. Unarmed and with their hands extended in friendship, they entrusted their lives (by choice this time) to the locals of Rutba.

HOW TO TRAIN
YOUR DRAGON

Archbishop Desmond Tutu

An Iraqi child in the rebuilt but not fully functioning Rutba General Hospital (2010). Photo credit: Jamie Moffett

Let the children lead us. If we grownups would only allow it, even our ani-mated movies with mythical Viking worlds could show us the way.

Take the DreamWorks Animation film *How to Train Your Dragon.* The moral of the story isn't as the title might suggest: slaying or training dragons. Rather, it's about taming our deepest fears in order to slay the prejudices we inherit. Fear and prejudice—*those* are our dragons. When the protagonist of the film, a boy named Hiccup, stares into the soulful eyes of his flying, fire-breathing nemesis, he sees something vastly different than the violent gospel of his Viking village.

"Three hundred years and I'm the first Viking who wouldn't kill a dragon. I wouldn't kill him because he looked as frightened as I was," Hiccup confides to a friend. "I looked at him and I saw myself."[1]

Hiccup and the dragon soon forgive each other's misunderstandings; they bond in delightful acts of cooperation and compassion. By the end, Hiccup teaches his warrior elders a lesson that is far more critical in the real world than in fictional 3D. In front of an audience of Viking peers and adults he drops his dagger and his shield, and he extends his hand in friendship, not fear. The fire-breathing dragon relaxes at this gesture and responds with kindness. "They're not what we think they are," Hiccup tells the unbelieving Vikings. "We don't have to *kill* them."[2]

These universal truths endure despite history's aggressive denial of them. They were true during the Holocaust, South African apartheid, Rwandan geno-cide; and they're true today in the factious Middle East. Tutsi and Hutu, Israeli and Palestinian, American and Iraqi, communist, socialist, and capitalist; no superficiality or conformity can ultimately withstand the genuine shock and awe of our shared, inherent goodness. It doesn't matter if you are a soldier or a freedom fighter; or if you have been branded a terrorist or a warmonger. It doesn't even matter if you pray to God, Allah, or to the sun; you possess the seed of the divine. And even as it yearns for our full attention and nourishment, it nourishes and attends to us. All of us. Compared to it, our earthly allegiances are silly thin veils, as shallow and transparent as the euphemisms by which we label war.

We *don't* have to kill. Simply, thou shalt not.

The story of *The Gospel of Rutba* illuminates universal truth. In its pages you will stare into the soulful eyes of a foe and recognize a friend. Keep looking and you will see that the friend is, in fact, family. Look deeper still and a reflection will stop you.

It's you, after all.

At our deepest best we are all rooted in a love that grows steadfast—genera-tion to generation. Like perennial flowers opening to spring's first caress, so too humanity grows toward light. Less graceful, and always groaning, but we are forever drawn to the peace of truth and reconciliation. *Agape,* and our love for our own children, demands that we provide a better inheritance.

The Good Samaritans and peacemakers of Iraq are torchbearers leading humanity to higher ground. Every major conflict generates extraordinary acts of compassion and courage that reveal the errors of our assumptions and stereo-types. In this new light we can see the shared and sacred path.

Once we are on this path we see that Christ had it right all along: To experience the blissful peace we call heaven we must become again as little children (Matthew 18:3-4; Luke 18:17). It is only through this kind of innocence and imagination that we see through the veil to the true nature of our flying, fire-breathing dragons.

The enemy is in me.

We are at war only with ourselves.

So follow the children's lead. As the great humanitarian Bono tells us in song and verse:

> *Every generation gets a chance to change the world*
> *Pity the nation that won't listen to your boys and girls*
> *'Cause the sweetest melody is the one we haven't heard*
> *Is it true that perfect love drives out all fear*
> *The right to appear ridiculous is something I hold dear*
> *Oh, but a change of heart comes slow.*[3]

PRIMARY SUBJECTS

SHANE CLAIBORNE: Christian author-activist, co-founder of the Philadelphia nonprofit The Simple Way. Shane resided with peacemakers in Baghdad during March and through the first nine days of the war.

CLIFF KINDY: Full-time member of Christian Peacemaker Teams. He was in Baghdad beginning in October 2002 and remained until being evicted by the Ba'athist government nine days into the war.

WELDON NISLY: Minister of Seattle Mennonite Church and a Christian Peacemaker Teams volunteer. He was in Iraq for four days beginning March 25, 2003. He was evicted with Cliff, leaving Baghdad March 29.

PEGGY GISH: Full-time member of Christian Peacemaker Teams who frequently works in Iraq. She was in Baghdad with CPT before and after the war in 2003. She was in the same convoy of cars driving from Baghdad to Amman when the convoy's rear car, a taxi carrying Cliff, Weldon, and Shane, wrecked.

LOGAN MEHL-LAITURI: Former Iraq combat veteran turned conscientious objector. He spent thirteen months in Iraq as an artillery forward observer or "fire support specialist" for the Army. He returned to Iraq as a student of peacemaking with Shane, Cliff, Weldon, and Peggy.

SAMI RASOULI: Iraqi-American who in 2004 moved back to his home of Najaf, Iraq, from Minneapolis, Minnesota, to help rebuild his country. He is the founder of the Muslim Peacemaker Teams. He was significant in helping to facilitate the return trip to Rutba for Shane, Cliff, and Weldon.

TIMELINE

November 11, 2001: Two months after the terrorism of 9/11, President George W. Bush tells Defense Secretary Donald Rumsfeld to review U.S. war plans for Iraq. "We needed to develop the coercive half of coercive diplomacy," Bush writes in *Decision Points*.

January 29, 2002: In his State-of-the-Union address Bush singles out three nations as global threats: Iraq, Iran, and North Korea. "States like these, and their terrorist allies, constitute an axis of evil, arming to threaten the peace of the world."

August 5, 2002: General Tommy Franks delivers to Bush a war plan intended to overwhelm Iraq with a "massive aerial bombardment" that would force Iraq's elite Republican Guard out of Baghdad. Franks tells Bush: "This is going to be Shock and Awe."

October 11, 2002: Congress gives Bush the authority to invade Iraq. Senator John Kerry explains: "When I vote to give the president of the United States the authority to use force . . . it is because I believe that a deadly arsenal of Weapons of Mass Destruction in [Saddam's] hands is a threat, and a grave threat."

March 5, 2003: Christian author-activist Shane Claiborne arrives in Baghdad to endure Shock and Awe alongside Iraqis and a team of activists assembled by Chicago-based Nobel Peace Prize nominee Kathy Kelly and members of the Christian Peacemaker Teams (CPT), including Cliff Kindy, an organic market farmer from North Manchester, Indiana.

March 20, 2003: The United States initiates war at 5:33 a.m. (Iraq time) with four 2,000-pound "bunker buster" bombs fired at one of Saddam's many compounds. Saddam is not there. The bombs explode primarily in the streets of Baghdad's Muslim-Christian Al Dora suburb. Fifteen hours later, Shock and Awe begins with more than five hundred bunker busters, missiles, and such fired into Iraq from warships, bombers, and jets. The heaviest bombing continued for twenty-eight consecutive days with fusillades totaling 29,199 aerial bombs.

March 25, 2003: Seattle Mennonite Church pastor Weldon Nisly arrives in Baghdad with Christian Peacemaker Teams. Included in the two-car convoy from Amman are peacemakers Jonathan and Leah Wilson-Hartgrove, students at Shane's alma mater, Philadelphia's Eastern University; Christian theologian, author, and peace activist James Douglass; veteran Middle East peacemaker husband-and-wife team Sis and Jerry Levin; and others.

March 26, 2003: Army Special Forces orders the bombing of a hospital warehouse in Iraq's rural western Al Anbar province. The warehouse is a suspected storehouse for Iraq weapons and ammo. The ensuing fire burns through Rutba General Hospital, killing two civilians and closing the only public hospital within 195 miles for tens of thousands of Al Anbar residents.

March 28, 2003: Eight foreign peacemakers are detained by Iraqi police after they are seen filming near the site of a bombing in Baghdad. Among the peacemakers are Cliff, Weldon, Jonathan, Leah, and Peggy Gish. They are released hours later, but ordered to leave Iraq.

March 29, 2003: Three drivers hired by the Ba'athist Party to take the peacemakers out of Iraq travel to Jordan on Iraq's East-West Highway 1. Shane Claiborne leaves with the evicted activists. The taxi that he, Cliff, and Weldon are in has a bad accident about an hour east of the Jordanian border. They are rescued by a truckload of Iraqis, who hand them off to other Iraqis, who then take them to a health clinic in nearby Rutba. There's no hospital. Rutba General is a smoldering pile of rubble.

January 2004-February 2005: Logan Mehl-Laituri serves in combat in Iraq as a member of the Army's Twenty-Fifth Infantry Division based in Oahu, Hawaii.

January 15, 2010: Weldon, Shane, and Cliff return to a little town in western Iraq to visit with the medical staff and locals who rescued and treated them. Peggy and Logan return with them, as do Philadelphia filmmaker Jamie Moffett, Jr., and print journalist Greg Barrett. The return trip was coordinated by me, the author, with invaluable help from Sami Rasouli. As a news wire reporter I was in prewar Iraq in January-February of 2003 and traveled from Baghdad to Basra with Iraq Peace Team leader Kathy Kelly. The lessons gleaned by me about the Iraqi "enemy" were counterintuitive . . . and lasting.

1

NO PLACE TO HIDE

Kill one man, terrorize a thousand.
> —sign at the Marine sniper school,
> Camp Pendleton, California[1]

Rutba children play on the rooftop of a bomb-damaged building next to Rutba General Hospital (2010). Photo credit: Greg Barrett

2003

They raced out of Baghdad heading west to Amman, an Iraqi driver, a Korean peace activist and three American pacifists—friends and strangers thrown together at the last minute like a game of pickup basketball. Squeezing into a car the size of a Kia, the color of a banana, they sped off. The five-hundred-mile trip negotiated through checkpoints, customs, and Iraqi bribery was always a test of endurance. Twelve hours one-way on the most peaceful and promising of days. And this day, the last Saturday in March 2003—a clear morning with blue skies streaked with war's black smoke—didn't offer much in the way of promise. Just the one, and it was being delivered even as the taxi accelerated down Abu Nuwas Street, past the Ottoman-styled houses and open-air markets, across the River Tigris on the Jumariyah Bridge, under a giant portrait of Saddam Hussein, left at Haifa Street, and then onto an eerily empty Abu Ghraib Expressway and Highway 1.

Shock and Awe. No place to hide. That was the Pentagon promise.

Before the plumes of smoke rising over Baghdad receded into the rear-view mirror, it was obvious that this was one of those rare political promises. Washington had kept it. Vans, sedans, pickups, taxis, tanks, buses, even an ambulance, lay dead on the roads, in the desert, and alongside the highway. Smoldering husks of fiberglass and steel, charred chassis, shattered windshields, blackened poles, and countless bits, pieces, shards and shrapnel of God-knows-what. An otherwise beautiful Saturday was trashed.

In the concrete rubble of a bombed overpass on Highway 1 shafts of rebar pointed skyward. Accusingly, as if to say, There, right there. Fighter jets streaked the sky, their wispy contrails dissolving into the day's dark residue.

Inside the taxi everything was silent—just the breathless whine of rubber on asphalt. The Iraqi driver, squat, middle-aged, and twitchy, his hands fixed at ten and two, pushed the accelerator. He was several hours west of Baghdad and moving steady at sixty-five, seventy miles per hour when a bomb or missile or grenade exploded in the desert, maybe one mile north of the highway.

Frightened, the driver punched the accelerator. Seventy-five, eighty miles per hour. Two hundred and sixty miles removed from Baghdad, he and his fare felt no safer than when they were in the capital's crosshairs. Littered with pieces of metal and shrapnel, Highway 1, the broad East-West trophy of Saddam Hussein's prosperous 1970s, was an autobahn loaded and explosive. For ten consecutive days Iraq had been showered with guided and unguided bombs. "Ordnance," the ground troops called them, radioing the heavens for support. That ordnance had fallen like hail, some 8,477 bombs and missiles[2] dropped in just the first nine days of Shock and Awe.

Any driver making a mad run for the border might not avoid all the leftovers—shell casings or dud ordnance from unexploded cluster bombs, some as small as D-sized batteries.[3] Allah knows he tried. He touched the brakes, swerved, accelerated; braked again, swerved, accelerated. Slow up, weave left, weave right, speed up. It was a slalom course. Eyes dead ahead, he was speechless. They were less than ninety minutes from Iraq's border with Jordan.

Ninety-five miles to safety, ninety miles, eighty miles, seventy-five, and then . . .

Boom!

The left back tire exploded.

The driver could speak a little bit of English. He shouted it.

"Bomb! Bomb! We're hit! Bomb!"

His car jerked up and forward. Maybe it struck something unexploded and no larger than a D-sized battery. No one knows.

He jammed the brakes, jerked the steering wheel left, right, left. Too far. The car skidded right, fishtailed, careened, flipped. Once, twice; no one is sure. It slammed to a stop on its right side. The radiator hissed. The driver moaned.

No guardrails protect traffic speeding to Jordan along the farthest reaches of Iraq's modern East-West Highway. Five or six hours outside of Baghdad, looking right and racing west, there are only desert hills and an irrigation ditch. A parched, deep trench. Nine feet down is a bed of cobblestone, a few tufts of dead grass, some trash. This is where the car as small as a Kia and the color of a banana came to rest. Violently. On the passenger side.

The driver was battered, bruised, hobbled, but otherwise okay. Same for the South Korean peacemaker Bae Sang-hyun, who at age twenty-eight was so full of optimism he thought he could stop a war. The American pacifists were also peacemakers: Reverend Weldon Nisly of Seattle Mennonite Church rode in the front passenger seat; Christian activist-author Shane Claiborne of Philadelphia, Pennsylvania, was in the left rear seat behind the driver; and rural Indiana farmer and Christian Peacemaker Teams veteran, Cliff Kindy, had wedged himself between Sang-hyun and Shane.

Weldon and Cliff were critically injured; one badly broken, the other cracked open. Shane, younger, taller, wiry and circus flexible, muscled a driver's side door open and wiggled free. His left shoulder was separated, his right leg was cut; but something more critical grabbed his attention: Three unarmed Americans were now stranded in an Islamic republic that was being attacked by their home team. It were as if three defenseless citizens of Japan had crashed on Oahu's Pali Highway on December 16, 1941—assuming Hawaii had been a state in 1941,[4] and the Japanese were in the ninth consecutive day of a bombing campaign that targeted sites civilian and military, and the Imperial Japanese Army had advanced guns blazing leeward to windward.

Shane figured that if any Iraqis were to peer into that highway ditch they'd stare wide-eyed at their very definition of terrorist: Anglo-American men carrying dark blue passports marked with a bald-eagle hologram. For the first minute or so, the bruised and hobbled, the badly broken, and the cracked open were invisible to the world in that blind spot of Saddam's trophy highway. Then Shane heard a familiar noise. The breathless whine of rubber on road.

The first vehicle to approach was on the opposite side of the highway, a pickup truck speeding east toward Baghdad, deeper into the gales of Shock and Awe.

It slowed, stopped, reversed. The driver parked on the highway shoulder. Three Arab men climbed out, craned their necks for a better view. They began jogging toward the ditch.

Turns out the Pentagon was correct. In Iraq there was no place to hide.

2

PRAYER FOR
A NEW DAWNING

*You have to understand the Arab mind. The only thing
they understand is force—force, pride and saving face.*
—Captain Todd Brown, U.S. Army[1]

*The Badiyat al-Sham Desert (aka Syrian desert) of the Al Anbar province
in western Iraq (2010).* Photo credit: Jamie Moffett

2010

Six or seven miles southeast of that hard ditch, some 270 miles west of Baghdad, there's a desert town named Rutba. It's the only city of any size between Ramadi, 195 miles east of it, and Iraq's western border to Jordan, 83 miles west.

American peace activists on the Amman-to-Baghdad highway never stopped there. Worst case, they sped through.[2] Fuel tanks and stomachs were refilled east or west of the Rutba exit, never off of it. It was the far western outpost of Saddam's Ba'athist Party; it was scrappy and Sunni, and to outsiders it had the reputation of a journeyman fighter. Cauliflower ears and pug nose, it's best to avoid those guys.

Short of an emergency, Americans didn't stop there.[3]

Seven years after their taxi flipped into a ditch, Rutba is where Cliff, Shane, and Weldon returned. It was January 2010. They arrived unexpectedly and with company: a former Iraq war combat veteran and conscientious objector; a Christian peacemaker who had been traveling ahead of them in an SUV when their taxi crashed; a Muslim peacemaker from the Shia city of Najaf, Iraq; a documentary filmmaker; and me.

They came back to tell a different sort of story about Rutba, and to return a favor.

We were the first unarmed, unprotected Americans to visit Rutba since March 29, 2003.[4]

In Rutba you awake each day to the strains of Arabic that rouse Iraq and all of the Middle East from slumber. The *fajr* (Islam's morning call to prayer) is encouraging if you understand it. But to Americans told ad nauseam that Middle East Muslims wish to harm them,[5] any Islamic chant or prayer breaking the quiet desert dark of a rural Iraqi town can sound at first like a battle cry. If you have also seen firsthand how everyday Iraqis suffer, and if you understand even a few of the reasons why,[6] the first morning or two you might open your eyes and feel unsettled.

> *Allahu Akbar*
> *Ash-had an la ilaha illa llah*
> *Ash-hadu anna Muhammadan rasulullah*
> *Hayya 'ala-salatt*
> *Hayya 'ala 'l-falah*
> *Al-salatu khayru min an-nawm*
> *Allāhu akbar*
> *La ilaha illallah*
>
> *God (Allah) is the greatest*
> *I bear witness that there is no deity except God*
> *I bear witness that Muhammad is the messenger of God*
> *Make haste toward worship*
> *Come to the true success*

Prayer is better than sleep
God is the greatest
There is no deity except God

The *fajr* (pronounced *FA-sheer*, meaning "dawn") marches to the beat of a half-dozen hard consonants. Each strikes like a prod or poke. If those don't chase you from bed, thirty minutes later it repeats. This snooze-control *fajr* is flatter, faster; its cadence quickens just enough to inspire a vague sense of urgency. The words are the same, but the sixth stanza—*Al-salatu khayru min an-nawm* (Prayer is better than sleep)—repeats. Up, up! it's telling the faithful. Come pray. Don't be lazy. Seize the day.

Returning seven years after Shock and Awe, Cliff, Shane, Weldon, and the group were housed in the second-floor staff quarters of the town's only hospital, a sprawling two-story, mud-brick compound known as Rutba General Hospital. Its name is deceiving. Early in the 2003 war, Rutba General became a casualty of the fight picked by Washington. And even after being rebuilt, hospital director Dr. Nizar Jameel Yaseen believes it will never be fully functional. With brackish water piped in from a dozen desert wells nine miles away, no constant source of reliable electricity, and only one functioning 70-watt, 280-amp diesel-fueled generator, the "hospital," he says, is only a clinic. Doctors can't store blood much less transfuse it. So surgeries requiring anything more than local anesthesia, and all injuries or illnesses needing something other than bandaging, stitching, meds, a cast, a splint or crutches are sent 195 miles east to the hospitals in Ramadi, the capital of Iraq's Al Anbar province. A drive one-way can take three to six hours, depending on that day's mood at military checkpoints and the girth of carnival-sized tractor-trailer convoys ferrying the nuts and bolts of war reconstruction. What Shock and Awe wrecked, crushed, incinerated, obliterated during a celebrated sprint through sovereign land is requiring more than a decade and hundreds of billions of dollars to rebuild.[7]

So for now, Rutba and its surrounding population of 25,000 to 35,000 residents wait. They have a hospital in name only, like a sick game of pretend. Rutba General's staff of ten doctors is half its prewar size; and its revered former director, Dr. Farouq Al-Dulaimi, left six years ago for Ramadi General Hospital. It's a real one with reliable electricity, labor and delivery, a trauma center, surgery, everything—just like Rutba General used to be. Another of Rutba General's top doctors moved to Baghdad; still another was killed in a car bombing in 2009.[8] But none of that matters to the viruses and disease that thrive in the stress and grief of war and reconstruction. On a typical day in 2010, Rutba General's staff examines six to seven hundred patients for minor problems such as joint pain, migraines, fevers, rashes, asthma, sprains, and fractures. Hallways are crowded with the sick and the injured, most of them waiting to see one of three general physicians. Three. Exams average only a few minutes before patients are handed off to nurses and medical assistants or, just as often, are referred to private medical clinics run by some of the same doctors.[9] Only occasionally does the pace slow.

Like yesterday, Sunday, January 17, 2010.

Fewer than twenty patients were examined by the hospital's staff. At 8:38 in the morning, three hours after the muezzin told the townspeople to wake up, seize the day, to pray, pray, pray, a war cripple's only generator groaned to a halt.

Rutba General closed for the day.

For all of this, the depleted staff, the deficient healthcare, the godforsaken drive to Ramadi, Rutba blames Washington.[10] In the first week of the March 2003 invasion of Iraq, Rutba General, a forty-bed public hospital offering free medical and maternity care to the poorest outposts of Iraq's largest governorate, the Anbar province, burned. The hospital's multibuilding compound was targeted by either an American F-16 jet or a B-52 bomber. No one seems sure, neither the Americans nor the Iraqis. To help explain why the United States bombed their only hospital in a war waged for freedom and the removal of WMD, the locals of Rutba confess: Iraq's Fedayeen Saddam paramilitary hid a mobile military communications center on hospital grounds. But it moved to another location just before two or three bombs exploded into the Rutba General compound.[11] There were so many secondary explosions even the Army major who ordered the attack cannot say for sure how many bombs were dropped on the night of March 26, 2003.[12]

Special Forces Major James Gavrilis did not witness the explosions until one month later when he watched a cockpit video of them. He never heard about a mobile communications center. He knew only what military intelligence had told him: a warehouse directly behind the hospital held Fedayeen ammo, and another to the east had been turned into a Fedayeen bunker. Locals say only that one was used as storage for the hospital; the other for agricultural supplies. Whether it was ammo and/or fertilizer stored in bulk, secondary explosions lit up the night sky in a way that could confirm either or both stories.[13] Flames taller than Rutba's low-slung downtown howled over interior walls and raced screaming through the main hospital. Windows burst, ceilings fell, a roof collapsed. Left in the ashes were beds, meds, and two people dead. Civilians, a boy and his father.[14]

Rutba General closed. Indefinitely.

The Army scratched one more target off its list.

Five days later, Washington claimed ignorance about it. An Associated Press story dated Monday, March 31, 2003, quoted from the Pentagon's boilerplate denial: "U.S. Central Command said Sunday it had no knowledge of a hospital bombing in Rutba. The U.S. military has said it is doing its best to avoid civilian casualties in its campaign to oust Iraqi leader Saddam Hussein."[15]

3

ONWARD CHRISTIAN SOLDIERS

Islam is as Islam does
            —bumper sticker on American family van[1]

Reverend Weldon Nisly, Cliff Kindy, and Shane Claiborne at the scene of the 2003 car accident near Rutba (2010). Photo credit: Jamie Moffett

2003

In the overturned taxi a drop of something hit Reverend Weldon Nisly in the chest, again and again, a steady drip smacking lightly against his blue-and-green slicker.

Thirty minutes earlier he'd switched seats with Shane, shifting to the front passenger spot from the seat directly behind the driver. With four men in a car the size of a Kia, riding shotgun was the only luxury. It also offered the only passenger seatbelt, and by everyone's account the harness crossing over Weldon's right shoulder snug across his chest had saved him. That was the initial consensus. But wrenched like he was into the dashboard and passenger-side door, stirring and moaning in a war and a ditch, survival wasn't a guarantee then or a sure bet for later.

Several miles ahead on Iraq's Highway 1, speeding out of view to Jordan in a GMC Suburban, were American friends Peggy Gish, a full-time veteran of the Christian Peacemaker Teams (CPT), and a young married couple from the same Christian college near Philadelphia that had sparked Shane's social-justice fire. Schooled in "Red Letter Christianity" by Eastern University professor Tony Campolo, a sociology Ph.D. with a Baptist pedigree in "wise-sassy-spitfire" preaching,[2] Jonathan and Leah Wilson-Hartgrove, same as Peggy, Shane, Cliff, and Weldon, chose to reside in Washington's war of choice because pacifists are not called to be passive. If evil prevails only when good people fail to act, as taught by people as diverse as Eastern's spitfire Baptist professor, a brilliant agnostic Jew, an eighteenth-century conservative British statesman, and a modern-day semi-fictional Hollywood gunrunner,[3] then inactive nonviolence is a guilty party to war. Without the scriptural cherry picking that attempts to rationalize violence and the sermons that keep congregants complacent, the highlighted Scripture in red-letter editions of the Bible—where the words of Christ are printed bold red—the Gospels leave no wiggle room on matters of Shock and Awe.[4] At least that's how Shane and some of the other peacemakers read their King James. No nation proclaiming to be Christian or a president boasting of rebirth should drop two thousand tons of ordnance[5] on a Muslim nation—or any population—without Christians on the hellfire ground testifying to the fuller story. Warfare is slander.

So when a half-million warriors gathered like a storm around Iraq in March 2003, Shane, Cliff, Weldon, Jonathan, Leah, and Peggy, as well as two dozen other peacemakers from North America, Europe, Asia, and Australia, gathered in front of it. They felt they had no choice but to endure the brunt of it with everyday Iraqis. That's not to suggest the decision was easy. Shane wrestled with it for a year. When he finally made up his mind that the decision stared him in the face written in red, his mother, a Tennessee Methodist with only one child, begged him to reconsider. He would phone to discuss and explain, but she would cry uncontrollably, forced to hand the phone off to Shane's stepfather.

It's just that when Scripture is read undiluted the bold red attributed verbatim to Christ emboldens or frightens, frequently both. Faith gets dicey.

Weldon couldn't move his left arm. It felt pricked by a million needles and paralyzed, like the dead weight of an arm slept on. His breathing was labored, each breath pulled through a snorkel. Goggles too—it was like he had a foggy pair on. Iraq was suddenly smeared in streaks and shadows. Steam rose from the car's banged-up radiator, but he only heard the hissing.

And the light smack of a steady drip—each drop a few seconds apart. He sure heard that.

Without glasses he's half blind, and his favorite wire rims had flown off somewhere between the exploding tire and flip landing. He knew the dashboard was crushed into his lap and the door into his ribs. He could feel those. The seatbelt credited with saving him still held on tight. Too tight. With only one arm mobile, he was captured. He began squirming, wiggling, anything to break free.

In a wreck and a war, close to blind with no way out, no help coming, no visible means of escape, there will eventually be panic.

Weldon felt the first tremors of it.

The taxi had been last that morning in a three-car caravan racing to Jordan. Non-Arab peacemakers and journalists filled the seats, leaving Baghdad by choice or deported by Iraqi officials.

The previous night an Iraqi Foreign Ministry officer named Zaid—kind, calm, professional Zaid—a favorite of the peacemakers for reasons other than the figs he gave away from his family's farm, angrily deported Cliff, Weldon, Leah, Jonathan, Peggy, and three other CPT members. Earlier that day the peacemakers were arrested after police spotted Cliff discretely filming near the site of a U.S. bombing. Photography and videotaping were transgressions of the highest order; filming anything war-related was strictly forbidden. The second was leaving the hotel without Iraqi government consent or a Ba'athist "minder." They were guilty of both. (Imagine if eight Japanese citizens visiting Oahu on December 7, 1941, were seen by police filming in the vicinity of Pearl Harbor.)

The CPT Eight[6] apparently couldn't help themselves. A few minutes before seven o'clock on the morning of the Muslim holy day, Friday, March 28, 2003, a $1 billion Northrop Grumman Corp. B-2 stealth bomber, the costliest and most high-maintenance jet in the U.S. Air Force's fleet of costly high-maintenance jets, dropped two 4,600-pound Raytheon Co. bunker-busting bombs on downtown Baghdad. A seven-story communications center and primary telephone exchange burned. Of Weldon's first three days in Baghdad, it was the closest strike yet to Al Dar Hotel, the mom-and-pop one-star where he had a room to himself, a stack of reading material, and spiral bound notebook. Written in its lined pages is this entry dated "26 March 03," his first full day in Baghdad:

"We have been duly warned not to go out anytime anywhere alone or to take photos anywhere outside or even from our windows. We could be arrested and taken away at any time."

There had been other explosions, plenty, but nothing like this. It traveled through them, up the spine, neck and into the temporal lobe. Even without the shimmy of floor and walls it would be enough to knock out an athletic 6'6" basketball player. Lesser bombs had. Hours after arriving in Baghdad on March 25, 2003, Jonathan and Leah, twenty-two-year-old rookies to the war-witness program, received a baptism of fire. The distant thunder of nighttime bombings resumed on schedule (soon after dinner and prayers) and then grew persistently louder, like strikes of lightning blowing closer to the capital. To help keep the windows intact, Jonathan opened the one in his and Leah's second-floor room at Al Dar, and then collapsed on the bed, exhausted. Seconds later, a blast flowed through his body "like a wave."[7] Eyes open and staring, he froze in place. Leah said they should take cover one floor down in Al Dar's makeshift bomb shelter, but Jonathan couldn't hear or move or respond to her intelligently. In dreams where he's playing basketball he's been given the ball and a chance to win the game, like Lebron James with five seconds remaining; but he freezes. His long legs are sandbag heavy; he can't move. This moment was like that. He regained consciousness and composure only after Leah towered over him crying and pleading, "Wake up, wake up!"[8]

Three days later, after the Northrop Grumman B-2 passed low and fast over Baghdad, they stood at the open window staring at dark smoke billowing lazily over the Tigris river. The peacemakers at Al Dar were scheduled to meet the Chicago-based Iraq Peace Team (IPT) at Hotel Al Fanar, another mom-and-pop one-star a few blocks away on the banks of the Tigris and a curb of Abu Nuwas Street. Most days Saddam's government minders took a combination of CPT and IPT peacemakers[9] on the Ba'athist-endorsed tour of bombing sites. But the troublesome CPT Eight, oddly emboldened by Raytheon's bunker busters, had other plans. Curiosity is a mad dictator. When no government minder showed up to drive them to Hotal Al Fanar, the peacemakers took off on foot.

"They did not want us going anywhere they didn't approve of beforehand or seeing anything they didn't want us to see. What were they hiding from us?" Jonathan wrote of the Ba'athist officials and their tours. "We weren't sure, but we knew we couldn't speak so firmly against the injustices of our own government while kowtowing to Saddam's tyrannical regime. We decided to leave our hotel without permission and go find where the bomb hit."[10]

On the way out Weldon foretold the future to his journal: "Zaid will be upset . . ."

Across the street from the demolished communications center an older Iraqi man waved to the Americans to come see his damaged business. The windows of his hotel/restaurant/home were apparently the victim of the same sonic blast that jarred him awake and showered shards of glass on him. As if proof was all he needed to ensure no American bombs hit so close again or, more likely, to ensure he would be reimbursed for the one that already had, he asked the Americans to photograph the damage. Cliff pulled out a video camera and turned his back to the street. A Baghdad police car pulled up behind him. Another stopped beside him, and then another and another and another. Pretty soon the peacemakers, looking like incompetent spies with cameras out in the open, were surrounded by a half dozen or so police officers.[11]

And that's why friendly, fig-giving Zaid was in no mood to forgive.

He gathered up the peacemakers at the police station, confiscated their cameras, and returned them to a worried and upset contingent of IPT and CPT peacemakers. He told the CPT Eight to get out of his country. Now. "They must leave now?" Iraq Peace Teams founder Kathy Kelly asked.[12]

As shocking as Shock and Awe was during the day, it was worse at night. F-16s, B-52s, B-2s and such are nocturnal creatures; the majority of U.S. bombings of Iraq occurred between evening and morning prayers. The B-2, with its tailless body, stealthy dark skin and wingspan stretching half the length of a football field, is even designed to resemble a bat.

"Yes," Zaid said sternly.

This was Kathy's twentieth trip to Iraq acting as a humanitarian on a par with Catholic saints. Her visits and diplomacy in support of everyday Iraqis stretch to the first Gulf War, when she camped with peacemakers in the demilitarized zone between Iraq and Kuwait. The ensuing twelve years of UN economic sanctions brought her frequently to Iraq with medicine, food, and toys for the poor who were most affected by Iraq's gutted economy. She had relentlessly lobbied Washington and the United Nations to end the collective punishment. One week after September 11, 2001, when the world still lit candles and mourned alongside Americans, it was Kathy who received Iraq's official letter of condolences.[13] Deputy Prime Minister Tariq Aziz, a Ba'athist Catholic,[14] bypassed the White House and faxed it directly to Kathy's Chicago home.

Kathy looked at Zaid pleadingly. The day was half spent. In a few hours the autobahn from Baghdad to Jordan would be dark—freaky dark considering the nocturnal creatures and all their baggage.

"That would mean they would have to drive through the desert at night," she said to him. "Couldn't they wait until morning to leave?"[15]

Over the years Kathy and Zaid had become good friends. He was well acquainted with her enduring persistence. Despite Washington's best efforts to intimidate her and block her stubborn diplomacy and gift-giving, she'd never stopped visiting Iraq.

Zaid nodded okay. "First thing in the morning."[16]

At daybreak three Iraqi drivers in a GMC Suburban and two taxis parked outside Al Fanar. They fidgeted with keys, cigarettes, and prayer beads, anxious and looking prefight serious, like three men headed into combat. And in a way, they were.

Professional, dependable, likeable Zaid was up early, his usual self, waiting at Al Fanar's curb. Returning the cameras police had confiscated the previous day, he leaned into a window of the GMC and said, "I hope you will have a safe trip to Amman and be able to come back to Iraq someday—under different circumstances."[17]

Behind him the sky over Baghdad looked sorely conflicted. It was a beautiful spring Saturday—sunny, cloudless, and marred by the dark belches of oil fires and air raids. The previous night American bombs woke Weldon several times until he finally gave up pretending. He rose early and prepared to leave.

"A restless fitful night!" he wrote in his journal at six o'clock that morning. Later, on the same page but sounding calmer and more reflective, he scribbled and edited: "God, what is the next step? I am prepared to leave today. But if there is no room in the cars I stay. Am I prepared for that? I go because of my family and church and the need to tell the story at home. God is with us. Amen."

Shane joined Cliff and Weldon in the taxi for similar reasons. At Kathy's invitation a year earlier he had come to Baghdad to meet, mingle, and basically just hang out in fellowship with the Iraqis who resided in the sanctions, cross-hairs, and, he suspected, blind spots of a militarized Christian-majority empire. To investigate this and to tell their stories, he blocked out from his schedule the month of March 2003. At the time no one knew for sure when the Pentagon would invade, but as the trip drew near it looked certain that he'd be right there in the bull's-eye. With the CPT Eight expelled and March drawing down—"the most beautiful and horrific month of my life," he recalls—he saw an opportunity to go west and tell the Iraqi side of this war story. Especially now, after Raytheon engineers and a Northrop Grumman sortie combined to eliminate Baghdad's primary means of communication.

So before a car the size of a Kia, the color of a banana, accelerated north on Abu Nuwas, west at the bridge, south on Haifa, west onto Abu Ghraib toward the airport, and then gun it to Jordan on the desert autobahn, Shane folded his lanky tall frame inside it. A couple hundred miles later the fuel gauge began to look more drained than the cabdriver. Thirty miles farther and it looked almost as desperate.

Ninety minutes east of Jordan, a few exits shy of Rutba, the three-car caravan stopped for the third time to refuel. Like the previous two, this gas station was closed and abandoned. Everything locked; pumps and electricity turned off.

The three drivers huddled to figure things out when a white van carrying students from the University of Baghdad rumbled into the lot. Out jumped a half-dozen Somali students headed to the UN Refugee Agency's Ruweished camp, a new $1.2 million tent city in Jordan's high desert, some forty miles west of the Iraq-Jordan border. Two hundred tents matching the dusky flat landscape and laid out in neat rows awaited their arrival. In the weeks, months, and years ahead, two thousand refugees—Iraqis, Palestinians, Somalis, Algerians, and Iranian Kurds—fleeing the war and its lawless aftermath would pass through Ruweished.[18] The Somalis would be some of the first.

Traveling in the opposite direction four days earlier, Weldon, Leah, and Jonathan had seen the camp with its family-sized tents, flush toilets, shower stalls, and Oxfam International's giant glistening water tanks. At least that's how news reports described it. From their Chevy conversion van speeding across Jordan's desert with Catholic Worker Movement veteran Jim Douglass riding shotgun, playfully bouncing to the driver's Arabian Techno music, they had only gotten a glimpse of Ruweished. It looked strangely vacant. Like a ghost town, Jonathan thought.[19]

The entire day had felt surreal like that, and not only because Ruweished was, for the time being, a refugee-less refugee camp. Arab men walked luggage-in-hand *toward* the Iraqi border, not away from it. Others had already crossed and walked in the middle of broad Highway 1, waving and thumbs out, asking, pleading for rides east toward Baghdad. Never mind the F-16s screaming overhead and American soldiers perched with rifles drawn on the highway's sandy knolls.[20]

All the while Weldon steeled his nerves in the backseat with a collection of Wendell Berry essays, *In the Presence of Fear: Three Essays for a Changed World*.[21] In the first months after 9/11, Berry, a prolific American author, activist, conservationist, farmer, and poet, cautioned his beloved nation not to overreact. Calm down; think this through. Like California hip-hop star Michael Franti sings, "You can bomb the world to pieces but you cannot bomb it into peace." Berry reminded Americans that terrorists and terrorism are defined by the eye of those terrorized. More importantly, he reminded us that "we are not innocent of making war against civilian populations." You don't have to track too far back in history to see it: Nicaragua, El Salvador, Laos, Hiroshima, Nagasaki, to name only a few direct or indirect hits of American-driven terror.

"National self-righteousness," Berry warned, is a sign of weakness and misleads politicians and their electorates. Any war declared by Washington on "terrorism" should be viewed with suspicion and sober examination. Keep it real, in other words. If there were to be a War on Terrorism with capital letters, we needed to see it for what it really was: the next chapter in a continuing saga of violence perpetuated by an economy reliant on the cogs and gears of modern warfare—weapons manufacturing, arms sales, military proliferation, and the deeply rooted fear that allows Congress to routinely pass gargantuan military and defense budgets. The plain-talking Kentucky farmer was just telling us the same thing our parents told us when we were kids, the same thing we tell our kids: You reap what you sow. Thank God Berry, age seventy-seven today and the winner of a 2010 National Humanities Medal, didn't leave us with only the bad news and baggage of our blatant transgressions. He provided answers and solutions. Just the fact that Weldon was barreling toward the latest Americanized war in a conversion van with Jim, Leah, and Jonathan proved he had studied Berry and graded ahead of the curve.

"We must not again allow public emotion or the public media to caricature our enemies," Berry writes on p. 8. "If our enemies are now to be some nations of Islam, then we should undertake to know those enemies. Our schools should begin to teach the histories, cultures, arts, and language of the Islamic nations. And our leaders should have the humility and the wisdom to ask the reasons some of those people have for hating us."[22]

Weldon began reading *In the Presence of Fear* before the sun had risen over Jordan's desert, before his seventy-miles-per-hour tour past Ruweished; he finished it the following day before a sandstorm painted Iraq's sky blood red.

In her book *Other Lands Have Dreams*, Kathy talks about "catching courage"—that ineffable and contagious strain of bravery that grows exponentially when spread among pacifists and peacemakers. Weldon was flush with it.

At 5:50 in the morning of March 25, 2003, just as he, Leah, Jonathan, and Jim were within earshot of Shock and Awe, Weldon wrote this to himself:

"I feel strangely calm as day breaks over eastern Jordan. We are forty kilometers from the Iraqi border."

The Somalis heading to Ruweished were unfazed by the problem that stumped three Iraqi drivers. In the lot of that abandoned gas station thirty miles east of Rutba, they jumped from their van and solved the problem.

In Saddam's Iraq few people dared to hotwire a fuel pump. Theft was punishable by amputation,[23] and gas cost as little as five cents per gallon. The Somali students, however, grew up improvising. They took the battery out of their van and used it to juice the fuel pumps. Within minutes free fuel flowed like beer from a fraternity keg. Everyone's gas tank was topped off, and after a round of whoops and hollers, handshakes and hugs, Americans and Iraqis sped back onto the highway with an enthusiastic second wind.

One more hour of safe travel. That's all they needed.

The drip, drip began to drip-drip-drip. Weldon couldn't see it, but a rivulet had spilled from a fold in his jacket and rolled down his chest. What had felt like a godsend from Somalia thirty minutes earlier now felt like a ticking bomb. Weldon feared the car was ready to explode.

Smashed into the door that was smashed into the ground, he wiggled, squirmed, twisted himself counterclockwise until he could reach across to the seatbelt. With his one good arm he unhooked it and began pawing across the dashboard like a one-armed pianist, frantic to find his glasses, something, anything to restore a sense of control. A car door slammed. He heard faint voices, a moan, footsteps. His hand landed on the wire rims; he slid them onto his face. They were intact. He looked around. He was alone in the wreck. Using his uninjured right arm and hand he began to climb toward the door on the driver's side, now above him. He managed to pull himself out of the vehicle and sat on the upturned side of the car.

Born three days before the June 1945 signing of the Charter of the United Nations (a decomposing document for all the good it did to stop the invasion of Iraq) Weldon was the eldest of the four peacemakers in the taxi. He would be the last to escape it. He didn't know the extent of his injuries, but judging from the million needles in his arm and shocks of pain firing through him whenever he moved, and even when he didn't, he figured he was critical. His breathing, too. He couldn't draw a deep-enough breath to cry out for help. Three years earlier his adult daughter was badly injured in a car accident in the foothills of Washington state. She suffered internal injuries, and she survived only because she was airlifted to one of the best hospitals in the U.S. Northwest. Weldon knew that no such help would be descending on the Iraqi desert.

Drops of blood pooled around the roof's interior light, succumbed to gravity, and fell, again and again, sailing perpendicular toward the crushed passenger-side door. Weldon's blue-green slicker looked like a Christmas ornament.

Before leaving for Iraq, Shane was taught what to look for if he or someone else suffered a fractured skull or any head injury resulting in a heavy loss of blood. Internal bleeding would likely stream down and around the brow as steady and crooked as a creek, and it would collect in the skull's gullies. These would be the soft tissue around the eyes.

"Raccoon eyes," it's called. You will know it when you see it. That's what Shane was told. In a cobblestone ditch of western Iraq, he knew it. Dark streaks tracked down both sides of Cliff's eyes and cheeks.

In the typical Iraqi taxi, back seats rarely have workable seatbelts. This taxi was typical. It wasn't enough to be wedged between Shane and the South Korean, Bae Sang-hyun, Cliff sailed upward as if fired from a cannon. He cracked his head on the interior light or perhaps his skull ripped open when it dribbled off the roof and the ditch's jagged hard ground.

Weldon's slicker was painted with Cliff's blood.

Cliff is a humble, soft-spoken, lifelong Church of the Brethren member with a curiously long beard (think Amish). He's also a bold, fresh piece of humanity who happens to have been born on the same 1949 day as Fox TV's Bill O'Reilly. (God's apology for Bill, I suspect.) To hear Shane tell it, just the sight of Cliff's cracked head would buckle the knees of lesser men. But Cliff is cut from the stock of country preachers, social activists, and Indiana farmers. Even at five-foot-nine he was durable enough to play fullback and linebacker on the Manchester (Indiana) College football team. With a mask of blood he wedged himself up and out of the taxi, stood briefly on the cobblestone ground, and then sat in the ditch. Towering over him at six-foot-three, Shane stared at him and thought about sitting too. The ground felt like it might spin. Through Cliff's thinning hair Shane saw skin peeled back like an open can, and looking closer he saw bone. But that wasn't the worst of it. A horror movie gurgled up from Cliff's crown, down his face, and onto his Amish-long beard. Shane did the first thing that apparently springs to mind when man or industry is faced with a gusher. He attempted to cap it. Retrieving Cliff's red cap with CPT embroidered on the front, he placed it on his head and told him to hold it firm, as if it were a tourniquet.

Cliff possesses the one thing that Washington and Wall Street should prize most in political candidates and CEOs: a quiet presence. He doesn't so much talk about helping the poor and the oppressed or the everyday people caught in war's crosshairs; he goes quietly into these far-flung hotspots and digs in, gets his hands dirty, leads by example. In my time around him he was always thoughtful, eternally composed. You would never suspect him of speaking just to be heard or complaining without good cause. Here too he didn't have any gripes. He nodded to Shane to indicate he was dandy fine with his mask of blood, and then the two of them turned their attention toward the wreck. There was one passenger still inside.

Weldon crawled his way to the driver's-side door and pulled himself up just as two Iraqi men scrambled down the hill. The engine of their pickup truck was running on the opposite side of the six-lane highway, and they looked to be in a hurry. Gripping Weldon under his armpits, they hoisted him up. That's the precise moment Weldon wanted to die. Bolts of pain fired from his broken ribs, broken sternum, broken thumb, and broken shoulder, all at once. He almost passed out. The men stopped. The hissing radiator didn't. They hoisted him again, harder, more urgently, never mind the loud moans through gritted teeth. With one arm over each of their shoulders, they carried him like a wounded soldier up the embankment, across the highway, and to their pickup truck. They sat him in the back of the truck's bed, sitting up with his back flush against the cab, and then they climbed in too and sat like bookends—one Iraqi on each side. Propped up like that in the bed of a pickup he could have been a trophy buck.

Cliff, Shane, and Bae climbed in behind them, and the taxi driver slid into the truck's cab. In the hurried Arabic flying back and forth Shane couldn't quite decipher the deal.

Were they just rescued? Or were they kidnapped?

Offering a clue, the truck took off driving east toward Baghdad. Toward war.

A couple of miles down the road it veered onto an exit ramp and stopped next to an idling station wagon. Another flurry of Arabic and the foreigners were transferred to the station wagon.

For all the Arabic Shane knew, they had just been sold.

The Somalis were the last to refuel and the last to leave. As the two Iraqi taxis and GMC Suburban gunned it west toward Jordan, the Somalis gave a thumbs up and finished topping off their gas tank. Only then could they retrieve the van's battery from behind the station and resume their pilgrimage to the refugee camp. About thirty minutes later, less than one hundred miles from Ruweished, they saw a car on its side in a ditch. It looked familiar.

Like the Iraqi men speeding east toward Baghdad, the Somalis stopped.

Thirty miles east of the Jordan-Iraq border, where Highway 10/11 splits, Jonathan, Leah, and Peggy pulled off to the side of the highway to wait. In the distance they saw a yellow taxi speeding toward them. It pulled off and waited, too. It's always better to go through the customs gauntlet as a team.

One car to go. Several minutes passed—too many for comfort. Then, on the horizon, a spray of sand and dust. Finally. But as the cloud drew closer it didn't look like a taxi was in it. The car wasn't yellow or the size of a Kia. It was white and as large as a van. Then they recognized their newfound Somali friends. As soon as the van braked next to the peacemakers several of the students began talking excitedly, pantomiming a missile and a car and an explosion. Another Somali interrupted. No, no, no, he said, speaking English. It could not have been a missile. Yes, the taxi was badly wrecked and smeared in blood, buckets of it, but the car was locked. Someone had thought to lock the car before abandoning it to a ditch.

People hit by missiles don't lock up.

En route to Baghdad from Amman, Jonathan, Leah, Weldon, and Jim had taken a detour around a bombed bridge. They raced as quickly as possible through a war-torn congested town where buildings were rubble and a charred tanker sat on the side of the road. Just outside of town, things had looked more apocalyptic. A burned ambulance van dead in the desert and a bus filled with the charred remains of passengers. Their Iraqi driver, Ahmed, had sped through Rutba, only slowing at the intersections but never stopping. Head down, foot on the accelerator.

It took a lot of coaxing but Jonathan, Leah, and Peggy convinced the driver of the GMC Suburban to return them to Iraq to hunt for their friends. Twenty minutes later they found the taxi in the exact spot and condition described by the Somalis: a couple miles west of the first exit for eastbound traffic entering from Jordan. Jonathan could see why some of the students thought a bomb had torn through it. Blood was smeared across the seats, interior roof, and around a spider-web crack in the windshield. The back left tire had a hole the size of a fist.

The Sunni town of Rutba was only six miles away. Any hospital in the area would have to be located there.

Past sandbag barricades, pockmarked buildings, and charred cars, the GMC crawled into town. This time the car stopped. The driver asked a man on the corner for directions to Rutba General Hospital.

Laisa hunak musteshfa.

Jonathan waited for the translation. There was more.

Lakad qasafa al Amerikeuon musteshfana bel qanabel.

The driver turned to the Americans and repeated in English.

"There is no hospital. The Americans bombed our hospital."

4

BOYS AND THEIR GUNS

War is either glamorized—like we kick their ass—or the opposite—
look how horrible, we kill all these civilians. None of these people
know what it's like to be there holding that weapon.[1]

—Marine Corporal Ryan Jeschke, age 22

Four-lane main road in downtown Rutba, Iraq (2010). Photo credit: Jamie Moffett

2010

During the time it took to rebuild the hospital into a shell of itself, the town's Ba'ath Party headquarters became Rutba General's stand-in. The same Army officer who two weeks earlier "dropped ordnance" on the hospital compound would handpick it. Located across the street from Rutba General,

21

it was large, clean, and freshly painted in a sunny hue of yellow.[2] The idea was perfect—even poetic. Special Forces Major James Gavrilis took one look at the posh offices and walled courtyard of the finest residence in all of Rutba—an audacious symbol of the totalitarian regime, he thought—and gave it to the desert-hardened citizens over whom it had been lorded. To the persecuted go the spoils of war. Clever. That way, Gavrilis explains, a "tool of the oppression" becomes an instrument for democracy. A new dawning. Out with the old, in with the new. Hello, Uncle Sam.

"It brought a tear to the [interim] mayor's eye when we talked about it," Gavrilis recalled for me many years later. "I left before we could actually do it, implement it, you know. While we were there they used a small clinic farther down the road as their hospital."

Gavrilis is expert at stage managing. Marching into the mess that he and his soldiers created,[3] he went to work to make things right. He convinced the manager of a bank he had bombed days earlier to reopen accounts. He helped coordinate a community-wide cleanup of Rutba's schools and then gave credit to the sheikhs and school principals. He loaned out his SAT phone to local vendors so they could order fruits and vegetables from Jordan and restock Rutba's markets. And when his battalion commander dropped in and city leaders insisted on hosting a dinner, Lieutenant Colonel Christopher Haas, Gavrilis, and a few other Army bigwigs showed their respect by eating like the locals—digging in with their hands. Looking up from a platter of goat and rice, Gavrilis saw that he wasn't the table's only diplomat. Rutba's new mayor, new police chief, and several tribal elders were smiling—silverware in their hands.

It was one of those lucid moments in the middle of war, the flash of clarity that defies all the fear-driven politics and (il)logic Washington uses to justify the world's largest "defense" budget.

The Iraqis noticed the Americans' gesture at the same time the Americans noticed the Iraqis'. They were eating outdoors in the courtyard of the police station, an old British fort one block from the remains of Rutba General Hospital. The Iraqis nodded, acknowledging the gesture, and everyone—American and Iraqi, soldier and civilian—began speaking in the world's universal tongue.

"We started laughing."

Gavrilis smiles at the memory. A good one. From a war zone.

"Both sides realized what the other side was trying to do. We wanted to reach out across each other's cultures. We didn't have to speak the language or talk about it. You could just feel it."

Special Forces are well schooled on the cultures and customs of the nations they invade, bomb, clean up, and occupy because when the killing stops sane minds ideally prevail. At some point dialogue resumes or begins; it helps if there is a semblance of deference and/or genuine respect. The First Battalion of the Fifth Special Forces Group was no stranger to Al Anbar's tribes, sheikhs, imams, nomadic Bedouins and warring past. History told them the locals had a fighter's heart, the type of dogged tenacity admired by Green Berets, Navy Seals and Marine Corps Recon. Al Anbar's embattled past dates back further than any high-tech weaponry branded American-made, further even than the New Testament.

No Special Forces officer would dare game-plan an invasion of Rutba without becoming a quick study of it.

Beginning in August 2002 Gavrilis and his Special Forces began reading up on Al Anbar and dress-rehearsing the invasion in simulated attacks coordinated with the air force in the deserts of Nevada and Jordan.[4]

By nightfall on March 19, 2003, they were digging across a one-story berm feeling taut like slingshots, eager to challenge Saddam's so-called elite Fedayeen fighters.[5]

Never generous in doling out life's comforts, the Syrian Desert (Badiyat al-Sham) forges resilient nomads, such as the Bedouins, and some of history's most stubborn fighters. Its rocky, sandy plains and dunes stretch out of sight to merge with lava rock in a frontier as harsh as it is vast. On average it draws only five inches of annual rainfall, thirty-six inches less than the U.S. capital region, two inches less than the most parched areas of Arizona, New Mexico, and Nevada. Spawned in the volcanic eruption of Syria's Jabal al Druze (Mountain of the Druze) thousands of years ago, it covers some two hundred thousand square miles (larger than the state of California; smaller than Texas). Its Iraqi border stretches to Syria, Jordan, and Saudi Arabia, with routes from all three flowing toward Rutba. This easy access long ago turned a desert outpost into a marketplace and watering hole for weary travelers headed east toward Baghdad.

The origin of the Persian word Anbar (rhymes with *care*) means arsenal or warehouse, reflecting the region's history of storing goods to sell and trade with nomads and foreign travelers. However, considering the battle scars left on it during the last century and as recently as spring 2008, when Marines from an artillery battery based in California's Mojave Desert shelled Rutba in firefights with the "last insurgent stronghold,"[6] Anbar (or arsenal) assumes a different meaning. Like the weapons cache that Gavrilis believed the Fedayeen had stored behind the hospital, Army and Marine officers would finger Rutba as a storehouse and refuge for "Al Qaeda."[7] A year earlier Camp Pendleton's Fifteenth Marine Expeditionary Unit said "the center of Rutba itself remained largely under al Qaeda's control."[8] Two years later, in spring 2009, three weeks before Shane, Cliff, and Weldon were first scheduled to return to Rutba with me, Jonathan Wilson-Hartgrove, and Iraqi-born American citizen Sami

Rasouli, a founder of the Muslim Peacemaker Teams, Rutba still resembled the gunslinger reference used by Marines to describe it. At the time its stone-fort police station wore fresh scars from rocket attacks; young men hid grenades in streets and alleys, and insurgents targeted Iraqi town leaders. "We're in the wild, wild West," said Marine Lieutenant Hamilton Ashworth.[9]

In April 2009 a friend of Sami's from Rutba phoned him in Najaf to relay a message: "Please do *not* bring the Americans here. Not yet."

Gavrilis had departed Rutba never to return on April 23, 2003, exiting like a Hollywood protagonist—driven to the edge of town in the middle of the night where a helicopter waited. Thereafter, control of Rutba had volleyed back and forth between American forces and insurgents—local, national, and foreign. In 2009 it was still difficult to know season to season who had dibs.

That's pretty much what Sami's friend was calling to say. In the spring of 2009 political factions supporting and opposing the new Iraqi government were clashing over a national referendum on an Iraqi-American security agreement that, among other things, promised to set a deadline for the withdrawal of American troops. Also, parliamentary elections scheduled (and later postponed) for January 2010 were already pitting insurgents and locals against one another. So, like a telegram arriving at the last minute by stagecoach, friends who knew about the peacemakers' planned return to Rutba passed along an urgent plea to Sami. A former Ba'athist village *mukhtar* (or mayor) who had been imprisoned and tortured by U.S. forces at Abu Ghraib prison sent a succinct, clear warning:

"Keep the Americans away. Rutba is not safe."[10]

Dangerous. God-forsaken. Mean. Unsafe. From the way the State Department, a British historian, some American peacemakers with years of experience in Iraq, and, now, a former Ba'athist official made things sound (in that exact order of adjectives and nouns), Rutba was cutthroat.

Sami said to heed the warning.

We waited several months before trying again to arrange travel into western Al Anbar.[11]

About the most flattering things you could read about Rutba in English-language books in 2009 were dated descriptions going back to the days of British colonialism. It was a way-station "to the crushed humanity in the taxis" and "a waterhole if never a leafy oasis."[12] To Anglos, then as now, Rutba and much of the Al Anbar desert seemed unapproachable. More crucible than oasis.[13] But to Islamist fighters hell-bent on defending Allah and country, Rutba's desert is a godsend. Eighty miles south of the city, where silt and sand marry Syria to Iraq, there are East-West passageways that can funnel insurgents directly into the fight. When Sir Winston Churchill invaded Iraq in the Second World War to secure its oil pipelines and to use Al Anbar as a staging ground to attack the

Axis powers, he underestimated the resolve of Rutba. Despite Britain's herculean superiority in troop size and weaponry, British ground forces could not secure the Syria-Iraq border outside of Rutba. British historian John Keay credited the scrappiness of a way-station that relied only on its police for military defense: "It was from across its desert border that relief (for British troops) was looked for, but never can a place have been so repeatedly retaken as Rutba. . . . It was reportedly recaptured several times a week."[14]

Only after Churchill ordered relief forces into the region that included a "flying column of 2,000 men" did Rutba relinquish its grip on the town and its borders. Some of the same squadrons of Royal Air Force fighters who had decades earlier helped carve a landing strip near Rutba for British Imperial Airways returned in May 1941 to repeatedly strafe the town until it bent to Churchill's will.

Similarly, the hardened fighters of Al Anbar would relinquish the fight in 2003 only after Gavrilis and an armada of fighter pilots and bombers strafed Rutba and the surrounding desert with modern-day high-grade American-made explosives.

Or, as Gavrilis puts it, "Yeah, unfortunately, we had to drop ordnance on the town."

Fourteen days after the only hospital in western Anbar province had burned, the elite soldiers responsible for its demise came marching into Rutba. At daybreak on April 9, 2003, the day the world watched Americans topple Baghdad's thirty-nine-foot-tall statue of Saddam Hussein with an American-made $2 million tow truck,[15] the day pollsters revealed to the world that Americans overwhelmingly approved of President Bush and his preemptive war,[16] the same day that Bush's hyper-hawkish Undersecretary of State wagged a finger at Syria and Iran as if they were next on Washington's list,[17] America's Finest from redneck[18] Fort Campbell, Kentucky-Tennessee, rolled into Rutba as if they owned it. For all practical purposes they did. No one dared challenge their unexpected Wednesday morning parade down main street. Scripted the previous day, it was a show intended to intimidate. Long, fat columns of customized two-ton Humvees outfitted with mounted M240 machine guns and Mk 19 grenade launchers growled east into downtown under a sky shaded by a B-52 bomber, F-16 jets, and an A-10 fighter roaring low, dropping flares, and then circling.[19] From Baghdad to Rutba that day Americans put on the best show that a $380 billion defense and military budget could buy.[20]

For three weeks, the First Battalion of the Fifth Special Forces Group had rocked the Rutba area from the city's outskirts to its congested core. The strategy was to incrementally "tighten a noose" from the perimeter of the city and either squeeze the "Saddamists" from its core or the life from the "Saddamists." Maybe both. The Saddamists, as Gavrilis called the enemy, could be the ominously black-clad Fedayeen paramilitary; Saddam's Republican Guard troops; members of the Ba'athist regime who fought back; foreign insurgents stealing across the border to take up arms for Iraq and Islam; or pretty much anyone in Iraq defending the sovereign nation.

The Saddamists never had a chance. They far outnumbered the six-dozen-member Special Forces teams assigned to secure western Al Anbar, Rutba, and the nearby airfield, but the Iraqis were outgunned, outwitted, and, from the descriptions of some of the firefights, their weapons were outdated.

Their first attempted assault on Bravo Company was launched by about forty Iraqis packed into four pickup trucks, resembling a formation of the Taliban. When they drove up the desert hill toward the Special Forces a single .50-caliber round striking a pickup caused an Iraqi fighter to toss his grenade launcher in the air and the driver to accelerate in circles.[21]

O n March 19, 2003, just after a 5:47 p.m. sunset in Jordan's easternmost desert, twelve hours before the war's official start would be marked with a failed four-bomb "decapitation strike" in Saddam's Dora Farms neighborhood, Gavrilis and his Bravo Company invaded the sovereign Republic of Iraq from Jordan's share of the Syrian desert.[22] In the face of overwhelming public opposition from Jordan[23] they crossed with a nod and a wink from King Abdullah II, a Western-educated[24] former deputy commander of Jordanian Special Forces. The following day and for weeks and months afterward, Jordan's officials would vehemently deny this assistance was given to the U.S. military.[25]

Gavrilis's first objective was, in effect, to protect Israel, Saudi Arabia, and Jordan.[26] In that order, probably. During the first Gulf War a dozen years earlier, Iraq deployed mobile Scud missile launchers in the western Anbar province to fire thirty-nine missiles at Israel, and more than forty at Saudi Arabia. The medium-range surface-to-surface Scuds resulted in only a few casualties, but they had terrorized the public. President George H. W. Bush's administration pleaded with Israel not to retaliate. Entry of the Jewish state into the first Gulf War—or this second one—could have fractured Washington's fragile coalition of Muslim allies. With the Arab world strongly suspecting that King Abdullah II sided with Washington in 2003, Amman and Washington feared that Saddam might target a third American ally.

Secondary to blunting the Scud threat, the First Battalion Bravo Company was to capture the H-3 airfield west of Rutba, the site of an immobile Scud launcher in 1991. Lastly, Gavrilis had orders to capture Rutba itself.

At the ready, dedicated solely to the needs and ground coordinates of six twelve-man Special Forces teams in western Al Anbar, was a diversified fleet of American air power: $15 million Lockheed Martin F-16 Fighting Falcons; $12 million A-10 Thunderbolt tank killers; $10 million Boeing B-52H Strato-fortress bombers; and, directing the circus of sorties, one $270 million Boeing E-3 Sentry, better known as an AWACS jet (Airborne Warning and Control Systems, providing surveillance and relaying coordinates). The acrobatics of it all had been practiced many times beforehand in the Mojave Desert north of Las Vegas. The plan was straightforward and standard fare: the Green Berets attack, capture, and/or kill up close from the ground; fighter pilots and bombers from the desert's magnificent cobalt sky; and some of the world's best-educated and highest-paid engineers from the sidelines several thousand miles away. Literally speaking, the Green Berets should be the only ones with blood on their hands.

Seeing the Fedayeen entrenched in downtown Rutba amid the sprawl of mud-brick houses, markets, mosques, schools, bank, hospital, and bureaucratic offices, Gavrilis wanted to apply his noose sooner than later. With the airfield abandoned and no Scud missiles found, the Special Forces moved into place on Rutba's perimeter in their Indiana-made Humvees[27] outfitted with mounted M240 machine guns from Columbia, South Carolina,[28] and Mk 19 grenade launchers from a touristy town in Maine.[29] Gavrilis's Bravo Company and five other dozen-man teams of Special Forces attacked from the edges of town to close the distance incrementally—east to west and north to south,[30] like hands squeezing Rutba's throat.

"The last thing we wanted to do was get in a giant urban battle in the city," he told me eight years later. "The Fedayeen had hunkered down in the schools, took all the desks and the furniture out, sandbagged the windows; they did that to a number of other buildings and even a mosque. Not the grand mosque, but the smaller mosque near the west side of town. And they were in the hospital. There was a storage house behind the hospital that they used to store ammo and there was another building on the other side of the hospital that they sand-bagged up and used as a bunker facing the east side of town. And then there was the Ba'ath Party headquarters that had been bunkered and sandbagged. They were basically fortified in the city."

Gavrilis and I are in two overstuffed chairs nursing green tea and bottled water at a Starbucks in Crystal City, an upscale neighborhood of Arlington, Virginia. It's a hot Friday in August 2011. The late-morning humidity has climbed to a suffocating 79 percent, like a layer of thick wool to anyone who hasn't saddled himself with forty-five pounds of Army gear in Al Anbar or resided there full-time with intermittent electricity and no air conditioning. A quiet hum of air conditioning washes over us while a mix of hip-hop and reggae soothes nerves and the pre-lunch rush. Add the scent of freshly ground coffee and the Starbucks calm begins to feel like something prescribed—lulling and subliminal. Four blocks south of us, directly across from another Starbucks (one of four on the crowded mile of Crystal Drive) is a sand volleyball court prepped for weekend cookouts and happy hours. In line ordering an iced Frappuccino a tall middle-aged man is dressed in what passes for Casual Friday in Crystal City: khakis and a white golf shirt embroidered with the name Lockheed Martin.

"Now," Gavrilis says, shifting his weight, leaning toward me to make a point, "You could sit here and say that we could justifiably have dropped ordnance on the schools because the Fedayeen used them for military purposes. And you could say [the same] even for the mosque because it is a protected site unless—*unless*—the enemy is shooting at you from it. You *could* say that."

I didn't. He is referring to the Pentagon's reading of the various articles and protocols applied to the Geneva Convention Relative to the Protection of Civilian Persons in Time of War, better known as the Fourth Geneva Convention. Adopted by the United Nations in the aftermath of atrocities suffered by civilians in the Second World War, it ideally safeguards populations against "total war" (i.e., open season on civilians and places where they congregate: their residential neighborhoods, houses of worship, schools, civilian hospitals, etc.). But war is messy. The logical thinking that gels naturally in the comfort and civility of UN council chambers doesn't always translate well in the visceral emotions of ground combat. There are shades of gray in the Fourth Geneva Convention, wordy attempts to differentiate between places that are purely civilian and those polluted by military objective.[31] Heard in the rush of fight-or-flight adrenaline is boot-camp clarity. "Kill, kill, kill!" military recruits shout.[32] There's no ambiguity in that.

But Rutba General Hospital was never targeted. At least not by Americans, Gavrilis explains, leaning forward to again explain his point: The hospital was a victim only of the Fedayeen fighters—their explosives, their collateral damage.

"We didn't drop ordnance on the mosques and we didn't bomb the schools either. We did, however, drop ordnance on a couple of places where they were firing on us from. But we tried to spare as much as we could."

Point made, he sits back, sinking into the soft Starbucks cushion.

"It was a delicate balance," he adds. "No one wanted to destroy that city."

He's smaller than he appeared to me in Linda Robinson's 2004 tribute to the Green Berets, *Masters of Chaos: The Secret History of the Special Forces*. Shorter than he seems in a long list of accomplishments and in his curriculum vitae: second in his division's Best Ranger competition; honors graduate in the Special Forces Q Course (the grueling, qualifying Green Beret test of endurance); bachelor's degree in political science from Penn State University, and a master's in international studies from Old Dominion University; senior advisor to the Center for Naval Analysis and chief of staff for a Top 100 defense contractor, DRS Technologies. Smaller in person even than in his many TV interviews as a military strategist and terrorism expert on C-SPAN and CNN.

Age forty-three now and a retired Lieutenant Colonel, Gavrilis's hairline recedes cleanly, front to crown, like a football player's after so many years of strapping on a helmet. If you're a fan of mixed martial arts and the Ultimate Fighting Championship, you would swear he resembles former welterweight champ Matt Serra. A couple of inches taller and maybe a dozen pounds heavier than Serra's fighting trim, but even in the soft recline of Starbucks you can see the sleeping dog. There are traces of a pit bull's squared shoulders and eager, bow-legged stance.

"Our posture the entire time there was like, 'C'mon Fedayeen, you want to fight? . . . Well, hey, here we are. We're right on the edge of the city. We're *right* here.'"

Recalling this, his right hand sweeps across his body as if he's welcoming someone into his house. Or maybe he's drawing a line in the sand. It's been many years since the firefights in and around Rutba. But the memory of battle sits him up straight; just talking about it is enough to secrete a rush of the ineffable high that lures punch-drunk boxers out of retirement and tempts soldiers with reenlistment.

"Yeah, okay, you want to fight, come fight us. That's what we were saying. C'mon out to the edge of the city. *Here* we are."

His hand sweeps across again.

"You want to be a *martyr*, then come be a martyr."

The Fedayeen in Rutba eventually followed the path of the Ba'athist regime. They fled. But not before Rutba's eight-story bank, a mechanic's garage, a factory to the east of Rutba General Hospital, an old British fort to the west of it, the storehouse directly behind it and another to the east of it, and the main hospital itself, including the children's ward, burned. And that's only the short list pulled from Gavrilis's memory eight years and two completed tours later.

Ask him about the boy and his father who died in the children's ward and he shrugs. It's not a callous gesture or sign of indifference. He looks exasperated. He didn't interview witnesses after every airstrike. It was war. Ordnance drops. People die. Compared to the bloody boots on the ground, U.S. civilians (and journalists) can be persistently, comfortably ignorant about the guts of it all. Like how those little bomblets the size of D batteries parachute down looking angelic and playful right up until their U.S. patented Wind Corrected Wind Dispenser sprays hot-molten balls of lead into anyone and anything that's nearby—parent, child, grandparent, pet, car, barn, house, playhouse. Do the brains who arm the jocks even understand this stuff?

"You didn't know?" I ask. "They say a boy patient and his father died. Apparently everyone else got out."

There was staff working in Rutba General that night, and there were other patients who were evacuated. The boy and the father were not alone; they just didn't make it out before the tsunami of fire swept in.

"No," he said flatly, "I didn't know anyone died in that fire."

His orders were to eliminate the threat of Scuds, secure the H-3 airfield, and squeeze the Saddamists out of Rutba. There were no orders for him to count Iraqi heads. So he never asked about casualties from the hospital fire. Or from the ordnance dropped on the bank. Or the old fort. Or the nondescript factory. Or the building suspected of housing Saddam's spy agency, the Jihaz Al-Mukhabarat Al-A'ma. Or the mechanic's garage near the medical clinic that treated Shane, Cliff, and Weldon.

"No one told me. When that ordnance dropped we were still outside of town. You couldn't see it from where we were."

It's not as if the hospital's demise was even the fault of the Americans. He had explained this to me already. The Fedayeen, they are the ones to blame. They forced the Army's hand, he said.

Crystal City is five miles from the U.S. Capitol, four from the State Department, two from Reagan National Airport; it's a military and business niche carved into Arlington. Literally. Above and below Crystal Drive's crowded four lanes trimmed in overpriced hotels, restaurants, and bars are offices coveted by defense contractors. Location, location, location. High-rent Crystal City is a draw for its intimate proximity to power. The Department of Defense has satellite offices here; the Pentagon itself is two miles north; the White House four miles; and all of the lobbyists of K Street are a straight shot and easy jog across the 14th Street Bridge.

Meanwhile, residing in or near its forest of fifty-five high-rises connected by a mile-long underground concourse are name-brand companies profiting from fat military budgets and perpetual war. Profits from not only the largesse of the U.S. military and defense budgets—by far the world's largest combined, at $707.5 billion in fiscal 2012[33]—but the violent bells and whistles of Washington's allies. The beneficiaries of American aid (e.g., Israel, Jordan, Egypt, Saudi Arabia, etc.). They receive the product too. The United States is the world's largest weapons' manufacturer and distributor (read: trafficker), and "defense" contracts arguably begin in the comfy and social confines of niche neighborhoods. The A/C, the music, the happy hours, the cold draught and fresh ground, these can help make things imperial feel impervious. In that way Crystal City is both a conduit and a buffer.

Four of the world's perennial top-five defense contractors based on weapons' contracts and annual revenue generated have addresses here:[34] Lockheed

Martin, Boeing, Northrop Grumman, and General Dynamics, in that order. The fifth, Raytheon (RTN), is only a hop and a skip away. Its Arlington office is equally close to the Pentagon and the U.S. Capitol; one mile closer to K Street and the State Department. In the decade that followed September 11, 2001, and the launch of Washington's War on Terrorism, the perennial powerhouses and their shareholders have resided in a growth industry—never mind the subprime mortgage crisis, bank bailouts, and a lingering global economic recession.

In the war's fleecing of Peter to pay Paul, the top five have managed quite handsomely.[35]

Gavrilis agreed to meet for coffee in Crystal City. Married and with a daughter, he retired from the Army in 2009. His company, The Gavrilis Group LLC, has an office in Crystal City. He's an international security and defense consultant. As with defense contractors, it pays for him to work in proximity to power.

The fight around Rutba and the ground war with Iraq began officially on Friday morning, March 21, 2003. All of the Special Forces teams that had dug their way across a desert berm from Jordan were not yet on Rutba's perimeter when truckloads of Iraqi fighters were seen leaving town and disappearing into a desert trench. Pickup trucks—Dodge, Datsun, Nissan are all popular in Rutba—drove to the town's southwest edge and disgorged passengers, again and again. A two-man Special Forces surveillance team on a hillside outside of Rutba radioed for help after counting one hundred fighters.[36]

Outnumbered but not outgunned, the Army looked to the sky.

In the ensuing four-hour firefight F-16s, B-52s, A-10s, and, even, a Boeing supersonic B-1 bomber[37] responded to Rutba's desert. For the next four hours, American-made bombs dropped indiscriminately. In her 2004 tribute to the Green Berets, *Masters of Chaos: The Secret History of the Special Forces*, Linda Robinson described a lopsided American advantage that sounded similar to Churchill's heavy-handed strafing:

> The immediate goal was to put enough ordnance onto the ground to shock the Iraqis into halting their advance, so no effort was made to match bomb to target. The planes dropped whatever they had, laser-guided JDAMS or dumb bombs, 500-, 1,000-, or 2,000-pounders. . . . The air force passed the team sortie after sortie of aircraft. At one point four planes were stacked up waiting to make bombing runs. The air force flew tankers into the area to refuel the jets. . . . The rain of bombs from above and the teams' heavy weapons tore up the hillside and reduced vehicles and Iraqi guns to smoking, twisted wreckage.[38]

Toward the end of four nonstop hours of shelling—with the Iraqis showing "no signs of surrendering"—a U.S. fighter pilot asked permission to go lower into the battle. From two hundred feet above the four-lane main road that cuts through Rutba (Business Highway 10) a 2,000-pound bomb was dropped onto a lone pickup truck armed with a machine gun. "The air force spared no effort or hardware in this, the war's first big fight," Robinson concluded.[39]

Special Forces remained on the perimeter of Rutba through March and into April, each week closing the noose violently, explosively tighter. The lopsided, heavy-handed treatment of the Saddamists ebbed and flowed until finally the townspeople had heard, felt, and suffered enough.

On April 8, 2003, two elders dressed in flowing *dishdashas* walked from the city and into the desert unarmed, hands open and outstretched, until they reached Gavrilis's Bravo Company. They had a single favor to ask:

Arjook ann tetewaquaffou min qusfina bil qunabel?

"Can you please stop bombing us?"

The men each draped a hand over their hearts, as if they were about to pledge allegiance to their newfound liberty and to the United States. But for Iraqis—Sunni, Shia, Kurdish, Christian, Agnostic, Atheist, etc.—a hand over the heart indicates a different sort of allegiance. It's a wordless greeting that says heart-to-heart I honor and respect you as a fellow human. It's similar to the Hindu Sanskrit *namaste*—three syllables that acknowledge the universal and flagless holy soul visible in one another.[40]

The elders explained that American bombs were frightening Rutba's women and children. The town's primary economy, a mile-long, dusty street normally crowded with stores, kiosks, and carts of fresh fruit, vegetables, cold drinks, and such, couldn't open. It was too dangerous to risk and, besides, shoppers weren't likely to leave the perceived safety of home. So, please, might he allow Rutba to get on with life.

Gavrilis was dressed for combat. In one hand he held his Colt M4 carbine rifle, one of 400,000 in service by the Army.[41] On his chest was a ballistic vest made from two ceramic plates bonded in bullet-proof thermoplastic composite. Neither could shield his heart. He considered the request for less than five seconds.

Na'am, he said. "Yes."

He told the elders that for twenty-four hours there would be no more bombs landing in or around Rutba. Children could sleep; women could go to market. "I told them, 'As a gesture to the people of Iraq . . . there will not be any ordnance today or tonight. . . . No one else is going to fire from around here—at least no other Americans.' Then I pulled all of our guys off and I gave orders to stay away from the city; no firing."

It appeared that most of the Saddamists had fled. At dawn the next morning they proceeded with their muscular parade of Humvees lumbering down Business Highway 10 like a train of elephants and the airshow reminiscent of Independence Day. The Americans had arrived.

During the fourteen days the Special Forces occupied Rutba, Gavrilis, in his mid-thirties then and freakishly accomplished in all things Army, appointed himself the town's de facto mayor. He put a good face on it and named an interim mayor (local elders confirmed his selection in a ballot election that was later contested, recast, and reconfirmed), but Iraqi lawmakers and lawbreakers still answered to the U.S. military. You can forget the PR about chummy relations and an initial flourishing of democracy.[42] Any good news circulated by Army Public Information Officers was relative only to the bloody resistance haunting Baghdad and the resurrected insurgency that soon marked western Al Anbar as the most dangerous spot on Earth. Years later, as the resistance in Rutba waxed, waned, and occasionally raged, the Sunni city—like many Iraqi cities Sunni and Shia—fell in and out of the Pentagon's loss column. So, naturally, the brief reign of Gavrilis and his Bravo Company would be recounted in books, magazines, and newspapers for its relative success.[43]

Don't swallow it. The bloom never fell off Rutba's rose. From the start it was just a weed finding light through a crack of concrete.

Gavrilis had the muscle, the guns, the tanks, the bombs, the airspace. Those crown kings. And dictators. But by all accounts, his and theirs, his tenure wasn't half bad as far as military occupations go.[44]

"Did they ever repair the [hospital] building and the grounds and everything?" he wants to know now.

It's been eight years and five months since he called in the strike that ultimately crushed the only local hospital for tens of thousands of desert-dwelling Iraqis. Since that fiery night of March 26, 2003, the pregnant women of Rutba have had to travel several hours to Ramadi for labor and delivery. With spotty electricity Rutba General can't risk the possibility of complications and C-sections; can't even provide a fool-proof Neonatal Intensive Care Unit. Appendectomies, hysterectomies, tonsillectomies, cardiac surgery, neurosurgery, any surgery; the patients all travel the same cursed two-hundred-mile route.

Within the sixty-four-mile radius of the I-495 Capital Beltway encircling Crystal City and the metropolitan area of Washington, DC, there are ten hospitals. Stretch the mileage in a straight line equal to the distance between Rutba and Ramadi and you go from Petersburg, Virginia, to just north of Baltimore, Maryland. On that congested route of interstate highway there are three dozen hospitals within easy distance of I-95 exit ramps.

No, I tell him, Rutba General's repairs have been mostly superficial. There is, however, a top-grade Japanese-brand ping-pong table in an otherwise empty hospital foyer. It's covered in dust and looks oddly out of place next to a broken sliding door leading to and from three parked Red Crescent ambulances.

Gavrilis shakes his head, disgusted.

"You'd think there would be a lot more actual reconstruction. Probably looks exactly the same. Jeez. That is something that's disappointing. . . . Now I wish we had stayed longer and could've done more to help them develop."

He thinks about that.

"But we had to do other things."

With a war to win, a dictator to capture, and WMD to hunt and gather, Gavrilis left Al Anbar after only five weeks. That's three weeks to shoot, bomb, invade, conquer; two weeks to occupy, befriend, rebuild, reconcile. Not unusual in war. Green Berets play first-string varsity; they keep moving, battle to battle. The jayvee comes in for mop-up and maintenance.

In Rutba that was the two-hundred-soldier Lightning Troop of the Third Armored Cavalry Regiment from Fort Carson in Colorado Springs, Colorado. A few of the Special Forces teams remained behind for two weeks longer, but, in effect, Gavrilis handed Rutba over to Brooklyn-native Captain Shawn L. Martin, another career military man, early thirties with fewer stripes and, soon enough, an Army court martial, three convictions, and a jail sentence for assaulting Rutba civilians. According to testimony from ten of Martin's own soldiers, including an Arabic-speaking Army lieutenant who worked as his interpreter, Martin carried an aluminum baseball bat nicknamed the "Iraqi beater" and bullied some of the same people Gavrilis had befriended, including the town's new police chief. The prosecutor at his court martial portrayed Martin as a vigilante like Buford Pusser of the 1973 movie *Walking Tall*. But that wasn't exactly fair. Not to the real-life Sheriff Pusser.

Martin was interrogating a Rutba welder suspected of having information about a buried cache of weapons when he bagged the man's head and drove him into the desert. According to testimony, he gave the welder a shovel and told him to dig up the weapons or "dig your own grave."[45] Saying he knew nothing about the weapons, the Iraqi began digging. He dug slowly, and as the hole grew deeper and wider he began to tremble and weep.[46] Soldiers testified that Martin ordered Sergeant Robert Cureton to aim his weapon at the man's head and fire a round over it. Cureton said he initially refused but relented under threats from Martin. Evidently, the welder was telling the truth. He was released from Army custody without being charged with a crime.

Captain Martin "thought the town of Rutba was his little domain," First Lieutenant David Minor testified. Even before the soldiers of Lightning Troop arrived in Al Anbar, he said, Martin was calling himself "King Martin" and boasted about how he would rule the town. Prosecutors referred to him as a "war criminal," and his time in Rutba as a "reign of terror."[47]

He was charged with eight counts of assault and one count each of obstruction of justice and conduct unbecoming an officer for his treatment of civilians and an allegation that he drew his .9mm pistol on Cureton. At his March 2005 court-martial hearing in Colorado Springs he faced possible dismissal from the Army and forty-four years in prison. He denied all allegations of assault and of threatening Cureton, and he said he carried a baseball bat only because he didn't want to always have to wave his pistol around at Iraqis. Overuse dulls the effect. "I never intended and never committed any violent offense against anyone," he testified. "I'm not a trained interrogator, but I do the best I can. If I used force, I tried to use reasonable force. You don't need to point a weapon at everyone."[48]

A seven-officer panel convicted him only of three counts of assault, including the mock execution of the Iraqi welder, and sentenced him to forty-five days in jail and a $12,000 fine. He was allowed to remain an Army officer. Afterward, Minor, the first lieutenant who first turned Martin in, declined to comment on the case's outcome. "Probably what I would have to say would be unprintable," he told reporters.[49]

Gavrilis had never heard about it. After stealing away to the desert in the SUV of Rutba's newly (s)elected mayor, he climbed aboard a $35 million Boeing CH-47 Chinook, clattered east toward Baghdad, and never looked back.

At Starbucks I handed him a newspaper clip about Rutba's very own Buford Pusser.[50]

"A U.S. Army captain forced an Iraqi detainee to dig his own grave and then ordered troops to pretend to shoot the detainee . . . ," the *Los Angeles Times* story began.

Gavrilis fell silent reading. A blender whirred, people chatted; the lunchtime Starbucks din sounded like a cafeteria, except for the music of Biz Markie and Booker T. Jones. They sang about love, lust, and youthful infatuation. Still, Rutba had closed the distance. The Al Anbar desert no longer felt six thousand miles removed from Arlington.

"This breaks my heart," he said, laying the story down. "Those people in Rutba, the vast majority of them, are good people, really good people. There are some bad apples, just like everywhere."

"Like here," I offered, "like Washington."

"Yes, exactly, like Washington. But overall the people of Rutba, like everywhere, I think, are good and decent people."

The prosecuting major at the court martial had asked the seven-officer panel: "Was it *King* Martin or Captain Martin?"

Gavrilis picked back up the news clip again.

"Really, man, I hate this. Breaks my heart."

5

BOMBS AWAY

You will be held accountable for the facts not as they are in hindsight
but as they appeared to you at the time. If, in your mind,
you fire to protect yourself, you are doing the right thing.
It doesn't matter if later on we find out you wiped out
a family of unarmed civilians. All we are accountable
for are the facts as they appear to us at the time.
— Lieutenant Nate Fick, briefing
his platoon in Iraq on the Rules of
Engagement[1]

Auto mechanic's garage near the Health Care Center in Rutba (2010).
Photo credit: Jamie Moffett

Bombs Away

2003

Downtown Rutba is ten minutes from the taxi's nine-foot-deep cobble-stoned grave, a mile or two east on the highway, three or four south on Rutba Road, and then left onto Highway 10/11, a main thoroughfare through downtown.

To Weldon those ten minutes felt like thirty. Placed into the Iraqis' station wagon flat on his back, like a pizza slid into the oven, his fractured body shifted with each start, stop, bounce, and bend in the road. Did the car even have shocks?

Long before Fort Campbell's Green Berets radioed for help and sortie after sortie showered Rutba's desert with 500-, 1,000- and 2,000-pounders, making no effort "to match bomb to target," the road leading south from the highway was bumpy and potholed. Now, Saturday, March 29, 2003, eight days after the United States put an old-fashioned indiscriminate strafing on Rutba and the Fedayeen, and just three days after Rutba General was crippled by collateral explosions, Business Highway 10, including the city and desert it threaded, resembled a crime scene. An oil tanker, pickup trucks, and a Red Crescent ambulance van were twisted and wasted; several downtown buildings looked like war amputees—bricks, roofs, windows, walls, and workers missing. A fighter jet cruised above the station wagon as if the pilot were looking for a target, a good reason, any excuse. The Iraqis grabbed white linens, probably sheets or pillow cases, and held them out the window. The pilot tipped a wing at the desperate flapping plea and broke off the trail.

Entering Rutba from Saddam's autobahn, driving south on the business route, Al Anbar's desert springs suddenly to life. Eyes have to adjust. What was a dusky blank canvas moments earlier sharpens into congested streets and desert neighborhoods; women in *abayas,* men in Western clothes, military garb and long, flowing *dishdashas.* Not a Norman Rockwell, rather a vivid but stark Layla Al-Attar.[2] Apartments, markets, offices, hospital, hotel, homes, all are in earth tones constructed from the same mud brick—the very mix of sand, mud, and clay on which the city sits. The whole of Rutba is dressed in desert camouflage.

A minaret towered over the station wagon's passenger side as the driver turned left off Rutba's main four lanes, and then left again through the entrance of a rusty iron gate. "Minaret" is from the Arabic *manārah*. It means lighthouse. This one was earth tone, of course, but as it stretched toward heaven there were ornate flourishes of color; and near the top of the conical dome was a coil of aqua fluorescent bulbs and a tiny silver crescent. Visible from anywhere downtown, the spire of the grand mosque gives Rutba its bearing. The station wagon drove toward it, stopping about a half mile away at the front of a pockmarked, mud-brick flat. Trimmed dark brown with bars on the windows, scratches and chips in the brick, and a scarred and dented green gate, it was a no-frills building. A place built purely for function, like a school or factory or a military barrack. Shane couldn't read the hand-painted Arabic on a sign above the gated door, but a sliver of a red crescent in the upper left corner was a universal good sign.

Ten days after Washington invaded Iraq with promises to shock, awe, and liberate its people, this is where the locals of Rutba and western Al Anbar came when they were sick or injured. A cramped, poorly stocked, poorly ventilated health clinic. The hand-painted sign above the green gated door read in Arabic, "The Heath Care Center in Rutba."

This is also where Sa'ady Mesha'al Rasheed, a burly, grandfatherly ambulance driver with forearms as thick as cordwood, scooped up one of the injured Americans, cradled him like a child, and carried him to a hospital bed. It's where locals stepped aside to let three Americans skip the line, even as Americans bombed them. It's where word spread that bloodied Americans had breached the town's border and where word spread just as quickly that these Americans were of the everyday variety, much like themselves—unarmed and civilian. It's where locals turned out armed with blankets and bottles of water instead of, say, knives, guns, and grenades. It's where locals objected when it was translated to them that one of the Americans needed a ride back to the irrigation ditch on Highway 1. Shane wanted to retrieve the luggage and passports locked in the taxi's trunk.

La, la, la, the locals protested. "No, no, no."

With fighter jets patrolling the desert and its roads he would be killed. White linen can be a hard thing to see in the noon glare. Instead of a ten-minute ride to the taxi's grave, he was offered a place to stay. The way it was translated to him by the driver of the taxi, this offer from the locals wasn't for an overnight accommodation. It was open-ended; he could stay in the homes of the people of Rutba for as long as he wanted.

This is also where twelve years of U.S.-endorsed, UN-enforced economic sanctions had choked off supplies of local anesthesia, anticoagulants, and other staples of medicine. So a debonair physician's assistant with the name of a prophet and the bearing of a surgeon stitched the ugly gash in an American head apologizing with each push of the needle. Like all medical students in Iraq, Jassim Muhammad Jamil knew proper procedure for suturing wounds: inject the surrounding tissue with 10 mg/cc of lidocaine or bupivicaine or some other numbing agent. But nothing in Rutba was proper ten days into the 2003 war. Nothing had been proper since Saddam invaded Kuwait twelve years earlier and the United States and the UN security council teamed up to punish the whole of Iraq.

Asif, asif, asif, Jassim whispered into the ear of an American Brethren with the long beard of the Amish. "Sorry, sorry, sorry."

The linoleum-floored corridor was mostly empty, but curious Iraqis crowded into the clinic's courtyard. Shane gripped his only tangible protection, played it like a Get-Out-of-Jail-Free card. The Magic Sheet, as peacemakers called it, was composed by Kathy Kelly and carried by Iraq Peace Team members. It explained in English and Arabic why pale-faced foreigners were traveling in Iraq's crazed war zone, In short, it said, We are here to work for peace and to stand as brothers and sisters with Iraqis in this time of war. It almost always elicited the same response: a grateful smile or nod accompanied by a hand placed over the heart.

A doctor wearing khakis and a button-up shirt approached as the Magic Sheet still circulated. He gave it the once-over but didn't seem overly impressed. When Dr. Farouq Al-Dulaimi, the director of Rutba General who would depart for Ramadi one year later, opened his mouth a question fired from it as if it had been spring loaded since March 26, 2003, the night his trauma ward, maternity ward, and children's ward were gutted quicker than you can define— much less find—WMD.

"Why, why, WHY?" he demanded in English, his voice revving before he jerked it back into neutral.[3] "Why is your government bombing us?"

N ot counting Gavrilis's Special Forces, the invasion of Iraq had begun on Thursday, March 20, 2003, in the predawn of the Middle East. In Crystal City and across the 14th Street Bridge into Washington it was 9:34 p.m., Wednesday, March 19. Iraq's snooze-control *fajr* had just finished chiding Islam's faithful to get up, don't be lazy, prayer is better than sleep. Cast against a hazy sky streaked blue, just as a crowning of sherbet orange rose opposite a full moon, two stealth jets, four American warships, and two submarines christened war on the sovereign Republic of Iraq.[4]

Forty-one minutes later President Bush interrupted our regularly scheduled programming:

> My fellow citizens, at this hour American and coalition forces are in the early stages of military operations to disarm Iraq, to free its people and to defend the world from grave danger. On my orders, coalition forces have begun striking selected targets of military importance to undermine Saddam Hussein's ability to wage war. These are the opening stages of what will be a broad and concerted campaign. . . .[5]

Four of Raytheon's most profitable laser- and GPS-guided missiles, each weighing 2,000 pounds and carrying payloads more powerful than what coal mining uses to sheer off the tops of mountains, were fired by F-117A Nighthawk stealth jet pilots toward Saddam's Dora Farms palace in Baghdad's Muslim-Christian Al Dora suburb. The bombs were nearly identical to the bunker-busters that had twelve years earlier destroyed a cavernous Baghdad bomb shelter in a similarly misguided attempt to target Saddam and his Iraqi officers. Saddam and his men were not where the Pentagon predicted in the first Gulf War either. On February 13, 1991, Public Shelter No. 25 in Baghdad's upper-class Amiriyah suburb burned. Bunker-busters are frequently armed with a warhead prized by war-makers because of the intense heat vortex they generate on impact. When they penetrated the reinforced concrete of Public Shelter No. 25, doors melted like wax, and Iraqis on the first level were trapped and cremated. On a lower level, where large boilers and water heaters made shelter living more tolerable for Baghdad's wealthy, scalding water rushed over families trapped underground, mostly women and children given the shelter's coveted spots. They cooked in the boil. More than four hundred civilians died.[6]

On March 20, 2003, the Air Force doubled the number of bunker-busters to four, and the Navy piled on with thirty-nine Tomahawk cruise missiles launched from the Red Sea and Persian Gulf, each carrying 1,000-pound warheads as explosive as the Oklahoma City bomb.[7] Like with the Amiriyah shelter bombing, neither Saddam nor his regime officers were where the Pentagon predicted for the opening strike of Operation Iraqi Freedom. But when two Nighthawk stealth pilots from small towns in New Jersey and Pennsylvania snuck into Baghdad's airspace they knew only to follow orders.[8] They let fly four "precision GPS-guided" bunker-busters preset with Dora Farms' satellite coordinates. Contrary to the hype generated by Washington, the Pentagon and Raytheon, precision bombs are imprecise. The satellite coordinates, or Satellite Constellation Geometry, directing the newest Enhanced Guided Bomb Units (EGBUs), or any GPS-guided weaponry, is handicapped by geometric matrixes such as satellite elevation angles, receiver algorithms, and terrain shading.[9] Even the most sophisticated smart bomb launches toward its target with the pilot's fingers crossed.

The attack on Dora Farms was no different. The four bunker-busters were close, but missed. They shattered only homes, families, and Dora's morning calm. Afterward, and following each aerial barrage until Baghdad's electrical grid was bombed in early April, Baghdad's mosques cued up Islam's call to prayer, blaring it from minarets like a rebuke to Washington or, maybe, just a plea for wiser, more prayerful minds to prevail.[10]

At the same time that imams were encouraging people to pray, the Pentagon encouraged Iraqis to celebrate. During and after the bombing of Al Dora, American forces pirated Iraqi airwaves and spread Washington's song of liberation, a message that would attest to the Bush administration's profound misperceptions about war and the willingness of Iraqis to reside in it. Cruising far above the arc of cruise missiles, Lockheed Martin transport propeller planes, refit for psychological ops (PSYOP) with radio transmit and jamming gear, hijacked the frequencies of Iraqi state radio channels 100.4 FM and 690 AM. Six weeks after Secretary of State Colin Powell delivered to the United Nations Bush's most passionate case for invading Iraq (to disarm Saddam of WMD) the PSYOP team trumpeted only the case for freedom. Curiously, the operation was run by an Air National Guard unit from Pennsylvania Dutch country, a popular home for peace-loving Amish and Mennonites.[11] In the midst of misguided bombs and civilian casualties the Arab-language broadcasts sounded alarmingly absurd: "This is the day you've been waiting for! . . . The attack on Iraq has begun!"

The announcement played even as a school-age boy from the Dora neighborhood was rushed to a hospital wearing pajamas soaked crimson. Carried frantically to the ER, he stared wide-eyed as doctors huddled over him and nurses attempted to avert his attention. Piled at the boy's side on the hospital gurney was what looked like a coiled rope of sausage links—his intestines.[12]

Meanwhile, six thousand miles away in Washington, Bush was still talking to TV cameras from the Oval Office desk named Resolute, a historic dark oak gesture of peace given to the White House in 1880 by Queen Victoria of England. It's the same desk where President George H. W. Bush told Americans in 1991 that the first Gulf War had begun. Now, the eldest son was bellied up to it, flanked by photos of his wife, Laura, and his daughters, Jenna and Barbara. Behind him were the stars and stripes of the American flag and the dark blue presidential flag, turned to show the eagle's left talon, which grips thirteen arrows, instead of its right talon, holding an olive branch. Off camera Bush had pumped his left fist in the air and declared, "I feel good!" Now he continued to peddle his war like a circus barker waving Americans into the strongman's tent:

> To all of the men and women of the United States armed forces now in the Middle East, the peace of a troubled world and the hopes of an oppressed people now depend on you. That trust is well placed. The enemies you confront will come to know your skill and bravery. The people you liberate will witness the honorable and decent spirit of the American military. In this conflict, America faces an enemy who has no regard for conventions of war or rules of morality. Saddam Hussein has placed Iraqi troops and equipment in civilian areas, attempting to use innocent men, women and children as shields for his own military; a final atrocity against his people. I want Americans and the world to know that coalition troops will make every effort to spare innocent civilians from harm. . . . We come to Iraq with respect for

its citizens, for their great civilization and for the religious faiths they practice. We have no ambition in Iraq except to remove a threat and restore control of that country to its own people.

Fifteen hours later, Washington unveiled Shock and Awe. Twenty-eight U.S. warships, two British submarines, and an aerial armada of F-14 Tomcats, F-16 Fighting Falcons, F-18 Hornets, B-52 Stratofortress bombers, and F-117A Nighthawk stealth bombers loosed the demons of high-tech warfare.[13] On the night of the first day, not long after the four bunker-busters had exploded in Al Dora, more than five hundred bombs were dropped onto some of history's most storied real estate—geography sacred to the narratives of Islam, Christianity, and Judaism.[14] The heaviest bombing continued for twenty-eight days, with fusillades totaling 29,199 bombs[15] that were laser-guided, satellite-guided, unguided and misguided. In concussive bursts of fireballs, shrapnel, and the kind of blast-wave pressure that ruptures lungs, eardrums, spleens, and intestines, Washington's weapons of choice inflicted mass destruction. American-made exports would shear, shred, collapse, pulverize, and incinerate Iraqi flesh, bone, bridges, roads, tanks, taxis, ambulances, mosques, schools, markets, bunkers, homes, hospitals, sons, daughters, fathers, mothers, ammo dumps, fuel depots, electrical grids, water sanitation plants and phone exchanges. Not since the 1945 annihilations of Hiroshima and Nagasaki or, perhaps, not since American and British jets dropped "a mere 305 weapons"[16] on Baghdad in the first Gulf War, had adjectives been rendered so useless, language so muted.

Witnesses in Baghdad and abroad were speechless. As live TV news broadcasted Washington's doctrine of Might equals Right, the world could see fireballs as large as city blocks mushroom into humongous dark clouds again and again and again, a veritable strafing of a Muslim capital crowded with millions of residents living in concrete flats, townhomes, and low-rise apartment buildings. Even hawkish *New York Times* correspondent John F. Burns, an unabashed convert of the war, described its opening night as "a cauldron of fireballs and drifting smoke, with one huge building after another erupting in a fury of flame and obliterated granite, marble and steel."[17]

Beginning at 8:59 p.m. Baghdad time on March 20, 2003, CNN's Wolf Blitzer watched silently on air for seven and a half minutes as Raytheon's bombs lit up Baghdad with successive, violent explosions. Seven minutes into "A-Day" (Pentagon parlance intended to amplify Iraqi fear) the shelling accelerated into a sickening string of choreographed blasts that evoked America's founding—the rockets' red glare, bombs bursting in air. It was as if Washington were giving American viewers a bang for their tax buck. Or the Pentagon was just taking a bow.

Blitzer finally spoke. "Remember," he began, reporting from a studio 350 miles away in Kuwait, "[Baghdad] is a city of five million people. We can only imagine what terrifying state most of those people are presumably in right now as they see this huge, huge round of airstrikes going after selected targets in and around Baghdad. . . . . In the thirty years that I've been covering these kinds of stories I've certainly never seen anything like this, of this magnitude, on live television and maybe not even on not-live television."

CNN military analyst Major General Don Shepperd, approved by the Pentagon for CNN's war coverage,[18] interrupted: "Wolf, let me make some points to you. As we're looking at this through soda straws [meaning the narrow perspective of TV cameras] it looks like this is the bombing of downtown Baghdad. This is *not* what is going on. These bombs are confined to the military area of Baghdad, as far as [what] I'm watching here."

Within an hour, Baghdad's hospitals began filling with the civilian victims of American-made "smart bombs."

Manufactured in a nondescript weapons factory in Tucson, Arizona, the Tomahawk Cruise Missile helped make Raytheon Missile Systems the largest employer in Southern Arizona and the world's largest missile dealer. Several days into Shock and Awe much of the Western news media seemed to be more enamored with the wizardry of U.S. weaponry than with the war's errors, costs, and consequences. In sterile business jargon that belied the facts and flesh on the ground, media described the Tomahawk as if it were the latest offering from Apple. A story on the AP wire dated March 25, 2003, began, "The manufacturer of the Tomahawk cruise missiles that have pounded Iraq for a week plans to replenish the U.S. Navy's arsenal with upgraded versions of the low-flying, laser-guided rockets. . . . The fact that it's performed as well as it has, and it has a great reputation already being reinforced in the current operation, will be good news for Raytheon, said Robert C. Martinage, a senior defense analyst at the Center for Strategic and Budgetary Assessments, a nonprofit think tank in Washington."

The online edition of *USA Today*, similar to the war graphics of CNN.com and other content-savvy news sites, developed interactive media that allowed readers to launch simulated versions of the Tomahawk. With six clicks of the mouse, readers could launch a virtual cruise missile from a warship and watch it travel cleanly from sea to land to roaring, bull's-eye explosion, no errors, no blood, no intestines, no puddles of bodily fluid or severed limbs of collateral damage.[19] If it were a video game, the Entertainment Software Rating Board (ESRB) would have stamped it PG. Maybe G.

Wall Street sounded just as giddy with its sunny forecasts for investors of America's No. 1 missile maker, and the good news and profits continued the following year when the U.S. Navy awarded Raytheon a contract to build as many as 2,200 additional Tomahawks. The contract dangled the promise of even more Tomahawks for the long term, giving Raytheon a shot at another $1.6 billion in U.S. defense spending. Afterward, a Raytheon spokesman said that for a $3.5-billion-per-year company, the Navy contract was critical for business. In other words, war would "keep things rolling" in Tucson, he said.[20] Ditto for the good fortune of Lockheed Martin, the largest employer in family-oriented, pocket-protector-hip Palmdale, California, the L.A. County home to the $43 million Nighthawk stealth jet; and for Textron and Boeing and General Dynamics, the brains behind the brawn of America's bombs, missiles, tanks, helicopters, and fighter jets.

Contrary to what critics of free trade often argue, not all U.S. manufacturing jobs have been lost to inexpensive overseas labor. Together, the largest defense contractors in the United States had ensured that the White House and the Pentagon could deliver on the threat of Shock and Awe.

At Baghdad's Al Kindi General Hospital there was no disguising or spinning the offenses of "defense technology." Seen up close, unfiltered by the soda-straw perspective of TV cameras and Pentagon analysts, the sins of aggression are at best undeniable; worse, perhaps, unforgivable. On March 24, 2003, some of the same American peacemakers who would five days later be rescued by Iraqis met "one of the first targets of the U.S. war." That's how Dr. Osama Saleh, the director of Kindi General's medical services, described a four-year-old girl from the Dora neighborhood. Kindi is a scarred, musky-smelling teaching hospital on Palestine Street in Baghdad's gritty east side, and in its three hundred and thirty beds were dozens of civilian casualties and conscripted soldiers.[21] In a metal crib lay a small girl, limp but smiling, a bushy haired preschooler paralyzed from the waist down by one of the Nighthawk jets' precision-guided bunker-busters. The bomb's thermobaric warhead is state-of-the-art, a pride of defense technology. It disperses explosive gases prior to detonation and uses a pyrotechnic delayed fuse and the target area's oxygen to create a bloated blast field. Detonation gives birth to a fireball heated to 2,500-degrees Celsius that gorges on the swollen fumes and erupts with furious sprays of hot shrapnel engineered for maximum hurt.

Missing Saddam, his palace, his family, his officers, the smart bombs that hit Al Dora, falling immediately after the *fajr* of March 20, triggered an inferno of projectiles firing across the well-tended streets and homes of Muslims and Christians.[22] Fragments of scorching hot depleted uranium shrapnel became embedded in the Dora girl's back. But she was lucky, Dr. Saleh explained to the American peacemakers. She was fortunate to just be alive.

Dr. Osama Saleh is tall, robust, and soft-spoken, a forty-eight-year-old father of four young children, and a surgeon fluent in Arabic and Spanish; semi-fluent in English.[23] Looking at the Dora child he called "Dora," and at Kindi General's other pint-sized patients wounded in the Dora Farms bombing and A-Day blitzkrieg, he could count a half dozen or more heads, chests, arms, and legs in gauze and casts. He began to weep. Perhaps from the exhaustion of working days and nights or from a doctor's innate empathy for maimed children or from his longing to be home to protect his own children, tears began to silently streak his cheeks. He emitted no sobs or screams, no outbursts of any kind. But he had a question for the Americans. It would foretell the frustration expressed five days later by Rutba General's Dr. Farouq Al-Dulaimi.

"Why bomb? For what?" Dr. Saleh asked, throwing his hands in the air. "This is for a country that has lost its imagination. . . . What has become of America?"[24]

In the war speech scripted for America's primetime, Bush assured the world that the United States was a kind and noble nation, and he stressed again the imminent threat posed by Iraq's WMD. Contrary to the opinions of the United Nations, the WMD search teams, the International Atomic Energy Agency (IAEA),[25] and, if judged by editorials and public protests from North America to Europe, a majority of the free world, Bush depicted the war as something unavoidable:

> Our nation enters this conflict reluctantly, yet our purpose is sure. The people of the United States and our friends and allies will not live at the mercy of an outlaw regime that threatens the peace with weapons of mass murder. We will meet the threat now with our Army, Air Force, Navy, Coast Guard and Marines, so that we do not have to meet it later with armies of firefighters and police and doctors on the streets of our cities. Now that conflict has come, the only way to limit its duration is to apply decisive force. And I assure you, this will not be a campaign of half measures.

The following three weeks served witness to Washington's full measure and the Pentagon's gratuitous execution of it. Collateral and direct casualties and the resulting orgies of blood and pillaging nearly crippled Kindi General and several of Baghdad's two dozen other hospitals. Still others, in desert outposts such as Rutba, closed indefinitely with hardly a mention in the foreign press.[26] So many bombs, so much destruction, so many wounded and killed, there was simply more to report than there were journalists willing and able. The same day that bombs hit Rutba General two other missiles dropped through a blinding sandstorm to burn through a Shia area of northeast Baghdad. Fireballs raced across stall markets, a crowded main street, auto repair shops and low-slung apartment buildings. BBC news reported craters in the middle of Abu Taleb Street in the poor Al Sha'ab neighborhood and, next to them, corpses wrapped in plastic and stacked in the bed of a pickup. BBC correspondent Rageh Omaar told viewers, "On either side of the road . . . I saw several destroyed houses and apartment blocks. I saw human remains, bits of severed hands, bits of skulls."

Pentagon officials would admit only that its jets had been bombing Iraqi military sites near the slums of northern Baghdad at about the same time that Al Sha'ab had burned, but they said the missiles that hit Abu Taleb Street could have been anti-aircraft shells fired at U.S. jets by Iraqi forces. As with the bombing of the Amiriyah shelter in 1991 and the Dora suburb on March 20, 2003, and, six days later, Rutba General Hospital, which burned the same day as Al Sha'ab, neither the Pentagon nor Washington apologized.[27] War is ugly and most everyone from the West to the Middle East knew Saddam's ploy of placing weapons and soldiers next to and in civilian neighborhoods, markets, and hospitals.

Were Iraqis being killed and injured by U.S. missiles launched defiantly in the face of this sick strategy or by the inevitable crossfire of war?[28] In Baghdad's emergency rooms, doctors were too busy trying to staunch the flow of dead to entertain conjecture. They quickly tired of reporters' questions. Dead is dead, they told the press, and only one country had spoiled for this fight.

"War indeed is about the total failure of the human spirit," wrote Robert Fisk of Britain's *The Independent*, walking readers through a Baghdad hospital besieged by the consequences of Shock and Awe.

> A hospital of screaming wounded and floors running with blood. I stepped in the stuff, it stuck to my shoes, to the clothes of all the doctors in the packed emergency room; it swamped the passageways and the blankets and the sheets. . . . As I wandered amid the beds and the groaning men and women on them—Dante's visit to the circles of Hell should have included these visions—the same old questions recurred. Was this for September 11? For human rights? For weapons of mass destruction? In a jammed corridor, I came across a middle-aged man on a soaked hospital trolley. He had a head wound that was almost indescribable. From his right eye socket hung a handkerchief that was streaming blood on to the floor. A little girl lay on a filthy bed, one leg broken, the other so badly gouged out by shrapnel during an American air attack that the only way doctors could prevent her moving it was to tie her foot to a rope weighed down with concrete blocks.[29]

Hours after the March 26 midday bombing across six lanes of Abu Taleb Street, hundreds of Iraqis turned out in Sha'ab in loud protest of Washington's war, its bewildering idea of liberation and democracy and Zionist motivations—valid suspicion whenever American-made exports explode in the Arab world.[30] The Shia of Sha'ab wept and screamed and chanted in protest of the war and its errant bombs. In raucous homage paid to the latest martyrs of American-Israeli aggression, they jeered Bush and Israeli Prime Minister Ariel

Sharon while waving the shoes and clothes of, presumably, dead neighbors, friends, and relatives.[31]

The fifty-six-year-old Fisk, Britain's most decorated foreign correspondent, roamed wartime Iraq without embedding with the military. His eyewitness accounts produced the sort of raw copy not seen on America's family-friendly front pages. Witnessing the carnage of Abu Taleb Street, he wrote of "the severed hand on the metal door, the swamp of blood and mud across the road, the human brains inside a garage, the incinerated, skeletal remains of an Iraqi mother and her three small children in their still-smoldering car. Two missiles from an American jet killed them all—by my estimate, more than twenty Iraqi civilians, torn to pieces before they could be liberated by the nation that destroyed their lives. Who dares, I ask myself, to call this 'collateral damage'?"

A week later at Kindi General he saw more of the carnage he would later compare to the Crimean War, a nineteenth-century battle between empires for control of the Holy Land, some of the same Christian, Jewish, and Muslim hotspots that continue to draw grief and conflict today—Jerusalem, Palestine, Bethlehem among them. By early April, Kindi General was full of the knuckle-sized flies that favor open wounds, its bed sheets were stained crimson, and toddlers lay listless or writhing in blood-soaked clothes. "It looks very neat on television, the American marines on the banks of the Tigris, the oh-so-funny visit to the presidential palace, the videotape of Saddam Hussein's golden loo," Fisk wrote two days before U.S. troops claimed Baghdad as their own. "But the innocent are bleeding and screaming with pain to bring us our exciting television pictures and to provide Messrs Bush and Blair with their boastful talk of victory."

With coalition troops advancing on Baghdad, an increasing number of cluster bombs had begun to hit crowded, urban areas. In addition to Raytheon's 802 Tomahawk cruise missiles, 98 EGBU Paveway III bunker-busters, and another 19,048 smart bombs deployed by U.S. troops in the first three weeks of war, there were at least 1,508 cluster bombs delivered by U.S. fighter jets and 9,472 by ground troops.[32]

The Cluster Bomb Unit (CBU) comes in a variety of sophisticated makes and models, thanks to the higher education spent mulling over such matters from the glimmering offices of the tech parks that dot affluent suburbs from Northern Virginia's Dulles Technology Corridor to Israel's so-called Silicon Wadi (Valley). Subtle differences in shape, size, and payload aside, most share an objective: to produce broad strokes of death and/or destruction. In hawking its 1,000-pound CBU-105 model, a jewel of the U.S. arsenal because of its infrared and laser sensors, Textron Defense Systems boasted of the bomb's "superior lethality."[33] The best defense is a good offense, after all. Especially when defense industry CEOs and investment portfolios are served by war not peace. Assembled in part or in whole in unassuming factories like Lockheed Martin's missiles plant six miles north of Orlando's Sea World and Textron's leafy campus fifteen miles from Harvard Law School, the models favored during Shock and Awe by the U.S. Air Force were the CBU-103 WCMD (Wind Cluster Munitions Dispersion) and Textron's CBU-105 SFW (Sensor Fuzed Weapon).[34] Both models descend looking deceptively tame. A "mother bomb" pregnant with baby bombs no larger than pints of milk approach the target by parachute. Before landing, the mom bomb releases her bomblets, which sway down on their own tiny parachutes. In war zones accustomed to missiles the length of sedans, bomblets can look like toy GI Joe paratroopers. Before hitting the ground they explode with superior lethality. Exactly as Textron promises. High velocity sprays of gumball-sized lead (CBU-103) or charged molten copper disks (CBU-105), shaped like hockey pucks and accelerating to 930 miles per hour, destroy the target or targets. The CBU-103 can maim or kill anything and anyone within the span of an American football field. The CBU-105, guided by laser and infrared sensors, will ideally explode directly into tanks and other enemy vehicles matching preset height and engine-heat coordinates. Ideally. In a radius of thirty acres (roughly twenty-three football fields, or a swath of real estate on par with the Pentagon) the molten copper disks can mutilate troops or cripple seventy-ton tanks and everyone in them—or in the way.

By the time Fisk arrived at Kindi General in early April, U.S. ground forces were fighting in Baghdad. Dr. Saleh had moved his family into the hospital, and ambulance drivers were dropping the dead on the hospital lawn. The concrete path leading behind Kindi to a detached morgue was well traveled and splattered with blood. Fisk walked readers along it and inside to the hospital wards where victims of the bullets and CBUs were clustered like flies:

> Safa Karim [is] eleven years old and dying. An American bomb fragment struck her in the stomach and she is bleeding internally, writhing on the bed with a massive bandage on her stomach and a tube down her nose and—somehow most terrible of all—a series of four cheap and dirty scarves that tie each of her wrists and ankles to the bed. She moans and thrashes where she lies, fighting pain and imprisonment at the same time. . . . [The civilian victims] lay in lines, the car salesman[35] who'd just lost his eye but whose feet were still dribbling blood, the motorcyclist[36] hit by a shell fired at him by bullets from American troops near the Rashid Hotel, the fifty-year-old female civil servant,[37] her long dark hair spread over the towel she was lying on, her body pockmarked with shrapnel from an American cluster bomb.

Dr. Saleh showed signs of cracking. Speaking to reporters who had come to Kindi on the afternoon of April 8 to check on journalists wounded and killed when an American tank fired on Baghdad's Palestine hotel, he said that in his twenty-five years of medicine, which included the eight-year-long Iraq-Iran war and the first Gulf War, he'd never seen so much bloodshed and death. At least one hundred wounded civilians and military conscripts had been treated at Kindi that day. Three children had died in Saleh's arms; one was three years old. With restrained fury, he began asking questions of the reporters:

"Do you think this is justified? Do you? . . . That child that died could have been my own."[38]

A line of locals waited to see the only doctor, nurse, and medical assistant who had shown up to work in Rutba on March 29, 2003. Despite the loss of the hospital and no assurance of a paycheck, they had been working almost nonstop.

The Health Care Center in Rutba is a half mile north of Rutba General, across a sand and dirt road from a row of auto mechanic garages where Kia, Opel, GMC, and Nissan are scrawled on stone walls in Arabic and English. In 2003 the clinic had an exam room, a couple of tables, a few chairs, two or three beds, and barely enough drugs to fill the cabinet of an average American bathroom. One week after the start of Shock and Awe, three days after Special Forces bombed the bejesus out of a suspected ammo dump, this is where the locals of Rutba and of the western desert of the Al Anbar came when they were sick or injured. A cramped, poorly stocked, poorly ventilated health clinic.

Sa'ady Mesha'al Rasheed, the broad-shouldered and barrel-chested ambulance driver, is a retired Iraqi soldier who dresses in flowing, sandy brown, ankle-length *dishdashas*. He was the first to reach the station wagon. He opened the car door before the engine shut off. The driver told Sa'ady what Sa'ady already knew just by looking. People were badly injured; two were in desperate need of help. On that particular day, Sa'ady was hurting also. A nasty case of asthma was complicated by extreme fatigue. His strong and aging body had been weakened by the back-to-back-to-back shifts that he had worked after Rutba General closed March 26. All but a few members of the staff had gone home with no immediate plans to return. There was nothing to return to. Like the majority of Rutba General's patients, its staff lived outside of downtown Rutba and in the vast desert of western Al Anbar.

When Sa'ady leaned into the bed of the station wagon he stared at Weldon's blood-covered slicker. If he also saw Weldon's Anglo-American complexion, brown hair, and blue eyes, it didn't show. Years later he would recall only that he saw what he was trained to see: someone injured. He placed his bear-sized hands beneath Weldon's back and legs, shifted him forward, and then tried to lift him without putting too much pressure on the spine, limbs, and joints.

Sa'ady, a devout Muslim, cradled the Mennonite pastor. Pulled him close to his own chest. He carried him inside the clinic, beneath the sign with the hand-painted Red Crescent that read, in Arabic, "Health Care Center in Rutba."

On Sa'ady's heels Cliff had followed with his blood-soaked CPT cap and Shane with his Magic Sheet.

"Why, why, WHY?" Dr. Al-Dulaimi demanded.

He handed the Magic Sheet back to Shane, and when he looked up at the six-foot-three American, Shane saw tears welling up in his eyes. Something in Shane's pained expression or in the gesture of his right hand, now placed over his heart, softened the tension.

"Sir, I wish I knew," he responded in his East Tennessee accent. "But I don't know either."

All around them Iraqis were moving furniture and equipment to make room for the injured. A hospital bed was found for Weldon; a table or desk for Cliff.

"You are safe in Rutba," Dr. Al-Dulaimi told Shane. "You are our brothers and we will take care of you. We take care of everyone—Christian, Muslim, Iraqi, American. It doesn't matter. We are all human beings. We are all sisters and brothers."

On the eve of Shock and Awe, and on the heels and popular TV ratings of *Star Search* and *The Bachelor,* Bush had had the full attention of his Christian-majority nation. He stared across the desktop of the Resolute and out from our TV screens to deliver a four-minute speech crafted to reassure the U.S. electorate. By the end, however, it sounded only like a desperate attempt to manufacture a sacred narrative. It was as if Bush were reading from a children's fable. A born-again Christian, he invited (read: implied) God's favor on 1,928 tons of bona fide American-made Shock and Awe that strained against the world's better sense:

> My fellow citizens, the dangers to our country and the world will be overcome. We will pass through this time of peril and carry on the work of peace. We will defend our freedom. We will bring freedom to others. And we will prevail. May God bless our country and all who defend her.

6

AT WAR WITH WAR

It was not only shock and awe,
but one of the most precise air raids in history.[1]
—George W. Bush, *Decision Points*,
November 2010

Rutba children play on the bomb-damaged rooftop of a building next to Rutba
General Hospital (2010). Photo credit: Greg Barrett

2010

S o they returned belatedly to Iraq in 2010 to apologize.
Apologize? For what?

Lordy mercy. *For what*? For allowing a modern-day empire and Christian-majority nation to run amok. If for no other reason we want to apologize for the appalling hypocrisy that invokes Jesus Christ in all of our "God Bless America" politics and wars.[2] For that reason—and for all the others, including the more than five hundred thousand tons of bona fide U.S.-grade, American-made high explosives[3] dropped on a sovereign Muslim-majority nation—they ("we"[4]) are sorry. So very, *very* sorry.

"They" are a tall, gangly, dreadlocked gentle giant, the bespectacled thirty-five-year-old Shane, a native Southerner who speaks with the same Tennessee drawl I inherited from a childhood spent on the Virginia-Tennessee border. In high school Shane was the good-looking Christian kid who attended church on Sundays and glided effortlessly through all the teenage cliques—and gracefully into none. He was a competitive jet skier and water skier, a Levi's model, and the prom king for the Red Rebels of Maryville High, a Confederate-flag-waving[5] and Republican-party-leaning[6] public school twenty miles south from where I flunked my Army physical[7] in Knoxville, Tennessee. How an anti-establishment social revolutionary was birthed from such mind-your-manners conservatism God only knows. The divorce of his parents before age two and the death of his father just before his ninth birthday no doubt marked him. But for what? In the foothills of the Great Smoky Mountains folk always said he was the full-length mirror of his daddy, tall, lean, and fuzzy headed, but Shane never saw the resemblance firsthand. In all his memories of Ronald Allen Claiborne, a Vietnam War veteran crippled by the meanness of multiple sclerosis, Dad is confined to a wheelchair. Father and son would play games of pinball on weekends and holidays with Shane on Dad's lap, the wheelchair bellied up to the flippers. But as Shane grew and MS continued its unstoppable, incurable march, weekends became freighted more with chores than games. Bed sheets needed changing, clothes washing, drying and folding; a dying father needed his son's attention, love, and care.

I suspect such a childhood might incline a kid toward extraordinary sympathy for others. Or, just as likely, I guess it could cut the other way. The kid might see himself as the victim and turn all that sympathy inward. Maybe even wallow in it. An only child with no cousins paternal or maternal, and no father figure at home after his mother endured a second divorce when he was eleven, Shane Allen Claiborne leaned on his mother, Patricia (Claiborne) Lafon, in a way that would prop them both up. She was a special education teacher[8] who brought home children with Down syndrome and cerebral palsy; he was a teenager eager to help others unjustly stiff-armed by life. As far back as he can recall, and for reasons he still can't fully explain, he has always been drawn to people residing on life's unwashed margins.

"I think a lot of those things from early on contribute to who I am," Shane says of his Tennessee upbringing. "Certainly some psychotherapist or something would probably say those are the seeds of compassion."

At an age when children often pull away from their moms, Shane drew closer; and as he kept growing taller, thinner, smarter, wiser, his empathy shot up several sizes, too. By the time he headed north to Eastern University it was a youth extra-large; outsized, really, for any age. It was as if his mother had tailored it to fit him.[9] Today, all arms, legs, laughs, and easy smiles, if the six-foot-three Shane owned a Great Dane named Scooby or if Shaggy wore his hair in dreads and traveled the world to discuss how best to apply Christ's teachings to social injustices, you might mistake the two. As is, Shane doesn't own a conversion van (although he lived briefly in a VW bus after college) or even a car, and he is more likely to hang out helping orphans and lepers in Calcutta (twice so far at Mother Teresa's Missionaries of Charity) than to unmask ghosts and imposters—unless you count the often-toxic trappings of capitalism, the free market, prosperity, and upscale know-it-all religion, whose near-sightedness and heresy he is constantly exposing.

Shane and the other five peacemakers[10] in our group are diehard pacifists (four Christians and a Muslim among them) who believe that as long as governments and militaries invade, kill, and occupy countries and peoples, civilians must get in harm's way and fight a different sort of war. Theirs is waged hand-to-hand and on the ground, like Gavrilis's Special Forces, but the enemy doesn't wear camouflage. Not exactly. It doesn't work like that. For starters, it dresses up real pretty and uses hyperbole. From a loft of law and authority it evokes our collective death with acronyms such as WMD and catchphrases like Axis of Evil, and then attempts to wring all reason from sanity. Has to. How else do you sell a murderous idea like Shock and Awe as a way to win hearts and minds? To a Christian-majority nation, no less. Then, as the (depleted uranium) dust spreads and settles, and the memory of Iraq's uncounted corpses fades from our conscience (or is trumped by the sight of military caskets draped in American flags), the euphemism changes from Operation Iraqi Freedom to Operation New Dawn,[11] making the whole rotting farce sound like a new scent of air freshener. That little error about WMD? No biggie. Forgiven like a kitchen spill. Oops. Well, just clean it up. By any sane definition or diagnosis the whole thing is barking mad.

But the enemy of peace doesn't wear a suit on Capitol Hill or Wall Street. Nor is it in dress blues at the Pentagon. You can find the enemy in those places and in those clothes, no different than you can find it in the basketball shorts and T-shirt I'm wearing right now, but this enemy is rarely *ah-ha* obvious.

Rather it's so vast, so prevalent, so constant, persistent, and present it's like that expression about not seeing the forest for the trees.

Fear, that's the enemy—and humanity's core infection. Politicians and CEOs may stoke it for political and personal gain, but we own it. Or vice versa. If, as The First Epistle of John (and U2's Bono) tells us, "perfect love casteth out fear: because fear hath torment"[12] then humanity in general and, specifically, a certain Christian-majority military superpower, are living and dying tormented. Ultimately, that is what the story of Rutba reveals. It's a gospel about our fears and theirs, the artificial divide placed between us; the walls we manufacture, but also the bridges we make possible through peace. Sounds hokey, I know. But this fear has hummed in the background for so long it's become our white noise. Its incessant whisper distorts humanity's potential to connect in ways dynamic rather than explosive. Brick by frightful brick we construct walls literal and figurative, blind spots crafted from nationalism and racism and all sorts of other isms. Some of these walls you can't miss; they're topped with gun towers and coiled razor wire. Like those that divide Israelis and Palestinians. In spots they are as high as San Quentin and stretch for hundreds of miles through the Samarian valleys to Jerusalem, Bethlehem, and on to Mount Hebron and the mountainous region of Judea, a demarcation of land sacred to Jews, Muslims, and Christians. But these walls divide more than property, of course. They polarize governments and religions and peoples. Not only in Iraq, Jordan, Iran, and the rest of the Middle East, but in North America and Europe, too. Israel calls its walls "a security barrier." That's half right. They are a barrier—a barrier to everyday Israelis and everyday Palestinians discovering that they are more alike than they are different.

Our figurative walls are harder to see, but no less formidable. Fear of loss, fear of failure, fear of the unknown, fear of not having enough; fear of faiths and cultures and peoples different from our own. Fear of suicide bombs, smart bombs, dumb bombs, nuclear bombs, hijackings, kidnappings, beheadings. And a parent's greatest fear: the loss of a child. Left unchecked, fear metastasizes into stones and mortar, gun towers and razor wire; it can spread in pledges of national allegiance; in statements of belief read aloud every Sunday; and in political ideology that feeds on the fear until humanity turns on itself. Nazi Germany begins slaughtering Jews; Japan bombs Pearl Harbor; the United States ("one nation, under God, indivisible . . .") drops WMD on Hiroshima and Nagasaki; Israel walls itself off from the world.

Nine hundred years later and the Crusades rage on.

F ear. Shane had to swallow his share. By the time he arrived at O'Hare Airport in March 2003 to travel to Iraq with Kathy Kelly's Chicago-based Iraq Peace Team, he knew he was headed into a war zone. His mother was so sure that her only child would be blown to pieces by American bombs or hacked to death by angry Muslims she could no longer speak with him coherently. Every sentence choked her. Two friends of Shane who were scheduled to go to Baghdad with him and the Iraq Peace Team changed their minds in the final worrisome days, leaving Shane alone with his prayers and a team of veritable strangers.[13] A friend and neighbor of Shane is Johanna Berrigan, a physician's assistant and the co-founder of Philadelphia's House of Grace Catholic Worker House and its free medical clinic in the same impoverished neighborhood where Shane resides with his Simple Way charity. Berrigan had gone to Iraq with the Iraq Peace Team four times during the twelve years of UN sanctions,[14] and sometime after 9/11 she encouraged Shane to go also. He contemplated it, prayed on it, tossed and turned with it until Kathy Kelly phoned out of the blue. They had never met, but word about the tall white guy with dreadlocks and a good heart who lived and worked in the slums of Philly had spread. From Berrigan and others working for the House of Grace and the Simple Way, Kathy heard stories about "this amazing young man who made his own clothes from burlap, lived simply, loved being of service to neighbors, and cut quite a figure in dreads."[15]

In late February 2003, as his departure date drew near, some journalists reported on Washington's newly released war plans as if they were previews to an exciting new show that would replace spring's reruns.

"Modern warfare isn't only about killing—it's about inspiring mass terror. That's why on the first day of *Gulf War II: Die Harder*, the Pentagon reportedly intends to launch 300 to 400 cruise missiles at targets in Iraq—more than during the entire 40 days of the first Gulf War," read the *LA Weekly*.[16]

The *Philadelphia Daily News* read,

> It starts on a pitch-black, moonless night—quite possibly in two weeks or less—over the sands of the Iraqi desert. . . . By the end of 48 hours, as many as 800 Tomahawks will have fallen on Baghdad. . . . At the same time, Stealth bombers will strike as many as 3,000 military targets across Iraq. The Pentagon calls the proposed pyrotechnic display "Shock and Awe"—a new kind of psychological warfare technique aimed at forcing a confused and shell-shocked Iraqi military to collapse within two days, thus achieving quick victory.[17]

By then Berrigan was beginning to side with Shane's mom. Maybe March is not the best time for you to go to Iraq, she told Shane.

Before leaving he wrote a letter to his mother, to Berrigan, to his friends, and pretty much to anyone who was worried that the magnanimous twenty-seven-year-old leader of the Simple Way was suicidal. In an eight-hundred-word explanation he expressed his gnawing frustration with watered-down Christianity and American complicity in war.

Yes, he was risking his life for people he had never met. No, it should not be considered extraordinary. It's what Christians are called to do. In part, he wrote,

I am going to Iraq to stop terrorism. There are Muslim and Christian extremists who kill in the name of their gods. Their leaders are millionaires who live in comfort while their citizens die neglected in the streets. I believe in another kingdom that belongs to the poor and to the peacemakers. I believe in a safe world, and I know this world will never be safe as long as the masses live in poverty so that a handful of people can live as they wish. Nor will the world be safe as long as we try to use violence to drive out violence. . . . Thousands of soldiers have gone to Iraq, willing to kill people they do not know because of a political allegiance. I go willing to die for people I do not know because of a spiritual allegiance. The soldiers have incredible courage, courage enough to die for something they believe in. I pray that Christians would have that same courage. . . . In an age of omnipresent war, it is my hope that Christian peacemaking becomes the new face of global missions. May we stand by those who face the impending wrath of empire and whisper, "God loves you, I love you, and if my country bombs your country, I will be right here with you." Otherwise, our gospel has little integrity. As one of the saints said, "If they come for the innocent and do not pass over our bodies, then cursed be our religion."[18]

In Chicago he signed all the usual next-of-kin and in-case-of-death stuff that people fill out when they're about to do something crazy hazardous like drag race, skydive, fight in the UFC. Then, like a military recruit headed to boot camp, he sat in a barber's chair. Afraid that Shane's dreadlocks would confuse Iraqis unaccustomed to them, Kathy suggested that he cut them. So, before boarding the Iraq Peace Team flight to Jordan, he and Philly friend Scotty Krueger of the alternative Christian rock band the Psalters visited a small barbershop on Chicago's North Side. Everything suddenly felt pressing and real. Shane drew a deep breath. If he were to cancel the trip, like his mother was begging him to do, like Berrigan was now suggesting he do, if he were to play it safe and return to the city of brotherly love, the time to decide was now. Before the dreads fell to the floor. There would be no turning back after shearing off three years' worth of artfully tangled hair.

He arrived at O'Hare with a close crop and clean part, looking more the Baptist choirboy than the social revolutionary.

In Baghdad there was one more piece of paperwork to sign. A night or two before Shock and Awe began driving up the Nielsen ratings for CNN and Fox News,[19] Shane, Kathy, and the rest of the Iraq Peace Team discussed how best to handle their own corpses. If, God forbid, it came to that. They agreed that if any of them were to be killed in, say, Hotel Al Fanar, a neglected $9-per-night Baghdad hotel where the Iraq Peace Team was based, the deceased would not become a great burden to the team or to their Iraqi hosts. Peacemaker corpses were to be rolled into one of Al Fanar's tattered, stained drapes with as much care and reverence as possible, and the body cremated or buried as easily and as quickly as possible. No remains would be flown home to North America, Europe, Australia, or South Korea, or to any of the other peacemaker homelands. They all signed the following: "In the event of your death you agree to your body not being returned to your own country but being disposed of in the most convenient way." (*Disposed* of. At least the shroud of Hotel Al Fanar's drapes would be more respectful than the way Dover Air Force Base handled the remains of 274 or more American soldiers—dumped like garbage into a Virginia landfill.[20])

"I am going to Iraq in the footsteps of an executed and risen God," Shane had written in his eight-hundred-word letter of explanation.

> I follow a Jesus who rode into Jerusalem on the back of a donkey at Passover, knowing full well what he was walking into. This Jesus of the margins suffered an imperial execution by an oppressive regime of wealthy and pious elites. And now he dares me and woos me to come and follow, to take up my cross, to lose my life to find it, with the promises that life is more powerful than death and that it is more courageous to love our enemies than to kill them.

So, yeah, we are really sorry.

For Washington's arrogant disregard of your country, we're sorry. For the Pentagon's brute audacity to invade, bomb, maim, kill, bully, and occupy. Sorry, sorry, sorry, sorry, sorry, sorry. For eager trigger-fingers and hooah Spartan hubris. For counting our casualties but not counting your casualties.[21] For offensive euphemisms that pretend to veil the ghastly consequences of our military mindset (smart bombs, collateral damage, defense technology, Department of Defense[22]). For the electorate's complicity—*damn,* we're so sorry. How did we let this happen? Please forgive us, *insha'allah* (God willing).

Armed only with our best intentions (no guns, no security) and with our arms extended in friendship, we're asking to return to Rutba to, basically, say all of that. And more. We're also returning to say Thank you and to ask, How can we help?

"We" are also Operation Iraqi Freedom veteran and noncombatant conscientious objector, ex-Army sergeant Logan Mehl-Laituri, the youngest of our group at age twenty-eight, born Christmas 1981[23] and "reborn," as the newly baptized often say, on July 4, 2006. These dual birthdates frame perfectly the

God-or-country niche that would soon define Logan's activist-academic life. Today, at age thirty, in blogs, speeches, and new book,[24] his voice as a former American-soldier-turned-Christian-pacifist gains traction with the same general demographic that populates anti-war and Occupy Wall Street protests.

In the summer of 2009, several months before our rescheduled return to Iraq, Logan joined the group. At the time he was forming an upstart nonprofit, Centurion's Guild, that helps combat veterans reconcile with their faith and challenges easy definitions of Christian and soldier (and of "Christian soldier").[25] Also, in speeches and nonprofit work, Logan was attempting to help likely recruits find other ways to pay for college and avoid the de facto military draft. As author Joe Bageant says of military-economic conscription, "Money is always the best whip to use on the laboring classes."[26] To high school dropouts and graduates stuck living at home and/or on minimum wage or worse (unemployed and unemployable) the shiny lure of a signing bonus, room, board, salary, and some college money down the road helps camouflage the realities of a four-year enlistment. Like me, Logan graduated from high school without the means to pay for college. Unlike me, he didn't have the offer of a factory job. He enlisted in the Army in 2000 at age eighteen and reenlisted two years later, motivated by 9/11, college scholarship money, and an opportunity to transfer from Fort Bragg, North Carolina, to Schofield Barracks in Hawaii. That was in the summer of 2002. By then the United States was at war in Afghanistan, and Gavrilis's Special Forces was in the Mojave Desert prepping for Shock and Awe.

Logan asked Shane and Jonathan about the possibility of returning to Iraq with them, and Shane asked if we could include him. Contacting him in the summer of 2009, I invited Logan on the trip. Since leaving the Army he'd spent a month in Israel and the occupied Palestinian territories as a volunteer with Christian Peacemaker Teams, but he had never been to Iraq without air support, Humvees, and an arsenal of weapons. Three years out of the Army he was entering his senior year at Hawaii Pacific University with his sights set on graduate school and a masters in theology. A trip to troublesome Al Anbar—unarmed and as a pacifist—fit perfectly with his infantryman-to-peacemaker metamorphosis. When Shane mentioned the possibility of Logan returning to Iraq with us, Sami Rasouli and I, the two responsible for planning and logistics, thought it was a good idea. Why not? Experiencing the peace of Rutba through the eyes of a combat veteran could enrich our perspectives on war and peace.

Following a deployment to Iraq that stretched from January 2004 to February 2005, Logan returned to Hawaii feeling as if he'd lost something in Najaf, Samarra, or one of the many other hotspots that had drawn the ire and live fire of Oahu's Twenty-fifth Infantry Division. His innocence, his self-esteem, his moral bearings, his sense of self, something had not returned home intact.

With a Christian girlfriend and her churchgoing family encouraging him, he set out to find or replace whatever it was that was missing or broken.

On Oahu there are countless places to go soul searching: the surf break off Pupukea Beach; Kaneaki Heiau (temple); the vertical drop at Manoa Falls. Logan dove instead into the New Testament. It's there that the Apostle Paul writes from a Roman prison to the church at Ephesus to explain, "For we wrestle not against flesh and blood, but against principalities, against powers, against the rulers of the darkness of this world, against spiritual wickedness in high places."[27] It's also there, in the book of Acts, that Luke describes how the apostles were healing the sick and "performing many miraculous signs" in Jerusalem when they were jailed by the Sadducees. Peter, the apostle who denied knowing Christ three times after the crucifixion, redeems himself and boldly snubs Jerusalem's authority. The high priest of the Sadducees orders Peter to stop with all the miracle making and hullabaloo, to cease and desist teaching people about Christ. Peter and the boys square up to the high priest and tell him to shove it: They will "obey God rather than men."[28]

Seems clear that Scripture demands for the faithful to follow the lessons of Christ rather than decisions made in Washington. Right? No contest. Except for Paul's apparent flip-flop in Romans 13:1—the verse cited most often by Christian hawks. It's here you could argue that Paul endorses local politicians and the suits on Capitol Hill: "Let every soul be subject unto the higher powers. For there is no power but of God: the powers that be are ordained of God."[29]

Tune your ear to it just so, and then read it again in the Bible's bestselling English translation (New International Version) and it sounds like Paul says definitively that our elected authorities are to be obeyed at all times. Maybe even at all costs. Romans 13:1 (NIV) translates like this: "Let everyone be subject to the governing authorities, for there is no authority except that which God has established. The authorities that exist have been established by God."[30]

Applied to modern-day empires, that would mean Washington is infused of the Holy Spirit; omnipotent, omniscient, benevolent. Made sanctified like that you'd think Congress would be innocent, pure, wholly righteous. There'd be no lying, cheating, or stealing in Washington; no hanging chads, adultery, or sexting either. What a hoot, right?

Reading Scripture that way, believing in its inerrancy or in the inerrancy of its translations and interpretations, you can almost forgive a Christian-majority nation for reelecting a born-again president. Even if, God forbid, he were to sell a preemptive war and invade a sovereign nation using suspect intelligence. Never mind that eight verses later Paul sings a different tune: Don't kill, don't steal, don't cheat on your spouse, and most important of all, love your neighbor as yourself. This is how Paul finishes it: "If there be any other commandment, it is briefly comprehended in this saying, namely, Thou shalt love thy neighbor as thyself."[31]

You can cherry pick, nitpick, and tune your ear to Glenn Beck, but that verse still translates into love and peace—loving your neighbor.[32]

Logan avoided killing the "enemy" directly or up close—pulling the trigger, lobbing the grenade. Says he never pointed a gun at anyone, but he did fire ordnance; assaults from afar that shielded him from seeing the immediate, bloody results. In war soldiers discover things about themselves and see things in others that civilians are fortunate if we never discover or see. In the frenzy of combat the garden-variety adrenalin that governs our schoolyard scraps and pool-hall brawls gets insanely amped. Fight-or-flight becomes kill-or-be-killed. And in the grip of that mania humanity's hardwiring is exposed.

I'm guessing such a thing leaves a grim imprint. Face-to-face Logan is reluctant to say much about it. At least to me. We shared a room in Amman, Jordan, and again in Rutba, and we later shared some heated debates about his motivation for going to Rutba. He never opened up to me about the war—the one in Iraq or the one he's waging with his memories. In speeches and testimony at veteran events, antiwar rallies and in churches, he usually makes only vague references. For example, at Jesus, Bombs and Ice Cream, a peace event hosted in Philadelphia by Shane and Ben Cohen, co-founder of Ben and Jerry's Ice Cream,[33] he said he saw things in Iraq that "nobody should ever be made to see" and he "lost someone on the field of battle—myself," but he didn't elaborate. The testimony moved at a soldier's cadence, as if too many details or anecdotes might pry open Pandora's box.

"After coming home, I found war had infected my mind. Images and memories from Iraq would haunt my dreams and invade my thoughts," he said, reading from testimony he'd prepared. ". . . I had sacrificed more than I bargained for—a lifetime of mental health and well-being forever crushed by the heavy yolk I bore as a combat soldier."[34]

However, online (in videos, photos, blogs, audio recordings, interviews, and journals), from the distance and relative comfort of a virtual buffer, perhaps, he is less reluctant. For example, on a Mennonite Central Committee website[35] he describes how "the most provocative experience" for him in Iraq occurred during a rescue of soldiers injured when their Humvee rolled over north of Kirkuk. It was a bitter cold November night; and, while Army medics treated others, one soldier lay trapped under the wreckage. Logan tried to free him, but ultimately all he could do was sit in the mud and watch life drain slowly, silently away.

Army Specialist Daniel James McConnell, a quiet twenty-seven-year-old working-class father of two girls, ages five and two, would be the thirteenth soldier from Minnesota to die in Iraq.[36] Unable to find steady work, he had joined the Army two years earlier to provide a better life for his daughters.[37]

On November 23, 2004, one week after Logan sat staring at McConnell's feet sticking out from under the Humvee, his funeral in Duluth proceeded without a hitch—a textbook affair by military standards. From sunrise to sunset the state and American flags at the capitol in Saint Paul flew at half-staff. A brigadier general came from out of town and spoke of the deceased as if he knew him ("He was one of the finest soldiers. He represented our Army and our nation with his spirit . . ."). A hometown priest recalled McConnell as a Catholic schoolboy and added his two bits to the heroic narrative ("Our friend Dan was taken from us when he was called to bring peace to a foreign land"). A bugler played taps; rifles fired in salute; an American flag folded into a tight triangle went to the next of kin; red, white, and blue roses with red, white, and blue ribbons decorated the fresh mound of gravesite dirt.[38]

"All I've heard is that he was in a vehicle rollover," said his younger sister, Becky McConnell, the next of kin whose front door two military officers had knocked on with news of her brother's death. "They weren't able to tell us who was with him or how it happened."[39]

Logan was with him. In the mud and almost to the bloody end. It's a memory that still haunts.

"In the course of a few hours, I watched [McConnell] die slowly under the pressure of two tons of Humvee wreckage. Medics and others looked on idly, convinced that his chance of survival was slim," Logan recalled on the Mennonite website.

> Combat triage insists medics do not "waste" time by treating troops whom they deem unlikely to survive. I helplessly tried to find ways to free him without assistance, until Special Forces medics arrived with a crane from Kirkuk. When they reached him, he still had a pulse. Within the hour, he had perished, before they could reach the clinic. For nine nights I didn't sleep. I realized there was a great possibility that he died, hearing everybody around him, knowing that nobody came to his aid. I hated the medics for a long time, until I found reason to hate myself. Why had this death struck me so powerfully, and not the numerous deaths of Arabs I had witnessed? I would later compare this realization to waking up to find a KKK membership card in your wallet with your name on it.

Two months later, a soldier in Logan's First Battalion, Fourteenth Infantry put a gun to his own head.

Russian roulette, military investigators said.

Pretty sure it was suicide, Logan said.

Noncombat related injury, the Department of Defense said.

Noncombat related injury, the hometown newspaper read.

During thirteen months in Iraq with Oahu's "1-14 Golden Dragons" Logan was an artillery forward observer or "fire support specialist." Fire support specialists creep close enough to size up the competition and ascertain the who, what, where, when, and how many that define the enemy. Their reports and ground coordinates direct the mortar, artillery, platoons, and AC-130 gunships[40] that soon follow. In effect, Logan painted targets on people and places. He may not have stared down the sights of his M4 and squeezed the trigger, but in no way does he pretend his hands are clean. They are forever bloodstained.[41]

On its first deployment to Iraq the 1-14 was a Quick Reaction Force, meaning it responded anywhere, anytime, and to anything, never bunking for long at any one place. From Iraqi Kurdistan's Tuz Khurmatu (110 miles north of Baghdad) to Kirkuk (fifty miles north of Tuz Khurmatu) to Najaf (305 miles southwest of Kirkuk) to Diwaniyah (forty miles east of Najaf) to Samarra (195 miles northwest of Diwaniyah) to Mosul (174 miles north of Samarra) to Tal Afar (forty-four miles west of Mosul) to Hawijah (160 miles south of Tal Afar), the Golden Dragons rode roughshod through Mesopotamia. "The more and more we moved, the more damage we caused," Logan said. "I really began to wonder if this was really winning the hearts and minds."[42]

In July 2004 the embattled Shia city of Najaf, home to the golden-domed Imam Ali Holy Shrine, the third most sacred site[43] for the Shia Muslims, was overrun by the militia of anti-American Shi'ite cleric Moqtada Al Sadr. A popular critic of the U.S. occupation, Sadr and his Al Mahdi army of black-and-green-clad fighters were a relentless, formidable obstacle to Iraq's Western makeover. Not long after a truce between Sadr and coalition forces had been announced in June 2004, the Mahdi army kidnapped Iraqi police in Najaf and demanded the release of its imprisoned members. The Golden Dragons were dispatched to Najaf in July to help evict the militia even though the U.S. occupation of Iraq ended June 28, 2004. Officially—at least on the front pages of newspapers and thick parchment of government decree—the power of law in Iraq now rested with the interim Shia-majority government. It didn't sound that way to Logan. As the 1-14 Golden Dragons rolled into the holy Shia city to battle a militia comprised of Shia fighters their Rules of Engagement (ROE) were refitted for eager trigger fingers. "We were told anybody in black clothing with a green headband is fair game to shoot," Logan said. "I never experienced it, but it was made very clear that this is the uniform of the enemy, and you should feel free to take them out whenever necessary."[44]

Meanwhile, 180 miles north of Najaf in the Sunni city of Samarra, attacks on coalition forces had increased from five to fifteen per week.[45] So three months after pacifying Sadr's Mahdi army, the Golden Dragons stormed into the thick of Operation Baton Rouge, a brutal rout of a Sunni insurgency entrenched in the city and the government of Samarra. In the biggest U.S. offensive since

Shock and Awe, three thousand American soldiers teamed with two thousand members of the newly formed Iraqi security forces to eliminate an insurgency that numbered a few hundred Ba'athists, Saddamists, and foreigner fighters. Joining with American-trained Iraqis for the first time in battle, the Army described the operation as a mission "to kill or capture anti-Iraqi forces (AIF) and return the city to competent civilian control."[46] Samarra is a congested city, with mosques and shrines revered by Shia Muslims, like Najaf, but its population of between 200,000 and 300,000 residents is predominantly Sunni. And like the July firefights in Najaf, resulting in the second defeat of Sadr's militia, the Rules of Engagement in Samarra changed at the line of scrimmage.

"ROE is a system to define when you can and when you can't [engage in fire]," Logan said of their orders in Samarra, a fight that began just after midnight on October 1, 2004, with AC-130 gunships descending on the city. "We had a very permissive ROE that allowed us to do as much as we needed to, basically. . . . We were told before we went in, 'We've told the entire city that we're coming on this day, at this hour, and they have to stay inside.' And so ROE were open. It was almost a free-fire area."[47]

By 0830 hours on Friday, October 1 (Islam's holy day) the Pentagon's war logs recorded ninety-four insurgents dead, one wounded, and five detained. By 1200 hours, the four U.S. battalions and two Iraqi battalions had secured most of the city's key religious sites and government buildings. Victory moved swiftly across the city. But at what cost? By Monday, October 4, the Pentagon reported 127 insurgents killed, 60 wounded and 128 captured. War logs made no mention of civilian casualties,[48] but military officials later said twenty innocents died. Locals claimed the toll was much higher. Of the seventy corpses carried into Samarra General Hospital, the city's 150-bed public hospital, doctors counted twenty-three children and eighteen women; of 160 wounded brought to Samarra General, twenty-three were women, said Abdul-Nasser Hamed Yassin, a hospital administrator.[49] By the end of combat operations, roughly thirty-six hours after the AC-130s first attacked from the city's edge, Arab corpses rotted roadside in downtown streets and in the hallways of Samarra General. Families desperate to bury the dead within the traditions and rites of Islam complained that the road to the cemetery, just south of town, was blocked by soldiers.[50] Islam discourages (some would say "forbids") the use of embalming fluid[51] and requires the deceased to be bathed, shrouded, and buried within twenty-four hours. By Sunday, October 3, ambulance drivers searched neighborhoods to recover bodies that had been hastily buried in shallow graves in residents' yards.[52] Still, Iraq's interim minister of the interior, Falah Naqib, hailed Operation Baton Rouge as a victory and a "great day for Samarra," even as Iraq's Human Rights Ministry pleaded for urgent emergency assistance from Iraq's Red Crescent, asking for medical personnel to respond to the "tragedy" in Samarra.[53]

In Baghdad, the Association of Muslim Scholars, representing some three thousand Sunni mosques in Iraq, accused American and Iraqi troops of widespread atrocities in Samarra; leaders predicted that such excessive aggression would undermine support for national elections planned for January 2005. "The hospital is full of bodies, children are buried in the gardens, and there are bodies filling the streets," association member Muhammad Bashar al-Faidhi told the *New York Times*, repeating what he said were eyewitness accounts. "These [aggressive] policies will increase the anger of the Iraqi people, and if the government insists on resolving the crisis in this horrible American way, then we expect that the Iraqi people will not cooperate in any forthcoming election or any other political program."[54]

Logan and his unit were among the eyewitnesses at Samarra General; also among the dead. They were tasked with identifying the killed Iraqis before their corpses decomposed. A half dozen years later, in testimony given at the Truth Commission on Conscience in War inside New York City's famous Riverside Church (where Dr. Martin Luther King, Jr., delivered his historic "Beyond Vietnam" speech in 1967), Logan described how the horror of combat affected both the killers and the killed. "I had smelled death, tasted the acrid carbon powder of the gun smoke, and heard the cries of mothers outliving their children. Sitting outside a hospital in Samarra in October of 2004, little did they know I wept with them, safely hidden from my platoon members, who would have seen the raw emotion as a liability. I had seen bodies outnumber available bags, draped over one another in an exterior storage room. My mind wandered recklessly and I saw my own father's face peer out at me from behind a thick black zipper of an open bag."[55]

From Logan's perspective in the hospital and atop a school, where he was perched alongside snipers, the ROE (or lack of one) had loosed a veritable turkey shoot. "On the second day on the roof of a school we had set up a security position and one of the snipers . . . saw a man crossing the street with a bag in his hand and shot him," Logan said. "[That was] within the ROE, but I don't think that for me that would satisfy my ethical kind of restrictions."[56]

Immediately after the battle, even as families and ambulance drivers excavated the dead from neighborhood yards, the Pentagon began beating the "good news drum" in a push to stay ahead of any bad press.[57] During the offensive the Army released daily upbeat press releases and gave embedded reporters access to American and Iraqi soldiers. As soon as the killing stopped the Pentagon moved Iraqi security forces out front to take the bow and "quickly paraded [them] in front of CNN cameras to tout a successful *Iraqi* [emphasis added by author] solution to the Samarra problem."[58] The PR sleight of hand drew mixed results from the Western media, but seven months later the operation's commander, Major General John Batiste (now retired[59]), described the operation's use of embedded reporters as "invaluable," and he portrayed the heavy-handed offensive as a blessing for Samarra. "Although Samarran Sunnis are still apprehensive about their role in the new Iraq, insurgents and criminals no longer hold Samarra hostage," Batiste wrote in the May-June 2005 issue of *Military Review*. "Operation Baton Rouge instilled hope of a brighter future in Samarra, and there is no turning back."

But sixteen months after Batiste's blitzkrieg of Samarra, the city's golden-domed Al Askari mosque, another of Shia Islam's most revered shrines, was bombed by Sunni insurgents dressed as Iraqi security forces. Tens of thousands of Shia Muslims railed against the attack and were still demonstrating and rioting[60] two days later when President Bush urged Iraq to calm down. He advised Iraq's leaders to step up and do as Washington says (certainly not as Washington does): practice restraint, foster unity, "reach out across political, religious and sectarian lines."[61] Halfway through a 2006 version of his years-old War-on-Terrorism speech, this time given to the American Legion at Washington's Capital Hilton on February 24, 2006, Bush condemned the bombing of Samarra's "Golden Shrine" and called it "an affront to people of faith throughout the world."[62] He concluded with Washington's usual invocation: "May God bless our veterans. May God bless our troops in uniform. And may God continue to bless our country."

The American Legion stood and applauded.

Logan emerged from his dive into the New Testament with his Independence Day baptism and a strong conviction: His allegiance to Washington, the Pentagon, and to their wrongheaded wars was wrong. Spiritually, morally, vitally wrong. God comes first; God before country. His newfound clarity didn't necessarily fix what was broken or missing, whatever it was he lost in Iraq, but it provided direction. So when the Twenty-fifth Infantry was ordered back into the fire of Iraq, leaving August 7, 2006, Logan balked. He asked if he could deploy without a weapon and go into combat unarmed. Sounds nutty, I know. What kind of infantryman goes to war without his Army-issued M4? Consistent with his demeanor, Logan was dead serious. He didn't want to renege on his commitment, he says, but he also didn't want to be cornered in combat and have to kill another person in order to save himself or others. Death by degrees, he had already lost part of himself. Enough already. He insisted on laying his gun down to follow the teachings of Christ rather than the orders of the Pentagon. You can't truly repent for an act knowing that you're getting ready to repeat it.

The Army dismissed his request as hooey; his platoon commander accused him of aiding the enemy, and his pastor said he was assisting the extremist Muslims that he was sworn to fight against. The Army reassigned him to a unit that wasn't deploying, and eventually it set him free with a reluctant but honorable discharge.

On the fifth anniversary of his Christian rebirth Logan woke early. He scrambled some eggs, showered, shaved. He dressed in his Sunday best (in this case, blue jeans and polo shirt), gave thanks to God for the new day, thanks for his health, thanks for his family, and thanks for the opportunity to testify. He was 5,500 miles east of Schofield Barracks, 7,000 miles west of Iraq. He got his usual fix of caffeine (medium roast coffee with nutmeg and cinnamon) at the Beyu Caffe in downtown Durham, North Carolina, and then drove to a small church six miles from his new home near the campus of Duke Divinity School, a bastion of ecumenism long grounded in Duke's motto, *Eruditio et Religio* (Knowledge and Faith). From Carroll Street to Chapel Hill Street, south on the freeway, Alston Avenue to Holloway to Lynne, the city was dressed like much of the nation: lampposts trimmed with ribbons red, white, and blue; the occasional balloon tied to fences, doors, trees, and car antennas; American flags hung from porch awnings. This was Independence Day weekend 2011—a time to celebrate the very same liberties and freedoms that Washington and its military industrial complex were doling out to others.

Three hours west in touristy Blowing Rock, North Carolina, where I visited with in-laws, the annual Fourth of July festivities reveled in the usual expressions of unquestioned patriotism. "God Bless America" blared from the beds of parade pickup trucks, and fireworks exploded in sprays of red, white, and blue; again and again, higher, broader, brighter, louder. It's the same oh-wow spectacle every year. Encouraged by kegs of beer, an open bar, and gluttonous bounties of grilled meats, the crowd at Blowing Rock Country Club stays up way past its bedtime to stare skyward. The fireworks shock and awe us.

On Sunday, July 3, 2011, Logan made his way to church. Then into the pulpit. Then he steadied his knees, cleared his throat, drew a deep breath. A first-year divinity school student at Duke, he was about to deliver his inaugural sermon. In that way, it was another Fourth of July baptism for him. If he had not made peace yet with the war in Iraq and the roles he'd played in killing and occupying an Arab people, a sovereign Muslim republic in blessed Mesopotamia, it was not for lack of tossing and turning, effort and study. Staring out at the silent smiles that lined the pews of Durham Mennonite Church, he began:

> America and I have a complicated relationship; it's one of those love-hate relationships. Sometimes I can't decide which it is. I love the freedoms that we enjoy here that many other nations don't have. We can speak our mind openly without much fear of retribution. If we choose to, we can contribute to the electoral process by voting. There are plenty of things that I love about America. . . . But there are things that I hate about America too.

Long before ten members of Logan's Twenty-fifth Infantry Division died in a helicopter crash in northern Iraq,[63] one year after they'd left Logan behind in Oahu, all of Schofield Barracks and every American—islander and mainlander, soldier and civilian—knew the deal about Iraq. Washington's prewar intelligence wasn't intelligent. Good chance it was only propaganda. All that sure-fire certainty about WMD? Bogus. But if you feed your anxious citizenry a steady diet of apocalyptic fear you can secure a blank check and a blessing to go and kill "the enemy." To kill en masse. You can even kill in the name of the Christian God. Later, when your justification to kill-kill-kill changes from a matter of imminent national security to some godly responsibility to spread democracy, no one makes a fuss about the obvious bait-and-switch. Heck, we're over there now. Finish the job. *Git 'er done.* God bless America.

"I hate that our government steals resources [needed] for education, healthcare, and jobs from the poor and gives them to corrupt banks and military budgets," Logan continued, reading from his notes to prevent himself from rambling. He reminded himself to slow down, to alternate pitch and volume, to look up and around, side to side, front to back. "I hate that national policy favors rich, white religious men. Sometimes I wish I were not American."

A few years back at one of those Blowing Rock Independence Day celebrations, a bumper sticker on a parade pickup truck read: "Rome did not create a great empire by having meetings. They [*sic*] did it by killing all those that opposed them." Inside the town's best barbecue joint, bumper stickers crowd the door of a vault-sized freezer behind a crowded small bar. Next to the orange and black #20 Dale Earnhardt decal, and directly below another sticker that declares, "Upholding the Constitution is NOT terrorism," there's an American flag bumper sticker. It states matter-of-factly, as though we're still fighting the Revolutionary War, "Without the Home of the Brave . . . There would be no Home of the Free." Next to it, a smaller sticker asks, "Why can't we shoot 'em?"

"I know all the passages about war and peace. I can cite a great number of them, most Christian soldiers can," Logan told the Mennonites of Durham. He continued:

> They can become weapons we wield against one another to advance the frontlines of our own ideological camp. [But] that is not the spiritual battle Paul wrote about to the church in Ephesus, or the good fight he describes to Timothy.[64] A proper Christian political stance loves God first and foremost, and tolerates Caesar. The only way to love our country is to recognize the inherent limitations of any and all nations to provide peace or ensure security. We must love our country, but we must do so as Christians, as people whose love for Jesus and for one another defines and orients all our other loves. If Caesar tells us to harm our enemies, we must not stop at Romans 13:1 and merely

be subject to his authority. We must continue on to Romans 13:10, in which we are reminded that love causes no harm to its neighbor.[65]

In Logan's apartment, one-half mile from Duke's West Campus, and less than one block from North Carolina's oldest mosque,[66] he keeps a prayer closet, a personal, private space no larger than a confessional. In it he's hung an image of the American flag. It's upside-down. Stripes atop stars can be discombobulating; throws the natural order off balance. Just the sight of it will stop you in your tracks and make you (re)think what it all means. That's the point. In the legal sense, and in maritime tradition, an upside down flag is a signal of distress—the silent, universal 911. At the start of the 2007 movie *In the Valley of Elah*, military father Hank Deerfield, played by Tommy Lee Jones, gives this definition of the inverted flag: "It means we're in a lot of trouble, so come save our ass because we don't have a prayer in hell of saving ourselves."

The day Logan preached at Durham Mennonite the church printed in its bulletin a photo of the American flag upside-down. The particular image in the bulletin, same as the one in Logan's closet, is from Philadelphia's alternative Christian rock band the Psalters. (You know, Scotty Krueger, the guy who flew to Chicago with Shane in 2003 and was with him at the barbershop when his beloved dreads fell like rope to the floor.) Atop each stripe of the Psalter's upside-down flag, and framing its margins, are the words of Christ as quoted in the Gospels. The first stripe shoulders Matthew 26:52: "If you live by the sword you die by the sword." The second and third carry John 18:36 and Matthew 6:24, respectively: "My kingdom is not of this world" and "No one can serve two masters."

On that Independence Day weekend in Durham, Logan explained that true patriots are not prideful Americans who love their country so blindly that they ignore egregious conduct. True patriots are like good parents. They keep vigilant watch over their children's growth and correct their flaws, blunders, missteps, and errors. The difference is as significant as building your house (or the nation's housing market) on sand or on rock. "The Psalter's flag reminds me that in the end, the nations, even our own, will crumble around us," he said, finishing his first-ever sermon. "It has been said that in those moments, the fallen will mourn and the angels will rejoice. What will we be doing? The challenge will be to love God more than country—to have one master, but many friends."

Logan and his platoon had bunked briefly in Samarra General Hospital during Operation Baton Rouge. He waded among people killed by his country—civilian and insurgent. The dead spilled from the morgue into the hallways. He slipped in crimson puddles and stepped around piled corpses.

Understandably, he was not thrilled about our housing arrangements for the 2010 trip to Rutba—the partly reconstructed Rutba General Hospital.

7

FACE TO FACE
WITH THE ENEMY

*War is disgusting and horrific. It never leaves the people
who were involved in it. The damage is far greater
than the lists of casualties or cost in dollars. It permeates lifestyles.
It infects cultures and people and worldviews. The war is never
over for us. The fighting stops. The troops get called back.
But the war goes on for those damaged by war.*

—Jess Goodell, Iraq war veteran
assigned to Marines Mortuary
Affairs Platoon[1]

Shane and Logan cross from Jordan to Iraq in the back of an Iraqi major's Chevy pickup truck (2010). Photo credit: Jamie Moffett

2003

Then there's the "we" that's me, a former newspaper grunt and wire correspondent, dispatched from Washington to Iraq on Super Bowl Sunday 2003.[2] The run-up to war. By then, January 26, 2003, all of the major players— hawks and doves—were just going through their prewar motions, like some sort of locker-room huddle and prayer: UN weapons inspector Hans Blix was set to deliver his report on Iraq's missing WMD and plea for more time to continue the search; Bush's speechwriters were polishing a State-of-the-Union address that placed the onus for world peace in the hands of military industrialists; and Wall Street watched and waited, like children on Christmas Eve, eager to rip open the largest wrapping on the floor. "I think the market will rally once we do go into Iraq, maybe as much as a thousand points," New York stock trader Daniel Marciano told *Business Weekly*. "It's the uncertainty that's hurting the market now, and once something really happens, it will be a very positive catalyst. I'd much rather have the catalyst come from earnings, but we'll still take it."[3]

Ironically, while I waited at Dulles Airport to board my flight to the Middle East, American pop-rock band *No Doubt* performed during the Super Bowl's halftime. By then the world knew that all hell was about to be loosed on Iraq. It wasn't a matter of if—only when. Ten days later, Secretary of State Colin Powell told the UN Security Council that "leaving Saddam Hussein in possession of weapons of mass destruction for a few more months or years is *not* an option." The way he said it, with unblinking conviction, it sounded like he'd personally seen Saddam's hidden bunkers teeming with WMD. So everyone in Baghdad—including myself—braced for Raytheon's shiny new imports/ exports. No doubt they would be screaming into Iraq's capital sooner than later.

This was still several weeks before hard-core peace folk began to see funeral shrouds in the hotel drapery.

I'm neither a dove[4] nor a hawk. More of a chicken, really. I left Hotel Al Fanar for the safety of Amman in the second week of February 2003, about the same time UN employees began to pack up their Baghdad offices. I reasoned that I couldn't file prewar stories that were overly critical of Saddam from inside of Iraq, and that was absolutely true: phones were believed to be tapped; government spooks frequently hovered within earshot; email sent from the Internet cafe next door endured lags of a day or two; and almost no one local or foreign dared to even whisper the name "Saddam." To speak ill of the dictator was a capital offense in Ba'athist-ruled Iraq. But, even if there had been no obstacles, I never planned to stay. The assignment was to get in and get out; maybe a week to ten days in Iraq, tops. I wasn't supposed to plant myself (or be planted) in Baghdad.

Alongside Kathy Kelly and her merry band of peacemakers I crossed from Jordan into Iraq two days after the 2003 Super Bowl, the same day that Bush's State-of-the-Union address ("If Saddam Hussein does not fully disarm," he told Congress and the TV universe, "for the safety of our people and for the peace of the world, we will lead a coalition to disarm him"[5]) played live and on a loop in the Middle East. As dusk settled over the desert we pulled into little-known Trebil, Iraq—the westernmost entry point and customs station, notorious for shaking down foreigners for bribes. Iraqi border guards smiled weakly and ushered us into a lounge with fat, comfortable chairs and a life-sized oil painting of Saddam. They brought us sweet hot tea and turned on a small TV. A cartoon played in black and white. There was only the one channel; no options. In hindsight that seems fitting—given the grave farce Washington was directing.

There were ten of us: three journalists (photo, radio, print) blending as discretely as possible with the group of seven peace activists. I hoped that crossing into Iraq on a tourist visa rather than as credentialed news media would free me up to talk to everyday Iraqis without the shadow of Saddam's Ba'athist "minders." As expected, our Iraqi drivers/interpreters were hit up for bribes, but even after they refused to pay we were allowed to pass. At midnight our two GMC Suburbans parked outside Baghdad's Hotel Al Fanar, a crumbling eight-story boutique on the banks of the River Tigris, across the shallow, murky water from Saddam's Republican Palace. We had arrived safely. At Washington's target.

For one week I was on the ground with Kathy traveling from the sanctions-decimated neighborhoods of Baghdad to the fetid slums of Basra, 340 miles south. I had arrived in Iraq expecting government officials, and everyday Iraqis, to respond harshly to seeing someone of my persuasion—persistently pale, dishwater blondish, blue-eyed, crucifix-wearing. Anyone North American, European, or Australian would surely elicit scowls, anger, maybe violence. But the Iraqis I met—Ba'athist officials and Sunni or Shia civilians—apparently weren't so concerned with superficialities. Turns out my arms and hands were all that mattered. Extended openly and in friendship they provoked a decidedly different response than if I had been gripping an M4.

In Saddam's Iraq I suspect visitors were as safe as Saddam wanted them to be, and with war pending he probably wanted foreigners to remain unharmed—especially peacemaker foreigners lobbying Washington for peace. But on my first day in Baghdad I wandered away from Kathy and the others and, with no government minders, police, or protection in sight, I was soon lost in a crowd of Iraqis. I was at a popular weekly book fair near Baghdad's old Jewish quarter, on a road named for a bombastic tenth-century Arab poet. Al Mutanabbi Street[6] hosted a Friday ritual where Iraqis could peruse, buy, or sell used copies of magazines such as *Esquire, GQ,* and *Vogue,* and books as diverse as Agatha Christie novels, ornate hardbacks of the Qur'an, and E. L. Nagaev's *Physics of Magnetic Semiconductors.* The farther I wandered from the main thoroughfare, Al Rasheed Street, the more Al Mutanabbi narrowed into tighter and tighter clutches of Iraqis. I saw no one who resembled another person of my persistently pale, crucifix-wearing persuasion. I was alone in the ebb and flow of thousands of Iraqis living in the crosshairs and satellite coordinates of my country's weaponry. Every step invited another bump or brush, my shoulders, elbows, knees knocked against theirs. The enemy. Nods of apology—me to them and them to me—were always reciprocated, often with smiles. Through it all, from the mouth of Al Mutanabbi to its narrow opposite end, only one man laid a hand on me. It happened deep in the street's recesses, closer to the Tigris than to the main entrance. I was near a bend in the road that led away from a tea house favored by writers and poets. The man looked middle-aged, and he looked professorial in his tweed blazer and serious expression. I jerked reflexively when I felt his hand on my shoulder.

"The zipper, the zipper," he said in a thick Arabic accent.

It sounded to me like, "Da souper, da souper."

I didn't understand.

"Da *souper*," he repeated, this time pointing directly at my work satchel.

In the grind of Al Mutanabbi a pocket on my bag had come unzipped. Any deft pickpocket had easy access to a thick roll of money, exactly 34,500 Iraqi dinars in 250-dinar denominations. In the 1970s, before Saddam's long war with Iran, the invasion of Kuwait, the 1991 Persian Gulf war, and subsequent UN economic sanctions, that amount of Iraqi dinars would convert to tens of thousands of U.S. dollars. On Friday, January 31, 2003, it was worth $16.[7]

Leaving the book fair I stopped to browse a collection of books piled on the pavement like a pyre. The bookseller, an older Arab gentleman with no customers, studied me for several uncomfortable seconds before he made things even more uncomfortable. In English he asked me the question I dread most when traveling in Egypt, Jordan, Iraq, or the West Bank.

"What nationality?"

I smiled and nodded, but offered no reply, hoping he would think I didn't understand him.

He asked again. I placed a hand over my heart, a gesture of friendship and apology in much of the Middle East. I thought about faking a French accent or calling Canada my home.[8] Instead, I offered an abbreviation of the truth.

"U.S."

"U.S.?" he asked. "U.S.?"

Yes, you know, U.S. It's the nation amassing 423,998 military troops near your border. The nation that's coercing Britain to deploy 40,906 troops and squeezing Australia for a token 2,050. The nation planning to heap hundreds of thousands of tons of bombs on you. The nation that demolished your electrical grids and water treatment plants in the first Gulf War. The nation that promises to attack you so ferociously, so relentlessly, so mercilessly that you will have nowhere to hide. You know, the U.S. God bless America.

Of course, I didn't say any of that. But we both knew.

"America," I blurted, finally, putting a hand over my heart again. "I'm from America."

He seemed to notice my discomfort. He smiled and nodded as if to say, it's okay.

"Very good," he said kindly, but without smiling. "Very good then."

My wire stories leading up to the war described the decent, kind, hardworking Iraqis whose lives, livelihoods, and children were about to be thrown in front of the world's most powerful military industry. I described how Iraqi parents, similar to North American, British, and Aussie parents, similar to parents Jewish, Christian, Buddhist, Agnostic, Atheist, Hindu, and whatever, wanted the same things we all wanted: our children to grow up happy, secure, and successful. This utopia might not have been possible for all Iraqis living under Saddam's rule, but I didn't see how tons of bombs and untold numbers of Iraqi (and American) dead would do anything but terrorize a people. We were fighting terrorism with terror.

Back home, where Washington was playing to prideful American hearts and stoking fears of WMD, my wire reports were not always well received. Some letters to the editor, like one that followed on the heels of my story about Al Mutanabbi Street, were upset with me for pointing out all the wrongs committed by Americans on Iraqis without listing the wrongs committed by Saddam on his own people.[9] The writer thought I should just "stay in Iraq."[10]

One Sunday, soon after returning home to Washington, an elder of a church I attended infrequently approached me at the Sunday worship service. He's a jovial, outgoing leader of the Christian congregation, an all-around nice guy. But on this particular Sunday he didn't appear to be filled with the Spirit—unless you count fighting. "So," he said to me, staring and unsmiling, "when are you going back to report on *those* people?"

Those people would be folk like Sattar, the peace-team's driver in Baghdad, a handsome, middle-aged Iraqi father and husband who bore a strong resemblance to detective Adrian Monk of the TV show "Monk" (at the time I thought only that he looked like cabdriver Antonio Scarpacci of "Wings"). Sattar is a college-educated civil engineer fluent in English and Arabic, but he and a brother eked out livings by shuttling Western travelers back and forth between

Baghdad and Amman—the torturous twelve-hour one-way on Saddam's autobahn. On my return to Amman, when it was just Sattar and me alone for five hundred miles of conversation, I asked about the friendly people I'd met in Iraq. Specifically, I asked why the people my country was preparing to bomb into the preindustrial age had offered me food, drink, smiles, and, as best as I could tell, genuine friendship. Why, for example, had Baghdad traffic slowed or even stopped to allow me and other Westerners to cross busy Abu Nuwas Street every day outside Hotel Al Fanar. Or why they would offer up their seats at the Hotel Palestine's Internet cafe if there was nowhere else for us to sit.

"Mr. Greg," Sattar answered in perfect English, "you are in Iraq as our guest and so we welcome you and treat you like family. You are always welcome here—as a guest. But if you came to Iraq with a gun pointed at us . . ."

He paused to glance over at me, keeping two hands on the steering wheel of the GMC, his voice pleasant, his demeanor as warm as Monk's or Scarpacci's.

"Well, if you did that," he continued, hesitating and appearing unsure how best to express himself without offending me, and then evidently deciding there was no way to soften it. "Mr. Greg, I would want to kill you."

It didn't sound like the verb came naturally to him. He didn't growl it or spit it. More like a whisper, an apology. He stared straight ahead at the road when he said it . . . or confessed it.

Many of Sattar's customers were peace activists from North America and Europe, like those with Kathy's Iraq Peace Team.[11] Twenty times during the twelve-year-long economic sanctions of Iraq, Kathy had openly defied the State Department to carry food and medicine to Iraqis in need. During the first Gulf War she camped in the desert as a witness with other peace activists near the Iraq-Saudi border, and then helped coordinate relief efforts from Amman. Petite, patient, soft-spoken, with long hair and natural curls, she is deceivingly tenacious. Five-foot-two and barely one hundred pounds when I met her, she is a larger-than-life Catholic who has twice emerged from maximum- or medium-security prisons scrappier than when she was incarcerated.[12]

Citing her preferences for girlish sundresses and buckle shoes, *New Yorker* writer Jon Lee Anderson wrote of her in his 2004 book *The Fall of Baghdad*: she has "a certain Pippi Longstocking quality." And I agree, but for reasons other than her wardrobe. After interviewing Kathy in January 2003 in her simple, unadorned Chicago flat, and then meeting up with her two weeks later in Amman to travel into Iraq, I can attest to the Longstocking likeness. Similar to the fictional superhuman, Kathy's anger is not easily aroused or carelessly deployed; it's holstered for use against superpower governments and egregious offenses, like UN economic sanctions resulting in the deaths of countless children and preemptive wars resulting in the same. Also, similar to protagonists in real life and fiction, Kathy possesses an extraordinary but calm derring-do.

On the evening of the Pentagon's A-Day, moments before the bombings that silenced Wolf Blitzer's report from Kuwait, I phoned Kathy at the Al Fanar. She sounded mystically serene, despite knowing that she, Cliff, Shane, and others from Voices, CPT, and the whole of Iraq resided in the eye of a storm that had passed over Al Dora that morning. It was dark in Baghdad, and everyone knew what that meant: bombing would resume at any moment. Days earlier, after she had agreed to have her corpse shrouded in hotel drapery, she enlarged a photo of herself taken with one of her dearest Iraqi families, a widow and her nine children. In it Kathy is smiling and radiant, a resonance of peace in the face of violence. She mailed the photo to her mother in Chicago. This way, if she were to be killed, the radiant calm evident in the photo would be her mother's last image of her.

Bracing for Washington's threat of Shock and Awe, Kathy had begun a novel by Indian-born Canadian novelist Rohinton Mistry, his bestselling *Fine Balance*. Set in contemporary India, Mistry weaves a profound tale of children, outcasts, and the innocent who learn to glean hope in a culture being crippled by greed, thuggery, and corrupt politics. As Kathy explained the novel to me— with me back in Washington at one end of the spear and her having remained at the opposite and pointy end—Raytheon's exports/imports began exploding close enough that Al Fanar's walls shook.

The hotel lobby, populated a month earlier by foreign activists, journalists, and the hotel's mascot epileptic spider monkey named Coffee, was now crowded with family members of the hotel staff and the few remaining peacemakers. Peacemakers and staff—North Americans, Europeans, Australians, South Koreans, and Iraqis—had turned the musty basement into a shelter with cots, pillows, blankets, and "survival kits" (bandages, bottled water, power bars, and bags of M&Ms) crowded against the usual stock of cleaning supplies.

"Oh, it's coming now," Kelly said of the assault that would count 504 bombs on just that one night. "The bombing is beginning in earnest. There are huge explosions."

She paused and listened.

"People here are running to the shelter."

The first time I met Kathy she was living in a second-floor apartment with countless other peace activists (coming and going to and from Iraq—their numbers were too fluid to track) in the euphemistically named Uptown area of Chicago's working-class North Side.[13] This was right after New Year's Day 2003, less than a month before Kathy would take me and nine other peacemakers and journalists through the sorry muck of sanctions-decimated prewar Iraq. At the time she was fifty years old, with no reliable income; today she is approaching sixty and resides in the same apartment and the same tax bracket. None. She is on the road and out of the country more often than she is home; she accepts no salary and enjoys no predictable income. This way she has no income taxes to pay. Unlike "war-tax resisters," she considers herself a war-tax "refuser." Paying income taxes is not a matter of *resisting*, as if she were tempted to give in and pay. For her, it's simply not an option. She would return to prison first.[14] Then, as now, she lived day-to-day on get-by money doled out from online donations, personal checks, and petty cash given in support of her group's nonviolent activism. She had no checking account, savings account, retirement plan, or mortgage; no credit cards, stock portfolio, 401K, or rainy-day fund. And she had long ago made sure that there were no wages for the Internal Revenue Service or Department of the Treasury to garnish. She embodied the National War Tax Resistance Committee slogan: "If you work for peace, stop paying for war."[15]

Climbing a flight of creaky stairs and walking unnoticed through Kathy's unlocked front door in January 2003 I had stumbled headfirst into the guts of radical peace. In the months leading up to the Iraq war Kathy's apartment looked more like command central than the home of a former parochial school teacher. I counted nine, ten, and then twelve activists (moving targets always), sixteen computers, three phone lines, three beds, some castoff sofas and chairs, two fax machines, and two pint-sized dolls—President Bush and Saddam Hussein squared off wearing tiny boxing gloves. On her walls were photos of Dr. Martin Luther King, Jr.; on the fridge Mahatma Gandhi. On the gas stove, being reheated for the umpteenth time, were two platoon-sized pots of lentils and rice. Crowding the curb outside were cars parked bumper to bumper, but none were Kathy's. She didn't own a car or even a driver's license. She never had. Out front a blue Schwinn bike rested against what looked to be a gumball tree. It had a ripped seat, rusted fender, and two flat tires. That was hers.

Like many peacemakers living on scraps and the appreciation of supporters, Kathy didn't own much that she couldn't carry abroad. As war approached in 2003 that included her Sony VAIO mini-laptop and a master's in religious studies degree from Chicago Theological Seminary. Not much else.

In the early 1980s Kathy had been living a relatively normal activist life, volunteering in soup kitchens, protesting Reaganomics, and teaching religion at Chicago's St. Ignatius College Prep, a private Jesuit high school. But midway into President Reagan's first term (think tax cuts, slashed social programs, swollen national debt; massive military buildup; invasion of Grenada; funds to help El Salvador's junta government fend off an overthrow, and more funds to instigate an overthrow of Nicaragua's junta government) Kathy went to her bosses with an unusual request: Would St. Ignatius kindly and greatly reduce her salary? A 75 percent pay cut would drop her yearly income to an untaxable

$3,000. Washington and its burgeoning military would not get a penny of her teacher's salary. "I knew I didn't want to pay for weapons," she wrote decades later in a collection of essays titled *Other Lands Have Dreams: From Baghdad to Pekin Prison*.[16] "And I wasn't too keen on the CIA, the FBI, the prison systems, US intervention in Central America, and the almost complete failure of any governmental system to serve needy neighbors, many of them desperate, in Uptown.... [It] was one of the simplest decisions I've ever made and one of the easiest decisions to maintain."

The transformation from parochial school teacher to full-time radical activist had begun, in part, with her marriage in 1982 to social justice rock star Karl Meyer, a writer, editor, and overall sparkplug for the Chicago branch of the Catholic Worker Movement. Meyer argued that Washington forced Americans to collaborate in its corporate-driven warmongering in the same way that the Roman Empire had built its dominance—through heavy-handed conscription of soldiers and taxes. Like Logan's or those of Gavrilis and his Special Forces, the hands of every American taxpayer were bloodstained. In the 1960s his writings in the *Catholic Worker* newspaper had inspired a legion of war-tax resisters, and in a 1969 manifesto about beating the tax system, he upped the ante with Uncle Sam. He explained to readers how best to cheat the IRS: claim extra dependents on Form W-4.[17] It had worked for him. *Had*. Two years later he was convicted of tax evasion and would eventually serve nine months in federal prison. Similar to Kathy, it wouldn't be the first (or last) time he emerged from lockup with a stronger conviction than the one that sent him.[18]

Meyer's willingness to live impoverished, imprisoned, and in passionate cause with social justice soon became legend in the relatively small community of American pacifists and peacemakers. A veritable protégé of a saint, Meyer, at the age of twenty, had been groomed by and arrested with the revered cofounder of the Catholic Worker Movement, Dorothy Day.[19] In spite of the breathless wails of civil defense air-raid drills (or, rather, because of them) that shooed Americans old and young into fallout shelters, school basements, and beneath school desks, Day and her band of Christian anarchists would sit on park benches in defiance of what they saw as government propaganda. To them it was just one more lie in Washington's Red Scare anticommunist crusade. In civil defense public awareness commercials and even in a nine-minute children's film starring a frightened bowtie-wearing cartoon turtle named Bert,[20] Americans were bombarded with the idea that a nuclear attack was imminent and that they should be fearful of anything, anyone that didn't blend with, say, a Norman Rockwell *Boys' Life* magazine cover. In the 1950s civil defense film *Duck and Cover*, Bert the Turtle dives into his shell to escape an exploding stick of dynamite. He refuses to come back out. The accompanying children's song, composed in part by the same duo that collaborated on the popular "See the

USA in your Chevrolet" jingle, instructed American schoolchildren to remain alert and be ready at all times for an atomic attack:

> *There was a turtle by the name of Bert*
> *and Bert the turtle was very alert;*
> *when danger threatened him he never got hurt*
> *he knew just what to do*
> *He'd duck!*
> *And cover!*
> *Duck!*
> *And cover!*
> *He did what we all must learn to do . . .*
> *Duck, and cover!*

A children's comic book starring the same preppy reptile with the same stark warning and elementary ideas of self-defense was circulated by the Federal Civil Defense Administration to grade schools nationwide. "The atomic bomb is a *new* danger," it read, emphasizing in bold the novelty of a global threat the United States had unleashed seven years earlier.[21] "Things will be knocked down all over town, and, as with a big wind, they are blown through the air. . . . So, like Bert, you duck to avoid the things flying through the air."

As sturdy as they were, no school basement or Theo. Kundtz Company wood-grain and cast-iron desk was likely to shield students from nuclear explosion and radioactive fallout. Hiroshima and Nagasaki testified to that. At or near ground zero you can duck and cover or stand and stretch; it won't matter which. Your fate is sealed. Washington knew it, too.[22] In Studs Turkel's 2003 book about activist heroes, *Hope Dies Last*, Kathy explains the broader message of Meyer's and Day's park-bench sit outs: "What they were saying is there is no shelter from nuclear bombs, that the best way to find security was to stop paying for these weapons."[23]

Moments before Meyer's first protest in 1957 in New York City, resulting in his inaugural jailing, Dorothy Day schooled him on the Catholic Workers' modus operandi: "We plead guilty. And we don't take bail."[24] He took her words to heart and served a month for civil disobedience in juvenile lockup on New York's Rikers Island—a watershed moment in his rebellious life, he later recalled.[25] That month in Rikers jail and the time spent at Day's side would change Meyer from a liberal with pacifist leanings into a radical pacifist committed to nonviolent combat. Even as the Cold War between Marxists and capitalists fanned a collective fear that would ultimately blur (some say blind) the morals of American politicians and electorates, it produced a profound sense of clarity for the peace movement. In the decades bridging Meyer's first arrest and Kathy's introduction in 1981 to full-time peacemaking—through wars in

Vietnam and Korea, and CIA-backed revolutions, counterrevolutions, coups, wars, and assassinations in places such as Brazil (beginning in 1964), Congo (1965), Greece (1967), Laos (1968), Cambodia (1970), Bolivia (1971), Chile (1973), Argentina (1975), Afghanistan (1979), El Salvador (1980), and Nicaragua (1980)—military industrialists would inadvertently swell the ranks of radical activism. If a butterfly flapping its wings in Rio could theoretically alter weather patterns in Chicago, imagine the fallout from the Manhattan Project, Agent Orange, napalm, the Contras, School of the Americas, etc.

The Cold War seeded change. It still does.

The Dorothy-Day throw-yourself-on-the-grenade style of social justice spread from North America to Europe and Asia and beyond, armies of converts strengthened in size and conviction. Nonviolence turned aggressive. The Catholic Worker belief that every action (or inaction) affects everything and everyone with its infinite consequences good and bad became a call to engage. To act.

Dorothy Day preached personal responsibility.[26] That is, the only remedy to abject poverty and a raging brand of militarism being fed a steady diet of capitalist greed is a solution that shocks the status quo. It makes comfortable folk like me uncomfortable. In effect, Day taught us that the remedy is you. And me. Nonviolent peacemaking can work only if it is personal and participatory. People like Kathy, Shane, Cliff, and Weldon have to be willing to die for it. Even if it means sending Mom an enlarged, smiling portrait of yourself right after you choose drapes for your shroud.

Thus said Dorothy Day, Leo Tolstoy, Henry David Thoreau, Gandhi, Dr. King, and the Sermon on the Mount,[27] to name a few. Any Day-Tolstoy-Thoreau-Gandhi-King-Christ apostle will tell you that the antidote to the combustible coupling of Washington and Wall Street—to the unwarranted influence of the "military-congressional-industrial complex" referenced in the first drafts of President Eisenhower's farewell address[28]—rises from the yeast of long-enduring personal sacrifice. This includes poverty and prison. Even death.

Kathy's first of more than fifty arrests came at Meyer's side and urging during a hastily organized protest opposing President Carter's plan in 1980 to reinstate the military draft. She knew the drill. Plead guilty, no bail. As Chicago police arrested them, Meyer noticed Kathy trembling; he thought the rookie was afraid. She was. Many years later she recalled how she was completely and utterly frightened during her maiden handcuffing. But not of the police or jail. "I was terrified of saying something stupid in front of him!" she said of Meyer.[29]

Like Kathy, Meyer's demeanor and appearance (small, professorial, rimmed glasses, trimmed gray beard) belied his grit. For decades, the mild-mannered peace hero had been a marked man for Washington. Dating to at least 1960, the FBI had a file that described Meyer as "a pacifist with a martyr complex."[30]

Meyer explained that he couldn't be a martyr, per se, because he didn't personally believe humans were called to lay down their lives and die for one another. "But we are called to live our lives with and for each other—and our lives will be richer for that," he explained several months before the terrorism of 9/11.[31] "I might have been a pacifist with a Gandhi complex, or maybe a messiah complex. But not a martyr complex."[32]

If Reaganomics helped spark Kathy's activism, Reagan's foreign policy would ignite it. Early in Reagan's second term Kathy traveled to Nicaragua on a professional development grant from the Jesuits. It was at the height of the war between Nicaragua's Marxist Sandinistas, which five years earlier had overthrown the U.S.-backed Nicaraguan dictator Anastasio Somoza and the CIA-trained counterrevolutionaries (or Contras) who were attempting to retake the government. Two decades removed from the Cuban Missile Crisis and its scary collaboration between Cuba and the Soviet Union, Washington wanted to eliminate ties between Nicaragua's new socialist junta government (the Sandinista National Liberation Front) and Cuban President Fidel Castro.

During Kathy's seven weeks in Central America, Nicaraguans were torn between the socialist government of the Sandinistas (it was delivering on promises of a more equitable economy and improved literacy rates)[33] and the suspect promises of democracy tied to the violent Contras backed by Washington and the Mafioso Somoza dynasty. Midway into her visit, Kathy traveled to a town in a remote valley of Nicaragua's neglected northwest. San Juan de Limay is a poor village near the forested mountain border with Honduras, fifteen miles as the crow flies—or as the Contras hiked. Its population of ten thousand had no running water, only sporadic electricity, and the farmers had to rely on arid land for crops of coffee beans, corn, potatoes, and squash. Most of the year the only road leading into or away from the village was dusty, spine-jarring, narrow, and frequently deadly. The remainder of the year, during the rainy season, it was muddy, and even more narrow and deadly. The closest Nicaraguan city, Esteli (pop. 40,000), was a Sandinista stronghold that took two to three hours to reach by bus.[34] Hemmed in by mountains that ascended to 1,400 meters; stranded by an unpaved road and the confluence of rivers Queso and Negro, the quiet, humble villagers of San Juan de Limay found themselves trapped in the crossfire between the Sandinistas' socialism and Western-styled democracy.

In 1985 the Sandinistas began fending off the Contras with Soviet-made Mi-24 Hind gunships, heightening Reagan's fear that socialism might grow in the fertile poverty of Central America and break Washington's grip on the Americas. Two decades removed from the Bay of Pigs debacle and the apocalyptic near-miss of the Cuban Missile Crisis, Congress reversed its resolve to stop funding the murderous Contras and staked Reagan for another $27 million. With winks and smiles the legalese was tweaked to read "humanitarian assistance," but both sides of the aisle knew that Americans were anteing up for more combat, not charity.[35] Reagan's national security adviser, Robert C. McFarlane, made no attempt to disguise the motive. Washington would continue to assist the Contras until Nicaragua established a Western-style democracy, he declared. "There is the possibility that . . . the home-grown strength of the opposition [the Contras] and the persistent bloody-mindedness of the [Sandinista] government combine to give us a real chance [for victory] there."[36]

Two years earlier the CIA had given to Contra leaders a ninety-page manual published in Spanish and titled *Operaciones Sicológicas en Guerra de Guerrillas* ("Psychological Operations in Guerilla Warfare"). Its preface read as if the Christian Crusades were ongoing and burning through Central America: "This book is a manual for the training of guerrillas in psychological operations, and its application to the concrete case of the Christian and democratic crusade being waged in Nicaragua by the Freedom Commandos. Welcome!"[37]

In a PR campaign intended to portray the Contras as heroic defenders of Western capitalism and democracy, the Reagan administration referred to them as "freedom fighters." Over and over again, freedom fighters. As if repeating something false would somehow make it true. Speaking to thousands of political conservatives at the annual Conservative Political Action Conference (CPAC) on March 1, 1985, President Reagan had even described the Contras as "the moral equal of our founding fathers and the brave men and women of the French resistance."[38]

The 64-page CIA manual taught the Contras how best to intimidate, occupy, and hold hostage entire towns that were considered "neutral or relatively passive in the conflict." It endorsed the "selective use of violence" against Sandinista judges, police, and other officials as long as the targets were unpopular with the locals. Kidnapping and ambushes were okay, too. But to win the hearts and minds of peasant locals, the CIA coached the Contras on how best to manipulate language—use oratorical devices such as strong alliteration and repetition with religious and patriotic mottos (e.g., "God, Homeland, and Country") and slogans (e.g., "freedom for the poor, freedom for the rich, freedom for all").[39]

In anticipation of some Nicaraguans reacting doubtfully to the easy promises of American-made freedom, democracy, capitalism, wealth, etc., the CIA crafted a preemptive response for the Contras to deploy. Among Washington's many propaganda tools is a rhetorical device known as prolepsis. Successful politicians (and a certain Secretary of Defense[40]) are expert at using it. It works like this: just before a troublesome question or objection is raised, you raise the question or objection yourself. Theoretically, this enables the target of the objection/question to frame it in a favorable way—and then to promptly dismiss it. It fits with the hawkish belief that the best defense is a good offense. So the

CIA instructed the Contras to follow Washington's lead: invoke the Almighty when the heroic narrative of war is challenged. The manual advised the Contras to stay ahead of the doubters by shouting this into the public square: "Some will think [these things we offer] are only promises; they will say, 'Others said the same thing.' But no, we are different, we are Christians, we consider God a witness to our words."[41]

At that same time that the CIA manual was being handed around, Scottish lawyer Paul Laverty roamed the country as a human rights observer for a Nicaraguan NGO. His job was to travel to the alleged scenes of war crimes and attempt to corroborate eyewitness accounts. In the summer of 1985, just weeks after Congress approved $27 million in "humanitarian assistance"[42] for the Contras and with Kathy in San Juan de Limay, Laverty published the incidents that he had personally corroborated.[43] Quoting verbatim from his field notes and journals, he reported:

- In my first week in Nicaragua the Contras assassinated seven children, all under the age of 11. In my last week in Esteli—a northern town—I counted 18 coffins lined up outside the church, all road and farm workers, three of whom had been decapitated.
- April 4 [1985] I spoke with Ephraim today [a nurse in the hospital in Esteli]. He had a terrible day: the atrocities of the Contras are almost beyond comprehension. He had examined some of the corpses of youngsters brought in from San Juan de Limay. An 18-year-old had been castrated and his genitals stuffed in his throat. His eyes had been burned with battery acid, most of his teeth removed by a bayonet, and his tongue cut out. They left him that way to die."
- February 2 [1985]: I chatted with Laura Sanchez, a daughter of one of the Co-operative workers who explained how her uncle, aunt and four cousins were massacred. Each had their eyes pulled out, ears cut off, and intestines smeared against the walls of their farm. Laura is 17 years of age, a catechist in the Catholic Church and a member of the women's militia.

One month earlier Reagan had invoked the White House equivalent of God: an executive order. With it he forced a total U.S. economic embargo of Nicaragua until specific demands were met. In hypocrisy so over-the-top ridiculous that only a parent, a Hollywood-star president, or a third-world dictator could say it with a straight face, Reagan told the newly and freely elected[44] Sandinista National Liberation Front exactly how to behave:[45]

- Halt its export of armed insurrection, terrorism, and subversion in neighboring countries

- Stop its massive arms buildup and help restore the regional military balance
- End its extensive military relationship with Cuba and the Soviet bloc and remove their military personnel
- Respect, in law and in practice, democratic pluralism and observance of full political and human rights in Nicaragua

Emboldened by his landslide reelection, Reagan again became the Contras' most powerful lobbyist early in his second term. This time he played it straight: U.S. taxpayer money would be used for military aid to the Contras; not humanitarian aid. Reagan's "freedom fighters" were losing the war against President Ortega's leftist military and needed modern weaponry, not the vintage weapons of Iran-Contra infamy. Kalashnikov AKM assault rifles, German-type G3 assault rifles, Russian-made Kord 12.7 mm machine guns, RPG-7 rocket launchers, and SA-7 portable surface-to-air missiles, all the hand-me-downs that had been routed through the back channels, were not adequate.[46] In a joint letter to Reagan, two GOP leaders encouraged the president to back the Contras more mightily than before. House minority leader Rep. Robert H. Michel of Illinois and House Republican Policy Committee chairman Rep. Dick Cheney of Wyoming wrote to Reagan: "The most dedicated freedom fighters in the world cannot fight Soviet-made MI-24 helicopters with 'humanitarian' supplies of boots and bandages. The contras need a substantial amount of military assistance now."[47]

Foreign ministers from Colombia, Mexico, Panama, Venezuela, Argentina, Brazil, Uruguay, and Peru all asked the Reagan administration to stop aiding the Contras in exchange for an agreement from the Sandinistas to liberalize their policies.[48] Washington refused. A month later, beginning in March 1986, Reagan stepped up his campaign for Contra military aid by fanning American fears about "communist danger"[49] and predicting that a Contra defeat would create "a refuge for terrorism" in Nicaragua. According to Kathy, Reverend Jean Loison, Michael Glennon, Paul Laverty, the Americas Watch, and the esteemed judges of the World Court, that refuge had already been created. By Washington. Nicaragua and the adjoining hills of Honduras housed CIA-trained terrorists.

Lobbying Congress and the U.S. electorate for more Contra aid, Reagan cast the fight as a historical moment for freedom fighters and for freedom overall. Wooing some two hundred supporters[50] in the Executive Office Building on a sunny Monday morning, March 10, 1986, he sounded more charming than an Amway salesman:

"The importance of this moment cannot be underestimated," he said of the Contras fight for democracy. "Think what signal we'll be sending to the rest of the world when and if this aid to the freedom fighters in Nicaragua is passed. And wouldn't it be wonderful to someday see in Nicaragua the restoration of the democratic dream, to see in downtown Managua celebrations similar to those that we've seen recently in Queen's Park, Manila, and Port-au-Prince, Haiti. . . . I think it's there for the asking, and so, too, is the moral obligation."[51]

Three months later, one day before the World Court ruled that Washington had violated international law with its military backing of the Contras and should pay reparations, the House of Representatives approved Reagan's request for $100 million—$70 million in military aid; $30 million in nonlethal "humanitarian" assistance—for Nicaragua's freedom fighters. Approval from the Republican-controlled Senate was a mere formality.

Reagan, in Las Vegas for a GOP fundraiser when he received the news, responded jubilantly: "We can be proud that we as a people have embraced the struggle of the freedom fighters of Nicaragua. Today, their cause is our cause."[52]

In the spring of 2002, four months after Bush had defined for the world its Axis of Evil—Iraq, Iran, and North Korea—the born-again Christian and president began a European tour to drum up support (fiscal and physical) for the Iraq invasion.

Meanwhile, Muslim leaders were attempting to bring saner minds to the table. In contrast, Bush sounded almost rabid.

On May 20, 2002, seven months after the 9/11 terrorist attacks, the Cairo Marriott (having removed the American flag) hosted the annual World Islamic Conference.[53] Muslim leaders from sixty-five nations[54] attended the conference's opening address, given by Egyptian Prime Minister Atef Ebeid, who read a message from now-deposed Egyptian president Hosni Mubarak. In it Mubarak asked Islamic leaders to tone down their rhetoric toward the West and Israel, to please choose their words more carefully.[55] Mubarak, a controversially elected leader known more for brass-knuckled governance than gentle diplomacy, was, in effect, urging Islam to turn the other cheek—"to shed light on common denominators between the different religions and to spread a culture of peace among emerging generations."[56] Two nights later, in a speech aired nationally on Egyptian TV, Mubarak reiterated Islam's message of pluralism. This time he delivered it personally: "Islam acknowledges the right of every human being, whatever his religious or cultural background, to hold different opinions and to enjoy respect from others.[57] . . . Our differences with others in religion, culture and principles do not imply enmity to others."[58]

Same day, different continent, President Bush marched into Germany hell-bent on inciting fear. He needed Washington's European allies for the American-led "War on Terror." Or wars, plural. First stop: Berlin. At the same time that Mubarak and the World Islamic Conference were pleading with Muslims to be more thoughtful and less provocative, Bush was 1,800 miles away, closer to the frigid Baltic Sea than to Egypt's Mediterranean shore, attempting to light fires.

"Our generation faces new and grave threats to liberty, to the safety of our people, and to civilization itself," he told the German Bundestag, which was ordered back from a parliamentary break to hear Bush speak. "We face an aggressive force that glorifies death, that targets the innocent, and seeks the means to matter—murder on a massive scale."[59]

From Berlin to Moscow to Paris to Rome his language and tone sounded as apocalyptic as a tent preacher's. This was no time to mince words. European lawmakers should cork their wine and face the sober truth: Washington's effort to root out global terror needed more money, more militaries, more muscle. It required the yoke of two Christian-majority continents.

He didn't use the verbatim language of the Crusades, but it didn't take much tuning to hear it. Speaking from the well of Berlin's Reichstag building, a place gutted in 1933 by an act of arson that helped to solidify the Nazi Party's authoritative rule,[60] he said, "Together, Europe and the United States have the creative genius, the economic power, the moral heritage[61] and the democratic vision to protect our liberty and to advance our cause of peace."[62]

He was heckled by the German lawmakers. A few from the Party of Democratic Socialism unfurled a banner telling Bush to "Stop Your Wars." At the same time, members of Germany's conservative Christian Democrats party shouted from across the chamber demanding that the demonstrators be removed.[63]

None of this would stop Bush, though. He was on a roll.

"Those who seek missiles and terrible weapons are also familiar with the map of Europe," he continued. "Like the threats of another era, this threat cannot be appeased or cannot be ignored. By being patient, relentless and resolute, we will defeat the enemies of freedom. By remaining united . . ."[64]

He paused briefly until the ongoing protest and counterprotest calmed down, and when he continued a few members of parliament stood and walked out.[65]

"By remaining united, we are meeting—we are meeting modern threats with the greatest resources of wealth and will ever assembled by free nations. Together, Europe and the United States have the creative genius, the economic power, the moral heritage, and the democratic vision to protect our liberty and to advance our cause of peace."[66]

Much of the world along with tens of thousands of Germans protesting Bush's visit to Berlin already knew the Pentagon's objective: Invade Iraq.[67]

From the tiny balcony of my room at Hotel Al Fanar I argued for war. I probably sounded like a hawk, like Reagan, and I wasn't even playing the role of devil's advocate. Although I didn't think it was right for the United States to invade an Arab nation unprovoked, or for American and British soldiers to die for whatever it was that Washington was pursuing (oil reserves, Israeli security, more free markets, caches of WMD), I thought that the Iraqis I'd met from Baghdad to Basra deserved something other than the dictator. I didn't dare say his name. Or even the word "dictator." Those facts alone spoke volumes about the need for change, I whispered. Nobody in Iraq could have a candid conversation about Iraqi politics. No one could even discuss candidly why it was important to be able to discuss politics candidly. Criticism of Saddam or his Ba'athist cronies was a capital offense. To have this conversation, photojournalist Thorne Anderson and I stood on a balcony of suspect building-code compliance five stories above Abu Nuwas Street. Our hope was that the traffic below would muffle our words. Seriously. Spooks, bugs, and phone taps were everywhere in Saddam's Iraq.

Thorne was born in Montgomery, Alabama, and grew up the son of a Presbyterian minister in Cabot, Arkansas, a suburb of Little Rock. But he had none of the Southern drawl that Shane and I shared. At the time he resided in Serbia.[68] But as a freelancer for *Time, Newsweek, Los Angeles Times*, the *New York Times*, the *Boston Globe, Toronto Globe,* London's *Guardian,* and, during my time in Iraq, the Washington bureau for Gannett News Service and *USA Today*, he lived nonstop on the world's front lines and for its front pages. For several years he had been based in the Balkans photographing the consequences of war and conflict on civilians. From Yugoslavia, Bosnia, Macedonia, Albania, and Bulgaria to Tunisia, Tajikistan, Pakistan, Afghanistan, Israel, the Palestinian territories, and, now, Iraq, he had photographed the sort of violence that family-friendly newspapers frequently filter. Blood and gore scare the children and will spoil an otherwise good breakfast.

Like Iraq Peace Team member Charles Liteky, a Vietnam War veteran and the first Army chaplain awarded the Congressional Medal of Honor for valor in combat, Thorne had seen enough "civilian casualties" and "collateral damage" to appreciate what was at stake in Iraq. Euphemisms can't mask the reality of it for anyone who knows firsthand that there are no words—English, Arabic, or Hebrew—to describe war's carnage. It's ineffable. And it's one reason why combat veterans return home reluctant to discuss their nightmares with civilians who don't have a clue. It's also why, as Americans bounced to *No Doubt's* "Just a Girl" and cheered lead singer Gwen Stefani's halftime military salute, Thorne, age thirty-six, was en route to the Middle East, and Liteky, exactly twice Thorne's age, was packing to go.

Thirty-six years earlier, in a jungle of South Vietnam, Captain Liteky (aka

Father Angelo Liteky, his Roman Catholic ordination name) was helping search for a Vietcong mortar site when his battalion was ambushed. Machine guns clattered, rocket-propelled grenades streaked from the trees, claymore mines fired steel balls through the air and into flesh. Soldiers dropped screaming.[69] Liteky tried to help a young medic who had one leg blown to gristle and bone, carrying him thirty yards to an evacuation area, and then returning to retrieve another soldier.[70] And then another and another and another. According to Army reports submitted to Congress, the wounded eventually became too heavy to carry so Liteky flipped onto his back in the mud, pulled the men on top of him, and crawled backward under gunfire using his elbows and heels. By the end of the day, December 6, 1967, Father Angelo Liteky[71] had rescued twenty soldiers and administered last rites to several others. "At one point," writes Edward F. Murphy in *Vietnam Medal of Honor Heroes*, "after Father Liteky had given the Last Rites to a man who had a huge hole in his back, he came upon an abandoned M-16. He picked it up. For a moment he was ready to use it to defend the wounded, but then he thought better of it. If a priest is going to [die] today, he told himself, they won't find a rifle on him."[72]

One year later, in a White House ceremony, President Lyndon Johnson presented Liteky with the Congressional Medal of Honor. Eighteen years later, about one month after the House of Representatives caved to Reagan's pressure and approved an extra $100 million for Nicaragua's "freedom fighters," Liteky returned to Washington. He put the nation's highest military honor in a large manila envelope with a note explaining why he was renouncing it and its lifetime tax-free monthly stipend (amounting to more than $12,000 annually today), and he placed it at the base of the Vietnam Memorial. At six-foot-one, he looked gaunt, starving. For more than six weeks he and three other combat veterans had fasted in the nation's capital in protest of Reagan's Central American policies. "I find it ironic that conscience calls me to renounce the Congressional Medal of Honor for the same basic reason I received it—trying to save lives," he told reporters at the Capitol steps. But "this time the lives are not young Americans, at least not yet. The lives are those of Central Americans of all ages: men, women, vulnerable innocents of the conflict."[73]

Waiting in Baghdad for the 2003 invasion to begin Liteky sounded as calm and serene as Kathy had on the second night of the war. When the Ba'athist government extended his tourist visa on March 12, 2003, enabling him to remain for the war, he immediately phoned his favorite ex-nun. She was the person who three decades earlier had encouraged him to invest himself in social justice and, later, to go to Nicaragua to see firsthand the terror that Washington was seeding in the guise of freedom.[74] She was his wife, Judy Balch Liteky, a nun-turned-math professor. After telling Judy that the Ba'athists were going to allow him to remain in Baghdad, they continued talking across eleven time zones for forty minutes—twice saying goodbye and both times unable to hang up. Every morning since arriving in Baghdad in late February Liteky had phoned Judy at home in San Francisco, and with each successive call it had become more difficult to hang up. "I don't have a death wish," Liteky told me one week before the start of war. "I have everything to live for. I have a wonderful wife and a wonderful life back home." The day his tourist visa was extended Judy posted a question on the rear bumper of her car, and then went to work as usual at San Mateo County (California) Community College. "Attack Iraq? No," her new bumper sticker read.

Liteky knew how scary war could be, and he expected Shock and Awe to be insanely frightening. He knew the earth would shake and houses would fall dark and children would scream themselves hoarse. It's precisely why he was excited when he phoned Judy with the "good news" that he would be staying in Baghdad. "I'm here because I hear the children cry," he explained. "In my mind I imagine the bombing and the noise and the windows shattering and something coming down from the ceiling and children looking up and parents grabbing them and fear being transferred from parents to children."

Set by the door of Liteky's room at Hotel Al Fanar was a "crash kit" the size of carry-on luggage. It was packed neatly with bandages, antibiotics, water-purification tablets, three liters of water, dried fruit, canned tuna, biscuits, power bars, and a shortwave radio. Liteky planned to ride out the bombings in Baghdad's Orphanage of the Sisters of Mother Teresa, a twelve-year-old orphanage filled with Iraqi kids. Knowing war as only a combat veteran and Medal of Honor winner could, he said he felt compelled to at least try to quell the inevitable trembling of children. "The most beautiful thing that can happen for me is if I am permitted to be at the orphanage," he said. "At least I could pick the children up, hold them, and try to let my calm and love transfer to them."

On the balcony with traffic teeming below us, I explained to Thorne my just-war theory. It did not include American soldiers marching on Baghdad. The atrocities of Saddam and his regime were scores that needed to be settled by Iraqis and their Arab neighbors. Similar to the Shia uprising in 1991, after the first Gulf War, when Iraqis were progressing from Basra toward Baghdad and were winning the day. Washington had intruded there too. President George H. W. Bush turned a blind eye when Saddam's gunships took flight in defiance of the UN no-fly-zone and quashed the rebellion.

Thorne explained that he could see nothing good coming from war. Especially a preemptive war, a war of choice. Innocent men, women, and children would die; thousands, tens of thousands, more. No one knew for sure. The UN had predicted the deaths of 100,000 civilians.

The previous week, before Hans Von Sponeck, a former assistant secretary-general of the UN in charge of humanitarian affairs in Iraq, had left Baghdad, he scanned Abu Nuwas Street and told me solemnly, "Many of the people who walk the streets of Baghdad today will not be walking the streets of Baghdad after the war. This enormous price that the Iraqi people would have to pay in order to have regime change is totally unacceptable."

Like Liteky, Thorne planned to ride the storm out in Baghdad. In a way, you might say he had Logan's dream job: going into combat unarmed. In an email Thorne had informed his family of his intentions, and he expected some preaching from his minister father, maybe some pleas to reconsider and to use the common sense that God had given him.

Instead, the Reverend Eade Anderson was succinct in his reply.

"I've always said life shouldn't be wasted on the small things. Love, Dad."

8

BRAVEHEART

When we Christians behave badly, or fail to behave well,
we are making Christianity unbelievable to the outside world.
—C.S. Lewis, *Mere Christianity*[1]

A wall outside a Rutba primary school reads: "My religion teaches me. My prayers guide me. I must not steal at all. There is a God who provides." Photo credit: Jamie Moffett

2010

Seven years after their taxi flipped into a ditch, Shane, Cliff, and Weldon met up again in Amman, each flying separately into the cosmopolitan capital for Muslim-majority Jordan. Their rendezvous and return to Iraq would

90

begin, ironically, at a hotel named for the first wife of ancient Egypt's King Akhenaten, a rebel pharaoh known for defying his day's status quo—the religious and political establishments of the Eighteenth Dynasty.[2] The Nefertiti Hotel, a go-to in Amman for Christian Peacemaker Teams (CPT), is another one of those peacemaker mom-and-pop one-stars that aspires to be more. And in many ways it already is: It's more humble, more personal, more accommodating, more friendly, more threadbare and jerry-rigged than any multistar I've slept in. But at a nightly rate of $14 for a room warmed in January by an oscillating heater fan attached to a duct-taped extension cord stretched to a hallway outlet, it's ideal for the famously frugal peacemaker.

Full-time CPT members and many other peacemakers, including Shane, Weldon, and Cliff, take vows of poverty and live on stipends that keep them close to the U.S. poverty line.[3] Too close for comfort. Literally. Defined by the Department of Labor they could be among the ten million Americans counted by the census as "working poor."[4] Most social justice activists I've met during my reports from Baghdad to Bangkok—whether it's about the war on wars, war on sex trafficking, war on poverty, etc.—work tirelessly, have bachelor's or master's degrees, speak two or more languages, and travel to and/or reside in the world's troubled spots. Yet they enjoy almost no disposable income or material wealth. They live "poor" by their own jolly defiant choice. But observing them, interviewing them, going into third-world slums and "enemy" territories to hang with them for days and weeks at a time, you would never suspect it. The poverty, that is. It's not like they lack for anything. Nothing in the spirit sags. Underfunded, unheralded, and constantly outgunned by the influence of K Street, Wall Street, Washington, the Pentagon, Raytheon, and the rest of the moneyed lot, their buoyancy is unsupported by current-day circumstances. That, in itself, is a peculiar brand of defiance.

On that chill Jordan night when the Nefertiti's custodian offered an oscillating heater fan and a frighteningly frayed extension cord, they responded with smiles and multiple thank-yous. It was as if he had tucked chocolates under our emaciated pillows. The next morning when the Nefertiti's shower was cooler than the lobby's offering of tepid Nescafe or the day's high temperature (59°F), there wasn't one syllable of peacemaker complaint. Other than tea or coffee (instant and tepid is fine) and broadband or wireless (somewhere nearby works fine), the singularly focused peacemaker shuns comforts and amenities.[5] Honestly, in that way I dread traveling with them.[6] It's as if hot water and fluffy pillows are traps. Heaven forbid they should sleep late or linger in the privy. Mom-and-pop one-stars might be an economic necessity, given the self-imposed poverty and all, but I suspect they are also badges of honor—the social justice rebuke of our status quo.

After Ali Shalal Al Qaissi (aka Haj Ali) warned Sami to keep us away from Rutba in the spring of 2009, our return to Iraq was recast for January 2010. If an ocean's current is strong and unpredictable you toe the high-water mark and wait for things to calm. Ditto for the desert. We timed our sprint into Al Anbar for the ebb in fighting. With provincial elections planned and postponed, planned and postponed, Shia, Sunni, and the insurgency were jockeying for power. Iraq was like the United States during an election year, except instead of slinging mud they lobbed grenades. We hoped to get in and out of Rutba quickly, unannounced, and, for the most part, unnoticed except by a dozen or fewer locals. We would only be there long enough for Shane, Cliff, and Weldon to have a reunion with Rutba's Good Samaritans, and to get updates on how the embattled desert town was faring in the "new" Iraq.

That was our plan. But like a surcharge added onto any trip to Iraq, you plan for your plans to change. It's a given.

Rushing through New York's JFK Airport toward my January 10, 2010, Royal Jordanian flight into Amman I exchanged glances, a curious stare, and then a double-take with another traveler racing through Terminal Four. We were headed in opposite directions toward our respective airlines. He bounced toward Delta with a spring in each step, on the balls of his feet, and vaguely smiling, like a man lost and comfortable in his thoughts. Two Caucasians, we were a decided minority in crowded Terminal Four—JFK's dock that night for flights headed to the Middle East.

"Weldon?"

"Greg?"

We hadn't realized that our itineraries intersected; his originating in Seattle, mine near Washington, DC.

Weldon is smallish, bookish, and in his khakis, button-ups, turtlenecks, and near-perpetual cheer, he comes across like an activist earnest in his beliefs, bold in his peacemaking, and slightly more domesticated than the full-time, globe-trotting, war-zone peace activists. More Rick Moranis than Harrison Ford. But as a Mennonite pastor with a vow of poverty and a church and charity in Seattle's lower-income, higher-crime northeast, I knew there was grit behind the smile. I knew even before I read his personal journals from wartime Iraq. Doubly so afterward.

Writing at 8:45 p.m. on March 25, 2003, his first night in Baghdad: "I am deeply aware at any second we could hear terrifying bombing even in our building. The next moment could be the end—the beginning of life. In Christ we shall live."

The following night American bombs rattled the walls of room 101 at the Al Dar Hotel and sent happy-go-lucky Weldon screaming. Not in fear, or even out loud, but in quiet anger. "I felt a wave of outrage for yet another round of victims," he wrote in his journal. "In [silent] prayer I screamed at God and our nation's leaders to stop the horror, the evil, the killing, the sin of the nation and the church inflicted on the Iraqi people."

Just five hours earlier, with war flashing on the outskirts of Baghdad, he had penned, "Does one ever get used to hearing bombs in the distance? Does one become callous? Almost as callous as [people] sending bombs [from] the other side of the world. Does it take the moment of looking death in the face myself or the one beside me to transform me forever. Here my life has ended: Life as I knew it is over."

Weldon and I had met twice the previous year to discuss the 2010 return to Rutba: once at his Seattle Mennonite Church, located in a sketchy area of Seattle's Lake City; a year later, at a diner near Shane's charity and row house in a sketchy area of Philadelphia. Define sketchy? After Shane survived the bombing of Baghdad and the end-over-end crash on Iraq's Highway 1, he returned home to Philly where he was mugged in his Kensington neighborhood. His jaw broken, he couldn't chew or talk above a whisper.[7] That's my definition of sketchy. This, too: In its list of "Top 10 Drug Corners," the *Philadelphia Weekly* ranks the corner of Kensington and East Somerset streets (less than a mile from Shane's home) No. 1. As recently as fall 2011, row houses in and around Shane's home and Simple Way charity could be bought for less than the price of a new Toyota van. So, yeah, sketchy. Life on the margins. Social justice is the umbrella cause, and like revolutionary slum priests, nuns, and genuinely righteous nonprofits—not to mention a Jewish man called Jesus of Nazareth—many peace activists pitch their tents under the umbrella, which is downstream from the mainstream.

The same day that Weldon and I bumped into each other at JFK, Cliff rode the South Shore Line train out of Hammond, Indiana, where he had been helping Brethren Disaster Ministries repair flood damage, to Chicago's L train and into O'Hare Airport. Accepting the cheapest and most unpopular fare (for Americans, at least) between the Midwest and Middle East, he flew Turkish Airlines into Damascus, Syria, and then continued on to Amman. Two months earlier he had been in Haiti with Church of the Brethren helping to rebuild homes damaged in the previous year's hurricanes and tropical storms. One day after arriving at the Nefertiti, a 7.0 magnitude earthquake would split open some of the same slum areas that Cliff and his Brethren team had been repairing.[8]

Peggy Gish left for Amman from the Iraqi Kurdistan city of Sulaymaniyah, 185 miles northeast of Samarra, where she was working for CPT. In effect she left Iraq in order to return to Iraq. She arrived at Amman's Queen Alia

International Airport in time to share a cab to the Nefertiti with Weldon and myself. Three years earlier she had been kidnapped in rural northwest Iraq, but she was still working in Iraq. In a war zone. That's what full-time, globe-trotting, war-zone peace activists do—return to the scene of the crime; stubborn, defiant. The way I see it, if the most courageous peacemakers are analogous to soldiers in how they camp on the frontlines to do Wall Street's and Washington's bidding and heavy lifting, Peggy is Special Forces. Like Kathy. So I scanned Queen Alia Airport for the peacemaker's version of a rugged, skirt-wearing Army major. You know, James Gavrilis in a kilt. Instead, Weldon introduced me to a sixty-seven-year-old Church of the Brethren grandmother who was a little hard of hearing and surprisingly fleet footed. She wore an ankle-length skirt, sweater, scuffed black flats, and her long, flowing gray hair pulled into a ponytail. Her voice was so soft, her smile so demurring, if I'd not known about some of her Indiana-Jones derring-do I would have figured her for fragile. In 2003, for example, she had been one of a few CPT members (Cliff was another) to document six dozen cases of prisoner abuse committed by U.S. soldiers at Abu Ghraib prison, that dungeon of a torture chamber used first by Saddam and then by Americans. This was before Abu Ghraib became infamous in the United States. The work of the CPT was critical in bringing out the truth at Abu Ghraib. It fueled the investigations that led to magazine covers, front pages, scandal, outrage, arrests, courts-martial, and, I hope, change.

Ali Shalal Al Qaissi ("Haj Ali") was among the Abu Ghraib prisoners Peggy personally interviewed.

"He has a big heart for CPT," Sami answered when I first asked why a tortured prisoner like Haj Ali would warn us—Americans—away from Rutba. Why would he care if we were killed? "He doesn't hate Americans. Just the government."[9]

The youngest of five children, Margaret Ann Gish was born during the Second World War to Church of the Brethren missionaries working in Nigeria. She grew up in Chicago's East Garfield Park area after her father began teaching at Bethany Theological Seminary, the Church of the Brethren's graduate school then located on Chicago's West Side.[10] In the way my Southern Baptist upbringing emphasized church on Sunday and prayers on bent knee, Peggy, as a child of the Brethren, was immersed in the values of minimalist living and service to others. Our return to Rutba marked her fourteenth trip into and through Iraq. For years she had served everyday Iraqis on both sides of Mesopotamia's tormented modern history—Saddam controlled and American occupied. Even after she was kidnapped on January 27, 2007, and released unharmed two days later, she remained in Iraqi Kurdistan.

Returning to Sulaymaniyah (*Sue-lou-ma-knee*—rhymes with money and is an economic center for Iraqi Kurdistan) from an impoverished village near the

Sinjar Mountains, she was traveling with an Iraqi news editor, Iraqi interpreter, and CPT member Will Van Wagenen when they stopped for a roadblock they thought was a checkpoint.[11] Ten months earlier CPT had lost one of its most beloved activists, Tom Fox, a fifty-four-year-old Quaker and former Marine[12] from Virginia. Fox and three other CPT members had been taken from their van in Baghdad by insurgents on November 26, 2005. The three men who, in 2007, abducted Peggy and Will Van Wagenen, a twenty-nine-year-old Mormon and former Brigham Young University soccer player, carried guns and ordered the Americans and two Iraqis to follow their old Volkswagen sedan. They eventually pulled off the road and transferred the hostages into the Volkswagen, making everyone but Peggy ride with their heads between their knees.[13] Arriving at a family compound, Peggy counted three buildings located at the edge of a desert village. The kidnappers claimed they had crossed into Syria, but Peggy believes they never left northern Iraq. They had not encountered checkpoints, customs officers, or border patrols.[14]

The hostages were herded into a large sitting room with mats on the floor and told they would be shot if they tried to escape. It was the only threat. The four of them were left with one guard, a man who seemed frightened. Van Wagenen, a Harvard Divinity School graduate, son of Sundance Film Festival co-founder Sterling Van Wagenen, and the first-ever Mormon CPT member, speaks fluent Arabic. During servings of bread, rice, yellow pea soup, and, one evening, chicken and an after-dinner cup of hot tea, Van Wagenen told the guard about the work of CPT. He talked about Peggy's husband and how, at that very moment, Art Gish was in the West Bank working for Palestinian rights. Peggy knows a little bit of Arabic, enough to recognize that Van Wagenen was telling the guard about her full-time, globe-trotting, Braveheart peacemaker.

The CPT teaches its members that in hostage situations they should not wilt in fear; be strong but nonaggressive; cultivate friendship, sympathy, and understanding. Peggy reached inside her purse for a news photo she carried around like an amulet of courage. It was from an Associated Press story dated January 30, 2003, just two days after Israeli Prime Minister Ariel Sharon was reelected by a large majority. Sharon interpreted the victory as an endorsement of his hawkish policies (sound like any president you know?). He immediately responded with a heavy hand to any charges or suspicions or threats or hints of Palestinian violence. Two days after the election three Israeli bulldozers flanked by four tanks plowed through downtown Hebron destroying more than one hundred vegetable and fruit stalls.[15] In the AP photo Peggy carried with her, Art is planted firmly in the path of a tank. Arms outstretched as if his hands are nailed to a cross, his red CPT cap pulled snug on his gray head, he stares calmly, defiantly into the muzzle of what appears to be one of Israel's prized $4.5 million Merkava Mark IV tanks. Looking at the photo for the umpteenth time,

Peggy's eyes swelled with tears. Art was scheduled to visit three days later in Sulaymaniyah. Held hostage, even if by a relatively benign outfit of kidnappers, she was sure she wouldn't see him. The guard studied the photo and his eyes began to tear also.[16] He walked out of the room holding it. The hostages had been told earlier that day that their Iraqi interpreter would be freed the next day. That evening the guard returned and said Peggy would be leaving with the interpreter. She was free to go.[17]

Van Wagenen and the Iraqi editor who had invited CPT to see a village's abject poverty were released unharmed six days later. There were never any demands made of CPT or of the families.[18] While still a hostage, Van Wagenen had whiled away the hours reading the Book of Mormon, an Arabic dictionary, and an Arabic children's book about Jesus. He discussed the politics of Washington and Baghdad with the guard, and when the guard complained at night that he couldn't sleep for fear that Van Wagenen or the Iraqi newspaper editor might attack him, Van Wagenen saw an opportunity to explain the core tenet of pacifism.

"Man, we're peaceful guys," he told the guard in Arabic. "We're not going to do anything to you."[19]

Tom Fox and three other CPT members had been kidnapped by a group calling itself the Swords of Righteousness Brigades. It demanded the release of Iraqi prisoners held by the United States in exchange for the peacemakers.[20] Fox's corpse was found sixteen weeks later wrapped in plastic and in a garbage pile in an upscale neighborhood of western Baghdad. There were bullet wounds in his chest and head.[21] Two weeks later the three remaining captives, a British peacemaker and two Canadians, were found unharmed by a team of British, Canadian, and American military forces.

Peggy's kidnappers had dressed in the flowing robes of Bedouin nomads, but they said they were part of the Ba'athist resistance. Ba'athists are primarily Sunni, like Saddam. And like Rutba. Rutba had been a hub in Al Anbar for Saddam's Ba'athist Party. Still, Peggy asked if she could go with us.[22]

The day before Peggy, Weldon, and I arrived in Amman, Sami hitched a ride three hundred miles to Rutba from his home in Najaf, just to make sure the violent currents that had coursed through and around Rutba had relaxed. One year earlier, on Kathy Kelly's recommendation, I had flown to Minneapolis, Minnesota, to recruit Sami for the trip. He is the multilingual co-founder of Iraq's Muslim Peacemaker Teams, and, at the time, his work of promoting peace and reconciliation was split between Iraq and Minneapolis. Born a Sunni in Najaf, he is married to a Shia woman and lives today in the holy city gutted in part by the 1-14 Golden Dragons. Sami was the owner of a popular Middle Eastern restaurant in South Minneapolis, Sinbad's Café and Market, when his beloved adopted country began bombing his beloved native country. "I felt like

Sami the American was attacking, through this war, Sami the Iraqi," he says. His mother died in September 2003, and when he went home to be with family he was stunned by the destruction caused by war. He returned to Minnesota just long enough to sell Sinbad's and move to Najaf to help rebuild his city and his country. In 2005, that effort would launch the Muslim Peacemaker Teams.

In Rutba on January 10, 2010, Sami told only a couple of trusted locals about our plans, and then he caught a ride with a friend to Amman.

That same day at Los Angeles International Airport, Logan, after spending the holidays with family in California, boarded Air France flight 3886 to Amman. Following a layover in Paris, he began reading Kathy Kelly's *Other Lands Have Dreams,* and he relaxed into the Christian rock of the Psalters. Landing after midnight at Queen Alia and seeing the airport's armed guards and blockades, and with the musty scent of the Syrian desert wafting through the Airbus A320, the Middle East felt suddenly—and eerily—familiar.

The next morning, January 11, 2010, Shane boarded a Delta flight in Memphis, where he had been speaking, caught a connecting flight in Atlanta, and by that evening he was in JFK's Terminal Four waiting for Delta's flight to Amman. In the same congested area where Weldon and I stumbled into each other, he met up with Jamie Moffett, an Eastern University alum and co-founder of The Simple Way. For the return to Rutba, Jamie was our last-minute upgrade. He's a documentary filmmaker, well-grounded in the corrupting influences spread by the bedfellows of Wall Street and Washington. His 2010 feature-length documentary *Return to El Salvador* traces Washington's bloody and costly role in the twelve-year-long Salvadoran civil war. The film was in its final edits when Jamie grabbed his equipment and headed toward JFK on January 11. Like me, he was eager to better understand and attempt to shed light on the crazy violence that strikes us both as primitive. Sick, obscene, senseless, primitive, even to two nonpacifist journalists. If, as the late American writer and civil rights activist James Baldwin wrote in *Notes of a Native Son,* "People are trapped in history and history is trapped in them," then heaven, Christ, and Allah help us. Humanity must come together to find a light leading out.

As Jamie raced from Philly to JFK he was still editing the narration to *Return to El Salvador.* With Scotty Krueger of the Psalters band in the passenger seat (is it just me or does this guy have more cameos than Alfred Hitchcock?), quick glances at the script held up by Krueger, and with actor Martin Sheen patched through to his cell phone from a recording studio in Santa Monica, Jamie bridged two film projects while steering his Honda CRV north on Interstate 95.

"On March 15, 2009, what once seemed impossible happened in the small Central American country of El Salvador," Sheen begins in his famously scratchy tenor. "For the first time in one hundred and fifty years El Salvador elected a president of the people. . . ."

Through Pennsylvania and New Jersey Jamie and Sheen polished ten pages of narration. Finishing just short of JFK, Sheen caught his breath and asked, "So, what's next for you?"

"Funny you should ask," Jamie replied. "Right now I'm on my way to Iraq."

He told Sheen the short version of how a taxi had crashed on Saddam's autobahn during the first days of war; how two American peacemakers nearly died; and, the real shocker of Shock and Awe, how the very Iraqis who were being bombed mercilessly[23] by the United States had rescued and saved the injured Americans. The story surprised most Americans who heard it. Sheen was no exception. Iraqis pulling Americans out of a ditch during the horror of Shock and Awe defied Washington's easy definitions of terrorists and terrorism.

Sheen was silent for a moment.

"How are you paying for this?" he asked, referring to Jamie's two projects *Return to El Salvador* and *The Gospel of Rutba*.

Jamie wasn't sure how to answer. There was a long pause.

"You're self-funding, aren't you?" Sheen asked.

Deep personal debt is pretty common in filmmaking, especially documentary filmmaking.

"Yes, sir."

"Rip up the check," Sheen said of his $10,000 narrator's fee. "I want to help anyway I can."[24]

By January 12, 2010, the eight of us (Shane, Cliff, Weldon, Peggy, Logan, Sami, Jamie, and myself) had taken up residence in Amman with plans to go to Rutba ASAP. Or, as it turned out, NSF (Not So Fast). On November 19, 2009, I had hand-delivered our visa applications to the Iraqi consulate in Washington, DC, a large brownstone office one mile north of 1600 Pennsylvania Avenue. Consulate officials assured me that our applications were in order; our paperwork would be routed to Baghdad the next day and returned to Washington with visa stamps in three to four weeks. Never happened. As of this writing, two years later, we've not received them.

So, in Amman, we started the process from scratch.

The Nefertiti stands four stories tall on the cracked limestone sidewalk of a residential valley in the fashionable, San Francisco-hilly Shmeisani district in west Amman. From its porcelain-tiled lobby on Jahed Street it's only a five-minute climb to a McDonald's, a Subway sandwich shop, and a Donuts Factory kiosk designed to look blood kin to the Massachusetts-bred Dunkin' Donuts family.[25] From there you turn right onto Abdul Hameed Sharaf Street, right again at Al Shareef Naser Bin Jameel Street, go east toward two roads named for King Hussein's third and fourth wives—right onto Queen Alia, left at Queen Noor—then east-southeast on Al Istiqlal (Independence), right at

Al Jaish (Army), and, finally, at Jabal (Hill), Amman's first traffic circle, you're there. A few downhill strides west of 1st Circle Jabal Amman, you can't miss it. A golden plaque with black lettering hung on a stone building: Embassy of the Republic of Iraq Consular Section.

The embassy, and the route(s) we took to it, became familiar terrain. In the five to eight miles (depending on if the cabbie stretched the fare on us) of lefts, rights, merges, and roundabouts we passed or came close to passing three Starbucks, two Burger Kings, a Kentucky Fried Chicken, Pizza Hut, Popeye's, Little Caesars, Hardee's, Domino's Pizza, T.G.I. Friday's, a bankrupted and shuttered Planet Hollywood,[26] a Safeway grocery store, and an abridged roster of American hotel chains (Holiday Inn, Sheraton, Marriott, Four Seasons, Grand Hyatt, Days Inn, etc.). If not for Amman's uniformly limestone architecture[27] some areas of the city would look cut and pasted from northern Virginia. Ironically, this is especially true of Amman's western neighborhoods. To varying degrees you could say the same about areas of Cairo, Doha, Bahrain, Oman, Dubai, Abu Dubai, and Riyadh, major metropolises of the Arabian Peninsula. Commercial areas in much of the "Greater Middle East"—new geography[28] invented by the George W. Bush White House—dress in golden arches[29] and the pink and orange of Dunkin' Donuts. (Not Iraq, Afghanistan, and Iran, however. At least not yet. Give them time.)

But don't confuse love of the Colonel's secret recipe as enthusiasm for all things American made. Seven years earlier on these same potholed, palm-lined streets, thousands of Jordanians marched rain or shine, holy days and Saturdays, demanding that Washington, Israel, and their British wingman, U.K. Prime Minister Tony Blair, stop with the war making. Corralled by riot police who herded the throngs peacefully through Shmeisani's peaks and valleys, processions of protestors stretched a mile or so from King Abdullah International Gardens to Amman's UN headquarters.[30] In Washington's global War on Terrorism, and on protest placards and banners carried through Amman, Bush was the world's No. 1 "terrorist" and "America, Britain, Israel" were the Axis of Evil. Pressured by Islamist and political groups,[31] city officials temporarily lifted a ban on public demonstrations in the hope that Jordan's majority population (Palestinian refugees totaled nearly two million in 2003) would peacefully vent its pent-up frustration. From the perspective of that majority, and of other majorities in the Middle East (or Greater Middle East), Washington was (and remains today) an appendage to Israel; more the strong-arm of the Knesset than the heart and mind of a separate and sovereign political body.

So beginning on Saturday, February 1, 2003, and continuing each week until Amman Governor Abdul Karim Malameh reinforced the ban on public protests one week before Shock and Awe, demonstrations in one of the Arab world's most Westernized cities railed against the "American Zionists"—a redundant term to countless Jordanians, Iraqis, Iranians, Palestinians, Syrians, Egyptians, etc. It's why a year earlier, eight months after 9/11, when a police officer in Cairo peered inside the Jeep Cherokee that I was traveling in and took a long look at my pale Euro features, he scolded my unarmed Egyptian fixer-driver-interpreter:

Lazem te-sheel tabanga maak.

"You have to carry a gun with you."

It wasn't that he was concerned about any threat I might pose. He was worried about my safety (and, probably, about the bureaucratic paperwork my death would generate). It's just that baseball, apple pie, Chevrolet, those things don't poll so well in Bush's Greater Middle East. Or in Obama's Middle East.

On February 14, 2003, following Friday prayers marking the end of *Eid al-Adha* (Feast of Sacrifice), a Muslim celebration that honors Ibrahim (or Abraham[32]) and his obedience to God, protests from Cairo to Jerusalem to the Baqa'a refugee camp[33] north of Amman began to sound louder, angrier, and more than a little bit scary. Frustrated Muslims started pledging their loyalty to a crazed brutal dictator. They shouted of their love for Saddam. They carried large portraits of Saddam.[34] They gathered near mosques, marched down the narrow roads of refugee camps, and they stood in a cold, driving rain outside the UN offices in Shmeisani yelling, pleading, chanting for Saddam Hussein and Osama Bin Laden to join forces against the American Zionists:[35]

"Oh, beloved Saddam, bomb Tel Aviv!"[36]

"Oh, beloved Bin Laden, bomb Tel Aviv!"[37]

"Bush, Bush, listen carefully, we all love Saddam Hussein!"[38]

"Baghdad, we are all your soldiers!"[39]

"No to the American and Zionist embassies on Arab land!"[40]

"Down, down U.S.A., we don't fear the CIA!"[41]

"From Baghdad to Amman, kill all the Americans!"[42]

At this same time a song by Egyptian pop star Shaaban Abdul Rehim put to music what the Arab street was attempting to express. Rehim's hit, *The Attack on Iraq*, blared from cars and clubs across Jordan and through the Arab world: "Chechnya! Afghanistan! Palestine! Southern Lebanon! The Golan Heights! And now Iraq, too? And now Iraq, too? It's too much for people. Shame on you! Enough, enough, enough!"[43]

Seven years later, two cabs dropped the eight of us off five miles from where three thousand Jordanians had stood in the rain shouting "Terrorist Bush, get out of our land"[44] and "We don't want to see any American embassy on our Jordanian soil." At the Iraqi embassy, just down the hill from 1st Circle Jabal Amman, we were only a few miles from the large and well-fortified American embassy in Jordan.

Unfortunately, we were also several days removed from Iraq. It could have been worse.

"Six to eight weeks," said Mohammed Al-Hashimi, the Third Secretary to the Embassy of the Republic of Iraq in Amman. "That is the best we can do. Six to eight weeks."

Mohammed was a middle-aged Jordanian bureaucrat, a father and husband, clean-cut in a white dress shirt and dark tie. Even in the din of a crowded consulate, he remained jovial, frequently smiling and taking drags of a cigarette from behind the partition of Window No. 5. Sizing up Mohammed, liking what he saw, Sami leaned toward the partition's small opening and made our appeal. He replayed a version of the same story Jamie had told to Martin Sheen. Speaking Arabic and waving his hands, he spoke as if he had two minutes in an elevator with a Hollywood producer: the war, bombs, peacemakers, wrecked taxi, injured Americans, empathic Iraqis; Christians, Muslims, everyday people joining forces outside the prejudice and violence of politics and religion. In the moral of that story we see the ugly divide that separates the Middle East and the West, but we also see a way to bridge it.

Finishing, Sami stood up straight, arms folded. I didn't understand more than a few words of the Arabic, but I could tell from Mohammed's reaction that Sami's elevator pitch had been top-drawer. Like Sheen, Mohammed fell silent for several seconds. His head began to nod lightly, like water simmering, and then it moved vigorously. "Yes, yes, yes," he said, speaking English. "*That* is a good story. The media gets it all wrong, but this—*this*—is good!"

He smiled and looked at the eight of us.

"You *will* get your visas," he declared. "I will make sure of it."

We promised to bring him a notarized letter of invitation from our hosts in Iraq, and he promised to check on our visa applications with the Iraqi consulate in Washington, DC. The following day we returned to Window No. 5 with a hastily assembled but official looking and notarized letter from Iraq's Muslim Peacemaker Teams, the nonprofit co-founded by Sami. The letter was dated Wednesday, January 13, 2010, the same day Wikitravel.org updated its advisory on Rutba using bold letters and uppercase: "Ar Rutba remains *extremely dangerous* and is emphatically NOT safe for tourists. Those who are going there on business are strongly advised to consult their own government first, and have an armed guard with them. Otherwise, don't even think of traveling there."

Mohammed liked the letter, and he said he was expecting to hear good news for us. Soon, very soon. First thing the next morning we were back in the din of the consular office. Waiting and waiting. It was Thursday, the last day of the work week for Islam. With Friday being the holy day, it's the first day of the weekend for observant Muslim nations. If we didn't get our visas approved before the weekend we would not be going to Rutba on this trip to the Middle

East. We had airfares to consider, but, more than that, everyone had scheduled a specific block of time for the Rutba reunion. There were other commitments to consider. If Mohammed didn't come through for us then and there, the trip to Rutba would be postponed. Again.

Five hours later Mohammed motioned for us. We approached Window No. 5 feeling hopeful. He looked up; he wasn't smiling. For two days he had been checking and double-checking with Iraqi consulate officials in Washington and Baghdad. He explained that even with the notarized invitation from the Muslim Peacemaker Teams, he needed more. Specifically, he needed verification that our visa applications were in the pipeline of approval. No one could parachute into the approval process and expedite something that had no paper trail. All that he had needed were the numbers that would have been assigned to our paperwork when it arrived in Baghdad.

His eyes narrowed, he turned his head, exhaled a cloud of smoke, mashed his cigarette out in an ashtray. "Washington has been lying to you," he said, staring at Sami and me. "Baghdad never received your applications."[45]

We felt as deflated as Mohammed looked.

"There is nothing more I can do."

He sunk back behind his partition.

There is a wizard behind the curtain of every foreign consular office. A stroke of the wizard's pen is all you need. With it walls recede; draw bridges lower. It's the surest last-gasp way across any border.

Bureaucrats don't volunteer that information. Usually. Mohammed showed us pity.

"If—*if*—you could get in to see the ambassador," he said, shrugging, looking at his watch, and then looking doubtful, "that is your only chance."

It was 2:42 p.m. The embassy would close for the weekend in eighteen minutes.

The wizard in our case was Iraqi Ambassador to Jordan, His Excellency Saad Jassim Al-Hayani. Born and raised in Baghdad, graduated by Baghdad University, Al-Hayani, sixty-two, is a career diplomat. He served Saddam as an undersecretary in the Ba'athist regime and worked as his attaché to Iraq's embassies in Paris, Senegal, and Lebanon. In April 2004, the Coalition Provisional Authority appointed Al-Hayani to Iraq's Ministry of Foreign Affairs. In 2006, he moved to Jordan to oversee the Iraqi embassy in Amman. Four months before we met the sympathetic bureaucrat behind Window No. 5, Iraq's Supreme Criminal Court had issued an arrest warrant for Al-Hayani. There were vague allegations linking him to Saddam-era "Crimes against Humanity," but these charges apparently never stuck because he was still Iraq's wizard in Amman in 2010.[46]

Mohammed declined to phone His Excellency on our behalf, but he pointed us in the general direction.

Out the consular office door, past the golden plaque, up the hill toward 1st Circle Jabal Amman, a sharp left, you can't miss it. There is another plaque and another door. Sami, our veritable lock pick, talked our way through it. This led into a courtyard with marble fountains and a roundabout driveway made from stamped stone. On it was a shiny black Mercedes parked beneath an awning. Next to the sedan was a brick facade painted turquoise. Turquoise. Three stories tall, the aqua blue wall resembled the battlements of a castle—crenellations, ramparts, turrets with golden inlays of aurochs and dragons. The architect had spared nothing. A fanciful castle fronting the embassy of a tortured and war-torn nation, it looked odd, like something Disney had misplaced or an eccentric pop star might buy for his Neverland ranch. A closer examination, however, revealed origins that are political, not playful. Completed before the first Gulf War, the turquoise wall is a small-scale reproduction of the Ishtar Gate of Baby-lon.[47] It's a biblical icon—the main entrance into the capital of King Nebu-chadnezzar II, an Old Testament hawk who invaded Jerusalem 2,500 years ago, destroyed Solomon's Temple (ancient Jerusalem's main temple) and drove the Jews into exile.

Saddam used to boast that he was the reincarnation of King Nebuchadnez-zar II. The mad dictator of Mesopotamia fancied himself as the modern-day conqueror of Jews. A real Nazi in that way. The wall is a sorry tribute to Sad-dam's anti-Semitism.

Behind this not-so-fanciful façade, beyond the cascading chandelier and up two flights of a spiral staircase, the wizard was in his office. Forty minutes after our request to meet with him was carried to "His Excellency the Ambassador," as his assistant referred to him, the wizard himself greeted us. He could have been the Arabic twin of J. D. "Boss" Hogg from TV's "Dukes of Hazard," except the ambassador, standing about five-foot-six, was low key and overtly polite. He welcomed us into an office roughly the same square footage as my house, and as he waved us toward a parlor area of couches and chairs, he offered hot tea. Eight cups of tea.[48] He then went to his desk (roughly the size of my office) where there was a twenty-five-inch computer screen flashing our virtual common ground. Google. He phoned his assistant, ordered our teas, and only then did he turn to Sami and ask, *Keif mumkin an usa'adek?* "How can I help you?"

Sami responded in Arabic, walking Al-Hayani through the elevator pitch before explaining that "we are connecting people to people to begin repair-ing this relationship between American and Iraqi people. When people meet one another in person, looking in the eyes, exchanging the cultures, and they find out they are brothers and sisters, the Iraqis are no longer terrorists and the Americans are no longer infidels." The ambassador shook his head at this, waved his hand, and stopped Sami. "The Iraqis were never the terrorists," he said. "The U.S. allowed the terrorists to come into Iraq after the invasion."[49]

After the pitch, no differently than the actor and the bureaucrat, the ambassador sat quietly and absorbed it all. Looking up and directly at Sami, he said that Jordan's Iraqi embassy only provides visas for foreigners who reside in Jordan. Americans traveling to Iraq would need visas approved by the Iraqi consulate in Washington, DC. He was sorry that Washington had failed us, but exceptions to this rule are rare. Al-Hayani was speaking in Arabic, so seven of us didn't fully understand the bad news being delivered. I attempted to read Sami's expression; he was poker faced.

However, the ambassador continued, still looking only at Sami, "because this mission is for a noble cause, I will grant your visas."[50]

He returned to his desk and phoned Mohammed. Within the hour we had our visa stamps.

We were a motley band of Anglo-Americans and one Iraqi-American: ages twenty-eight to sixty-seven; four Christian peacemakers, one Muslim peacemaker, one Army combat veteran turned peacemaker, and two journalists (one print, the other film); beatnik to business casual; dreadlocks, close crop, ponytails; clean-shaven, mustaches, goatee, and one curiously long beard of the Brethren, Mennonite, or Amish variety.

Surprise, surprise, we caused a stir at the border.

Trying to cross from Jordan to Iraq with our special visas hand-signed by His Excellency was no skip in the desert. Rather, it almost turned into a walk in the desert. The day after we received our visa stamps we left the Nefertiti before sunrise and rode three and a half hours in two taxis[51] from Amman to the Al Karama border crossing on Jordan's Highway 10. But at the entrance to the customs zone, where signs ordered "Tanks & Trucks" into the right lane, "Cars & Buses" into the left, our cab drivers were turned back by a half dozen Jordanian soldiers. Our immediate destination, the customs office, was a teasing glint in the desert. If not for a middle-aged Iraqi who kindly stuffed eight suspicious looking hitchhikers into the bed and cab of his Nissan pickup, we would have walked the last two miles in the desert. Then, finally in line at the customs office, things got difficult. Each of us was pulled away at one point or another and questioned. I suspect Jordan just didn't know what to do with civilian Americans freewheeling it to Iraq as if it were spring break. We weren't contractors. We weren't military. We weren't armed. To gun-toting officers patrolling the border of a war zone those three facts added up to one conclusion: We weren't sane.

After an hour or so a plainclothes Jordanian officer walked like Joe Friday into the customs common area and asked us to follow him. Like baby ducks we obediently trailed behind him, out one door, around the corner, into an office. All eyes were on us; the Arab civilians, the Jordanian military, the border guards, many of them staring and whispering. Joe Friday shut the door.

Dressed in dark slacks, dark shoes, a blue pinstripe dress shirt with a semi-automatic pistol holstered high under his left shoulder, it appeared that he was exactly what he claimed to be: an officer with the Jordanian secret police. Major Nedal, he called himself.

"Sit, sit, make yourselves comfortable," he said; and in the way that his invitation had sounded like a command, and because he tilted his head like he was ready to interrogate us, I felt immediately uncomfortable. He moved to an armless chair behind a metal desk; we crowded around it.

Major Nedal asked about our travel plans and best intentions; the fundamental who, what, when, where, why of our trip. The elevator pitch, delivered ad hoc this time by different members of the group, had no visible effect. He didn't fall dramatically silent. Didn't pause even for a beat. He explained in so many words that it was his sworn duty to try and protect us from our own foolish selves. Special visa or regular-Joe visa, made no difference to him. Our plan was suicide. Speaking matter-of-factly in a thick Arabic accent, he walked us through what he believed would happen if we proceeded to Iraq unarmed and with no conventional means of protection: A corrupt Iraqi police officer or soldier at a checkpoint somewhere along the way would earn a fat commission by phoning kidnappers and alerting them to unguarded American prey. Our ground coordinates would become something of value. Easy money. That's just how things worked in the capitalist market of new and improved Operation Iraqi Freedom Iraq. We would be taken hostage, he was sure of it. In exchange for a ransom or media attention or some political concession, we might escape with our lives. Probably not. More likely, we would be killed.

"Decapitated," he said. He enunciated each syllable. Nothing matter-of-fact in that.

Six of the eight in our group had previously traveled and worked in Iraq unarmed and, not counting the taxi crash, unharmed. The lone hostage among us had been freed without a harsh word spoken to her. At one time or another everyone in the group had already swallowed this mental image of their own headless corpse. Some digested it better than others. I shifted in my chair, rubbed my palms against my jeans. The last thing my wife had said to me before the flight to Amman: "Be safe. Don't do anything foolish."

One of the first things that Nedal had said: "This plan of yours is not wise."

Not satisfied with the room's relatively calm resolve, Nedal repeated that last image he'd attached to his prediction. This time he leaned slightly forward for emphasis and chose a more visceral adjective.

"You understand, yes? *Beheaded*," he said. "You could be beheaded."

He picked up the phone and dialed the U.S. Army.

"Here, please speak to the captain," he said, handing the phone to me.

Captain William Don Foster asked to meet with us, and he used the same tone that Major Nedal had used when he insisted that we "sit, sit, make yourselves comfortable." We really had no choice in the matter.

Less than one mile east of the Jordanian customs compound is a two-square-mile buffer of dirt, sand, and asphalt road. It's where the flat rocky eastern desert of Jordan meets the flat rocky western desert of Iraq; neither side has jurisdiction on this middle ground. It's called No Man's Land, and that's where Foster "asked" to meet with us.

"I can be there in an hour and a half," he said.

"I'm sorry, but we really can't wait that long," I said. "We would like to get to Rutba before dark."

It was my weak attempt to spring us, although I wasn't entirely sure I wanted to be sprung. But I was also telling the truth. In Al Anbar the winter sun begins setting a few minutes after five o'clock. We still had to clear the customs gauntlet on the Iraqi side of No Man's Land before we phoned for our rides from Rutba. That roundtrip drive would cost us three to four hours, at least. It wasn't even noon yet in Al Karama, but I could see us running out of daylight. If driving into Rutba unannounced and unarmed is a foolish thing for Americans to do during daylight, surprising Rutba in the cover of dark would be barking mad.

"I'll be there in one hour then," Foster replied.

Nedal looked relieved. He stood to leave. He's nearly six feet tall, and with the gun holstered to his side, the pinstripe button-down open at the collar, a pack of cigarettes tucked in a front shirt pocket, and with the subtle swagger that comes standard-issue with all secret police, his credentials on matters like this were solid with me. He asked if we wanted him to phone the American embassy in Baghdad on our behalf. Shane, Cliff, and Sami responded quickly and unequivocally.

No. Thank you, but *no*.

The trip from Jordan to Iraq had already consumed five days, and we weren't even in Iraq yet. Asking another bureaucracy to get involved would just invite more trouble.

"I'm supposed to alert the embassy in Baghdad," Nedal said. "I should call, yes? You agree?"

"No."

He tilted his head again, stared at us, allowed a few seconds for everyone to reconsider.

"You sure?"

"Yes. We're good."

"Listen," he said, moving us toward the door, "I'm just trying to do my job, keep you safe. Personally, I don't care. It would be easier for me to just stamp your passports, stamp, stamp, stamp, and let you go through. No skin off me. But I'm trying to help you stay alive."

After we left Nedal's office he phoned the American embassy in Baghdad.

Ninety minutes later the U.S. Army accelerated past a long line of fuel tankers and tractor-trailers and rolled into No Man's Land intending to stop us before we crossed the deathly line in the sand. Foster climbed out of the lead Humvee; there were gunners in the turrets, five fresh-faced, chain-smoking soldiers, and one brawny, slightly graying Chicagoan named George, who served as the Arabic interpreter. Foster embraced Nedal, handed him a gift of truck reflectors for the reconstruction traffic that crawled into and out of western Iraq. Small talk, smiles, Foster to Nedal and vice versa, and then Foster turned to look at the nutty gringos responsible for the wrinkles in his schedule. He assessed us with a long and stern now-what-do-we-have-here look. As commander of the Army's 458th Movement Control Team, 14th Transportation Battalion, a critical part of Foster's job was safeguarding the military and reconstruction convoys entering and exiting Al Anbar province. That included keeping naïve Americans out of his war zone. He really didn't give a damn about special visas signed by His Excellency.[52]

Foster was forty-four years old, an Army reservist on his third deployment since 9/11; his third of Iraq if you count the first Gulf War. When he wasn't sweating in Humvees and ballistic vests he worked as a general contractor and church builder[53] from the quiet suburbs of Belleville, Illinois, the birthplace of Buddy Ebsen (Jed Clampett of "The Beverly Hillbillies"). Peace for Foster didn't always include the praying-hugging-sharing moments that often define peacemaking and peacemakers. Sometimes it was enough for him to just escape death threats and desert grit, and then to arrive home safely to his wife and children twenty miles east of St. Louis, Missouri. Lately, that peace had eluded him. He has four sons, ages fifteen, thirteen, twelve, and seven, all at critical stages of development. Because of this thing Washington called Operation Iraqi Freedom, his sons relied on Skype to visit with a father who was gone for twelve months at a stretch. Twelve months feels like twelve years when you're a kid of Little League age. Also, when you're a father six thousand miles away.

In October 2009, when Foster and his soldiers were packing to leave for six weeks of training before their next deployment to Iraq, photos of the sendoff ran in a local paper. Foster's face was clean shaven and winter pale; he had a father's slight paunch, and his youngest son clung to him like Dad was a favorite blanket being taken away. Foster's eyes looked hound-dog sad, maybe tearful. Now, just three months later, standing in the patchy nothingness of No Man's Land, he was tan and unshaven. In Army-issue reflective sunglasses and desert fatigues he looked fighting fit and a good bit ornery. He had too much diplomacy to come right out and say it, but I'm pretty sure he thought we were complete idiots. During his last tour in 2005 in Iraqi Kurdistan he lost three Arabic interpreters, Iraqis he'd grown fond of and considered as good friends. Each failed to show for work on the same day, and as if that weren't odd enough, the same three failed to show the next day. And then the next and the next. After a week of missed shifts he received an explanation delivered in the mail. It came by way of a video stuffed into an envelope. Five years later that video still ran the occasional gruesome loop in Foster's sleep.

On January 15, 2010, the overcast, chilly day that Foster found himself staring at some half-wit peacemakers and journalists attempting to cross the border all but naked, he dispensed with the storytelling and cut to the point. He'd seen in that bloody video what could happen in Iraq:

"People get their heads cut off. I know that for a fact. I have friends who've had their heads cut off."

At that same moment an Iraqi major drove up from the Iraqi customs office one mile away. He walked quietly from his Chevy pickup and stood alongside his military peers from Jordan and the United States. Of all the military men now clustered around us in No Man's Land, Major Mohsin was the only one without a weapon. And standing next to Foster's tan desert fatigues, he looked like he had dressed in hand-me-downs. His fatigues were jungle green. As Foster went over our plans for Rutba and our reasons for going, and then asked again about our decision to go into Al Anbar unarmed, as if he literally couldn't believe we were that stupid, Mohsin never spoke. Foster repeated Nedal's warning: kidnap, ransom, decapitation, the whole final act played out for us again. Sami must have sensed my rising hesitation or maybe he can smell fear, but he was suddenly agitated. Not at me, but at Foster and Nedal. He had heard enough, too much.

He turned to Mohsin, and, as one Iraqi to another, he asked: What do *you* think? Is Iraq too dangerous?

La, Mohsin said, shaking his head. *La, la, la.*

"No, no, no."

As long as we followed the advice and guidance of the locals in Rutba, Mohsin said each of us would remain safe. Rutba would protect us. He was sure of it.

That was good enough for me. The others had already been convinced. We thanked Foster and Nedal for their advice and concerns, but then we all piled into the bed and cab of an Iraqi major's white Chevy pickup. We would ride into Iraq looking like Jed Clampett's family.

"Well then," Foster said, "I guess I'll see you on your way back out."

He paused one beat.

Insha'allah.

"God willing."

9

PRO CHOICE

Degrees of separation allow us to destroy human beings
we do not know except as the enemy.[1]
—Shane Claiborne,
Irresistible Revolution

At Iraqi embassy in Amman: Jamie, Weldon, Cliff, Shane, Ambassador Al-Hayani,
Greg, Peggy, Logan, Sami. Photo credit: Jamie Moffett

2003

Cliff was given a choice on Jassim's table.
Life or afterlife?
Physician's assistant Jassim Muhammad Jamil was fitting Cliff's scalp back
on, tugging and stretching it over his bloodied, swollen skull as if he were

squeezing a size-34 waist into size-32 pants. By then Cliff's soul, his consciousness, whatever the spark is that fires our core, had leaped from his body. In the shadows of the unlit Health Care Center in Rutba, Cliff saw an Iraqi man threading sutures through the head of an American man. His head. He saw himself sitting at the edge of a table, his body bent slightly forward toward Dr. Farouq Al-Dulaimi or nurse Tarik Ali Marzouq or Jassim, the debonair assistant who would ultimately finish the job. They jumped around at first, moving between Weldon (fractured sternum, ribs, left shoulder, and left thumb); Shane (separated left shoulder); the Iraqi driver (cuts, bruises, limp),[2] and twenty-eight-year-old Korean peace activist Bae Sang-hyun (cuts and bruises).[3] By the time Cliff realized who and what he was watching, and from where (overhead), Shane was at his side, one hand resting on Cliff's back, another grasping one of his hands. Shane recalls looking into Cliff's "raccoon eyes," that red flag of internal bleeding, and wondering if he were slowly bleeding to death. From the inside out, rivulets of blood streaked Cliff's face like wet, running mascara.

Jassim settled into the task of sewing Cliff back together, pushing a needle through the scalp without the use of antiseptics or water to clean the wound. Because of war's constant shelling, the clinic didn't have electricity, running water, or anesthesia to numb Cliff's wound. Most of its supplies were buried in the rubble of the Rutba General compound, bombed three days earlier by order of Major James Gavrilis.

Asif, asif, asif. "Sorry, sorry, sorry," Jassim kept saying into Cliff's ear.

Cliff didn't respond. Shane saw a meditative, almost otherworldly, smile creasing Cliff's face, frozen in place even as blood streamed down the inside and outside of his head. Long before he would hear about Cliff's out-of-body experience, Shane described the expression as "this unbelievable Saint Francis-type of perfect joy."[4] Of all places and times, it appeared that the peacemaker had found peace during crisis in a Ba'athist and Sunni stronghold of Al Anbar.

Cliff doesn't often talk about it. Even to fellow activists and devout believers, it can sound bizarre. Shane and Weldon would hear the story for the first time when Cliff returned to Rutba in 2010, and I asked him about that joyful Saint-Francis-of-Assisi moment. He smiled at me, paused for two beats, and then said, "Well, you see, I had left my body. I wasn't feeling any pain."

In the utter bliss and grace of that moment, he recalled, "I floated out of my body; I was given a choice. It was very clear to me that I could choose to leave life right then or I could choose to come back."[5]

A baritone voice didn't whisper in his ear. No angels suddenly appeared. But a message was conveyed in a way that is ineffable to anyone who's never experienced spiritual phenomenon. Cliff knew he could remain outside of his body and ascend into light. Or, he could remain on earth and deal with this life. His call. He also knew that there was no wrong choice. However, the latter came with baggage (and missing luggage, as it were). He would be returning to war-torn Iraq without a passport (it was in his bag in the trunk of the wrecked taxi) and no obvious way out. He has a Church of the Brethren wife, Arlene, whom he married on her parents' front lawn in 1971. While he was with CPT in Iraq, she was with CPT in Colombia. Two hearts, one mind. They have two grown daughters, a comfortable home (a corncrib they remodeled into a two-story house[6]), and they share a seven-acre organic fruit and vegetable farm near North Manchester, Indiana, with another Brethren family. Cliff's parents lived on the property with them. To remain below the taxable income level of $13,850 in 2003 and avoid giving money to the military industry, Cliff and Arlene lived off the land, and off sales of the fruit and vegetables they sold at farmers' markets. They were happy and comfortable. In their peace work and travels, they have many close friends throughout Central America, the Middle East, Haiti, Puerto Rico, etc. In other words, Cliff was living large and enjoying a rich—if not wealthy—life.

So, to ascend or stay grounded? He weighed the options briefly. Five minutes or five seconds, he's not sure. This stuff always seems to happen in a vacuum of time that's unique to, say, serious car accidents and *The Matrix* movies. The light of that moment felt fireside cozy; it was tempting to just curl into it. "It wasn't like I had not lived a good life; it had been a full life," Cliff says of his decision making. "But something was drawing me back. So, I figured, eh, what the heck, I guess I'll come back and give it another try."

Instantly he felt the pressure of Jassim pinching the scalp together to push needle and suture through skin, blood, and strands of loose hair. *Asif, asif, asif.* But he didn't feel pain. Shane says the raccoon eyes began fading, almost immediately, as if someone tightened the knob of a drippy faucet. The internal leakage dried up, disappeared. Jassim finished with the last of one dozen or so stitches, and Cliff climbed off the table brimming with gratitude and vigor, eager to troubleshoot the life he'd just chosen.

The eldest child of a Church of the Brethren pastor, Clifford Lee Kindy was born into the world of social justice on September 10, 1949. The Reverend Dean Kindy and wife, June Zimmerman Kindy, met in 1947 at the Brethren Service Center in New Windsor, Maryland, where they helped World War II refugees. By the time Cliff was born they had moved to south-central Florida to help poor families populating the migrant camps in Pahokee, a farming town on the shores of Lake Okeechobee, the state's largest freshwater lake. Swampy Pahokee became Cliff's first home and playground, so, in that sense, you might say he was walking the social-justice talk before he could crawl. The family soon moved back to Maryland for eighteen months, and then to Chicago for three years while Cliff's father attended the Brethren seminary. Eventually, Cliff and his four siblings (two brothers, two sisters) moved four times, as the Reverend Kindy and June pastored Brethren congregations in small towns through Michigan and Ohio.[7] But if living on the church circuit was a hardship, Cliff doesn't recall it. What stuck were the Brethren lessons on minimalist living, maximum giving; a cultural revolution grounded in Romans 12:2: "Do not be conformed to this world."

In the '60s and '70s, as Washington and its electorate ignored President Eisenhower's 1961 farewell warning about the unchecked, unwarranted influence of a military-industrial complex,[8] and as U.S.-led or CIA-backed wars, revolutions, counterrevolutions, and coups burned through South and Central America, and Southeast Asia, Reverend Kindy lowered his income to the untaxable level.[9] Similar to Dorothy Day, Karl Meyer, and legions of others, Cliff's parents imposed poverty on themselves. They knew they might not live to see world peace or, even, a more humble, sober military industry; but they saw the sacrifice as down payment on a better future. Similar to Chief Sitting Bull's Iroquois Confederacy of Five Indian Nations, which required all counsel actions to weigh the effects on the seventh generation (the great, great, great, great, great grandchildren),[10] the greatest belief of the Brethren is selfless action. That is, walking the talk of the Gospel's teachings. Cliff's father died (or ascended) at age ninety on January 27, 2012, in North Manchester, and in obituaries from the funeral home and testimony from friends, the Reverend Robert Dean Kindy was remembered as a "peace and justice pioneer."

In this case, the organic apple had fallen especially close to the family tree.

Service and faith are vital to the Brethren Church, but these never included blind faith in service to Washington. In 1969, Cliff was entering his second year at Manchester College in North Manchester when his football coach brought him to register for the military draft.[11] At the time there were some 500,000 American troops in Vietnam, and President Richard Nixon was the newly elected Commander in Chief. Cliff was a five-foot-nine, thick-necked, muscular Midwesterner who once had envisioned himself as a Green Beret (no joking—remember, he was a linebacker and fullback in high school and lettered in college football) and, like countless teenagers of his day, seduced by the patriotic machismo playing on radios in 1966—a *Billboard* No. 1 hit single, "Ballad of the Green Berets."[12] But by 1969, a sober Cliff could see how the moneyed alliances, Washington and Wall Street, were driving wars and militaries; and he saw combat veterans returning home partly insane and wholly in caskets. He registered for the draft as a conscientious objector. Instead of a pawn for the Pentagon he would be a grunt for Brethren Volunteer Services (BVS). In August of 1969, four months before the draft's lottery system resumed, category five Hurricane Camille flattened coastal Mississippi with a storm surge of twenty-four feet and sustained winds estimated at 190 miles per hour. Cliff spent the next six months with the BVS cleaning and patching up Mississippi. While there he learned about the history of the federal telephone excise tax, created in 1898 to help fund the Spanish-American war. In the budding era of Vietnam protests, refusing to pay the 10 percent tax was a sort of starter kit for rookie peace activists.[13] With expenses mounting from its wars (Vietnam alone would cost taxpayers close to $700 billion[14]), Washington had repeatedly extended the phone tax to help pay bills owed to the military industry. The tax, on our phone bills at a reduced rate still today, had been set to expire in 1960 as part of the Tax Rate Extension Act of 1959, and, later, as part of the Excise Tax Reduction Act of 1965. Quietly, Congress kept reviving it until it had become an accepted add-on to the phone bill.

In his first act of protest, Cliff stopped paying it in 1969. All that was required was for him to tell the phone company that he refused to pay the federal excise tax, but, with each bill, he had to write a letter to the IRS explaining his reasons. Then as now, Cliff explained in each letter how he could not in good conscience pay a fee that goes to support wars.[15] For a full-time peacemaker, it seems decidedly counterproductive. So every month, even today, he or Arlene writes the same general letter and mails it to the IRS. This reduces the phone bill by about sixty-eight cents, give or take a nickel. It's a tedious, symbolic protest, a matter of principle. That's how Cliff explained it to the IRS special agent who visited him in Fort Wayne, Indiana, in March 1982. He and Arlene were coordinating the work and meals for fifty volunteers helping with flood relief when, of all times and places, the IRS decided it was time Cliff paid up. Right there in Allen County, Indiana. The streets of Fort Wayne looked like canals, and nine thousand people had been driven from their homes. By then Cliff hadn't paid a phone tax for thirteen years. The agent flashed a badge and asked him why. Cliff described how the tax was essentially an investment in war and how he couldn't justify its support. To ante up for war, even if it were less than one dollar per month, was like helping pay for a hit man to target your brothers and sisters. Cliff and Arlene have friends who are as close as family in hotspots all over the world, from the Congo to the Gaza Strip to Bogota. The agent frowned and fidgeted and argued; he said Cliff's reasoning wasn't good enough. Cliff said it was good enough for him. The agent eventually gave up and left.[16]

Toward the end of his volunteer work in Mississippi, Cliff, then twenty years old, graduated from the starter kit of phone-tax resistance to full-time peacemaking and self-imposed poverty. Like his father and mother, he made sure his income stayed below the taxable level. He also returned his draft registration card, hand-delivered it to Selective Services officers and politely told them to keep it. He didn't burn the card or steal off to Canada;[17] he simply said no to war. No means no. Like Kathy Kelly with her tax "refusal," he didn't see it as an act of resisting the pull of war. It just wasn't an option. He gave the card to officials in southern Mississippi and told them where he would be staying; gave them an address in Dayton, Ohio. If they needed to contact him with follow-up questions or, say, an arrest warrant, that's where they could find him. He then took off on a nonstop tour of the Midwest speaking out against the Vietnam War, wars in general, and the burgeoning military-industrial complex. He spoke at churches, colleges, high schools, any place that would have him. He's been doing it ever since.

When "The Phil Donahue Show" still taped in Dayton in 1971, one of its guests was then-Selective Services Director Curtis W. Tarr. Because of Cliff's speeches through Ohio, Michigan, Illinois, and elsewhere, Donahue, a critic of the Vietnam War, and his staff were familiar with him. The day Tarr was on the show, Cliff attended. Donahue referred to him, pointed him out in the audience to Tarr, and then he asked Tarr what Washington planned to do with men like Cliff, the draft-eligible Americans who flat refused to participate in Washington's war making.

Tarr warned that Washington would be coming for Cliff, and for the 200,000 other men like him.[18] That was four decades ago.

Shane walked from the Rutba clinic's dark corridor into the bright, dry Al Anbar afternoon. He had to find a way to get Weldon from Rutba to Amman, a drive one hour west on Saddam's autobahn, another four hours west on Jordan's desert highway. Cuts on the back of Weldon's head had been sutured without anesthesia by Jassim and Tarik, and Rutba General director Dr. Farouq Al-Dulaimi had placed his left arm in a simple blue sling. With no hospital and few medicines, it was the best they could do. The clinic wasn't set up for critical care.

His left arm in the same type of simple blue sling, Shane squinted into the daylight. The clinic's driveway, a concrete courtyard tucked behind a low-slung mud-brick wall and a sliding metal gate, was filled with Iraqis. A local sheikh and dozens of others, women, mostly, many of them covered head-to-toe in Islam's full-length *abaya,* brought blankets and glasses of water. Shane smiled, moved his right hand over the sling and his heart, and graciously accepted the water. He didn't dare drink it. Under the best circumstances the peacemakers avoided drinking Iraq's tap water.[19] In a town shelled by American ordnance, a desert outpost that had recently lost most of its electricity, the drinking water was highly suspect. Shane tipped a glass to his lips and pretended to sip.

A GMC Suburban with the Christian cross duct-taped to its roof turned into the clinic's drive. Shane's heart leaped. Moments earlier, the Baghdad driver had stopped on Rutba's main road to ask directions to the hospital.

Lakad qasafa al Amerikeuon musteshfana bel qanabel, he was told.

"There is no hospital. The Americans bombed our hospital."[20]

He pointed them in the direction of the Health Care Center in Rutba. "Go straight, veer left, straight again until you see a minaret behind a strip of concrete auto garages. Look left until you see the sign with a red crescent painted on it."

A big smile flashed onto Shane's face when he saw the SUV. He waved excitedly to Peggy Gish and to his Eastern University comrades, Jonathan and Leah Wilson-Hartgrove, welcoming them to the clinic like a newly anointed host. They immediately began brainstorming a way to Jordan or, at the very least, to the highway to retrieve their luggage and passports, but Shane was warned to stay off the roads.

La, la, la, the locals in the courtyard had responded, pointing skyward toward the contrails of military jets. "No, no, no."

Jonathan saw an ambulance parked next to the clinic with the emblem of the International Red Crescent. He asked Dr. Al-Dulaimi if they could transport Weldon to Jordan in it. He had the same response. "No," he said, "it will be bombed."[21]

That left one option. Everyone squeezed into the GMC Suburban to go to the accident site and continue on to Jordan. Eight people in an SUV is manageable. Eight people with luggage is doable. But Weldon, with multiple fractures, had to remain flat and still, stretched across the middle seats. At that point an SUV begins to resemble a clown car.

Leah and Jonathan folded themselves into the floorboard beside Weldon; Cliff burrowed into a blinding pile of luggage stacked in the front shotgun seat; the remaining three, Shane, Bae, and Peggy, were contortionists in the back.

The same burly, grandfatherly ambulance driver who had cradled Weldon and carried him into the clinic, an ex-Iraqi soldier named Sa'ady Mesha'al Rasheed, also helped to carry him out on a gurney. Sa'ady, Jassim, and Tarik gently fit Weldon and the gurney through the Suburban's door. It was awkward, all tight angles and balance. The sun's glare bounced on Weldon's face like a sniper's laser, and he squinted into it, unable to lift an arm to shield himself. A man's hand reached across to shade him. Weldon stared up into the smile of a redheaded, blue-eyed Iraqi in a flowing white *dishdasha*. He was bathed in sunlight. Weldon would later write in his journal, "I saw the glowing transfigured face of Jesus in that kindly Iraqi face that unforgettable day in the desert."

Shokran.

"Thank you."

Weldon could barely whisper.

Squatting on the floorboard, Leah helped slide Weldon across the seats and then closed the door at his head. The door reopened. The same redheaded Iraqi looked down at Weldon, still smiling gently. He leaned down and kissed him on both cheeks.

"Allah will take care of you," he said in English.

Shane collected all of the group's Iraqi dinar, the grossly deflated currency that would soon have value only as a souvenir. He asked Cliff, Peggy, Jonathan, and Leah to empty their pockets; let's give them everything we have. Before racing from Rutba to the highway, and then west to No Man's Land, he and the others hugged the ambulance driver, Sa'ady; they hugged the nurse, Tarik; they hugged the physician's assistant, Jassim; they hugged the doctors and the townspeople and the hobbled taxi driver who lost his car. From the way each of them tell it, those final moments in a desert of war-torn Iraq were a sappy love fest. Eyes pooled with tears. Hands were placed over hearts. Shane didn't count the money; it would have taken too long. Stacked and pressed together with two hands it was the size of three mud bricks.

"Here," Shane said, holding it out for Dr. Al-Dulaimi, "I don't know what we owe you, but we'd like to give you this."

Shane says now that it felt like the right thing to do. It felt very American.

The doctor stared at Shane for a few seconds. It felt like several minutes.

"No."

"But we *want* you to have this."

He looked at Shane as if he had just failed the quiz.

"We don't want your money. This is not why we took care of you. We cared for you because you are like our brothers and our sisters. You go on and keep doing this work of peace. That is payment enough. Just go and tell the world about Rutba."[22]

COMMON GROUND

If you come with us, you'll see a side of Iraq you've never seen before.
—Cliff Kindy to former Army
Lieutenant Colonel Nathan
Sassaman[1]

Reunion in 2010 at Rutba General Hospital: Cliff, Peggy, and Jassim Muhammad Jamil. Photo credit: Jamie Moffett

2010

The drive in the clown car from Rutba to No Man's Land was as uneventful as the drive in 2010 from No Man's Land to Rutba, although both had elicited similarly morbid predictions: The belief in 2003 that American bomber pilots would annihilate the GMC Suburban; and the belief, seven years later, that rogue Iraqis and/or foreign insurgents would kidnap and decapitate unarmed peaceful Americans.

That's not to say that either of these scenarios was impossible. It's just that neither occurred. And in their absence other scenarios were made possible. Courage defeated fear. Or, foolishness did. Either way, fear lost.

On Facebook I recently saw a graphic that looked something like this:

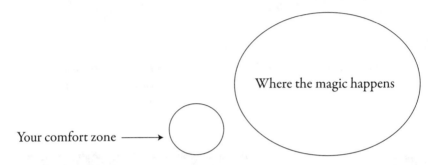

There were no discussions of comfort, discomfort, or of things arcane and magical, as we crossed into Iraq in 2010 in Major Mohsin's Chevy pickup; thank God or Allah, all the waiting and talking was over and the crazy troublesome border was breached. Hooah, right? Not exactly; not yet. As I watched Captain Foster and Major Nedal recede from sight, armed officers standing side by side next to two cocked-and-locked Hoosier-made Humvees, I felt a tug to return to the ugly, hard ground of No Man's Land. Like the Green Zone in Baghdad, it was the buffer between "us" and "them." It felt safe, comfortable.

The Iraqi border facility, no more than two miles from its Jordanian counterpart, was on the far side of a riches-to-rags arc. There were no lines of travelers waiting for visas to be processed. Only us. Eastbound tractor-trailer convoys running bumper to bumper ferrying food, gas, cars, and reconstruction materials into a war-scarred nation had their own express lane, like the I-395 HOV highway feeding into and out of Washington, DC. Civilian traffic veered left; Humvees and eighteen-wheelers right. Mohsin pointed us in the direction we needed to go, and then he disappeared. Inside the visa processing area there were four unmanned windows covered in dust, a four-seat bench missing one seat, and a four-legged chair missing one leg. It was noontime and the sidewalk, the offices, the waiting area looked ghost-town empty. Then we heard the haunting cry of the muezzin—noon prayers carried from a minaret one hundred meters away. We could see it through the office's filmy windows.

The *Dhuhr*[2]—the second of Islam's five daily prayers—was ending with the *Tashahhud* (what my Baptist family would call the doxology[3]):

At-taḥiyyātu lillāhi, waṣ-ṣalawātu waṭ-ṭayyibātu.
As-salāmu ālaikā ayyuhā n-nabiyyu wa-raḥmatu llāhi
  wa-barakātuh.
As-salāmu ʿalaynā wa-ʾalā ʿibādi llāhi ṣ-ṣāliḥīn.
Ashhadu allā ilāha illā llāhu wa-ashhadu anna Muḥammadan
  ʿabduhū wa-rasūluh.

All worshipping is for Allah.
Allah's peace be upon you, O Prophet, and His mercy and blessings.
Peace be on us and on all righteous servants of Allah.
I bear witness that there is none worthy of worship except Allah,
and I bear witness that Muhammad is His servant and messenger.

Only then did an officer from Iraq's Ministry of Interior escort us through the border complex and into an oblong, narrow office where floor-to-ceiling curtains were pulled shut. Faded and brown, the drapes matched the castoff couches and chairs which, in turn, blended with the facility's overall decor: electrical wiring hung from the walls and ceilings; a single bedroom choked on three single beds; hallways reeked of stale urine, like in the bowels of New York's Penn Station. The oblong office was warmed by an electric heater, and the officer in charge, a smiling, amicable Iraqi wearing a dark Adidas sweatshirt over a dark blue uniform, offered us cans of Pepsi. Like Mohsin, he didn't carry a gun. Neither did the officer who had three stars on his uniform and eight cans of room-temperature Pepsi. Similar to American Supermax prisons, where inmates would have little to lose if they attacked guards and stole their weapons, Iraq's border officers do not carry guns. The officer in Adidas explained to Sami that he owned only one pistol, total, and he kept it at home for his family's protection.

"Now," he asked, speaking Arabic and reviewing our passports with Sami, "what is it that brings them to Iraq?"

Before I'd left Washington, my wife and I made wallet-sized laminated cards with each of the peacemaker's names, city, and thumbnail-sized mug shot. With Kathy Kelly's advice and Sami's English-to-Arabic translation, I loosely mimicked the Iraq Peace Team's Magic Sheet, the Get-Out-of-Jail-Free card Shane had flashed in 2003 in Rutba to explain why unarmed Americans were in a war zone. My Magic Sheet v2.0 stated, "We represent a group of American activists dedicated to hearing the voices most affected by the U.S. warfare in Iraq. We are traveling, briefly, in Iraq, to visit with doctors and nurses who have given some of us hospitality and medical treatment in the past. When we return to our homes, we will work on behalf of a just and lasting peace."

It was repeated in Arabic script on the opposite side.

The officer wearing Adidas turned it over, read it, and then smiled, presumably at our best intentions. Or maybe at our naiveté. Regardless, he shook Sami's hand and wished us Godspeed, telling him, "I'm impressed that you represent not only the old generation, but the new generation for peace."

Ninety minutes after Islam's noon prayer and "doxology" had concluded, cars sent by Sami's friend in Rutba, seventy-eight miles east of No Man's Land, arrived at the border complex. Two Opels, one dark cherry with tire retreads, missing hubcaps, a cat's paw prints down the dusty back window, and Arabic pop music on the stereo; the other, sleeker and gray, with mud flaps, spoiler, and a yellow "taxi" sign on the dashboard. The previous night in Amman we'd purchased tourist-priced $7 *kaffiyehs*, the headdress worn as turbans by many Arab men. We wrapped them clumsily around our Caucasian heads as the Iraqi officers walked us out a side door to the idling Opels. Two young Iraqi men—one, Ali, the son of Sami's friend—drove us east on Iraq's Highway 1 (formerly, Saddam's autobahn) with Peggy, Weldon, Cliff, and Sami in the gray Opel; Shane, Logan, Jamie, and me in the other. Passing oil tankers and tractor-trailers, and stalled briefly in traffic, we drew similar reactions—drivers strained for a better view of the Anglo-Americans wrapped in *kaffiyehs*. They stared, not in an aggressive manner, just curious.

From Highway 1 we merged with Highway 10/11, an empty straightaway into Rutba. Barricades, the same waist-high blocks of concrete that cordon off 1600 Pennsylvania Avenue, funneled us to the city's guarded entrance. To our left was a garrison the size of a football field flanked by a cocked-and-locked Hoosier-made Humvee bearing Iraqi plates and Iraqi flag. Directly in front of us were two guards, one holding a cigarette in his mouth and an AK-47 in his hands; the other dressed in desert fatigues with an Iraqi flag patch sewn onto his right sleeve, an American flag onto the left, and, strapped to his chest, brass knuckles.[4]

We pulled over.

Evidently, everything was going exactly as Sami had planned, because, at 4 p.m. on a Friday, Rutba was surprised to see us.

A sleepy looking two-guard station swelled immediately with three, four, five guards and multi-uniformed officers—military and police. Looking back now at video and photos, I count four camouflage color schemes worn by the Iraqi officers surrounding us. All are from the U.S. military's closet of Battle Dress Uniforms: traditional Army combat fatigues with patches of tan, gray, and green; urban combat with a blend of dark shades; desert combat with patches of tan, brown, and pale green; and the Airman Battle Uniform, an old pattern based on the Vietnam-era tiger stripe. By the time I climbed out of the Opel and found my Magic Sheet, an officer with the Ministry of Interior had driven up in a full-sized blue Chevrolet Silverado pickup with police lights and a missing front headlamp. I now counted ten uniformed Iraqis inspecting our Opels, our passports, our visas, our story, our motives. It was as if we were trying to board a flight bound for Washington's Reagan National Airport. The Ministry of Interior officer didn't understand the Magic Sheet, so a younger guy in street clothes read it to him. A scrum of fourteen people, us and them, huddled in the wind and chill for the first-ever public reading of Magic Sheet v2.0.[5] The officer, middle-aged and graying at the temples, listened intently, leaned in, and nodded as if to say, Yeah, yeah, I understand, but he never smiled or placed a hand over his heart or acted as if Rutba might offer us eight cups of tea or warm cans of Pepsi. The reading completed, he looked up, nodded to Sami and me to hold tight, and then he returned to his truck and, I suspect, phoned the mayor or someone. A moment later he motioned for us to follow; he revved his Chevy engine and blared his siren.

In a parade of cars and trucks we followed him from Rutba's bland, dusty outskirts to its tired, dusty downtown, past concrete walls decorated with graffiti of palm trees, cityscapes, the Iraqi flag, etc.; past an elementary school wall spray painted with an Arabic prayer ("Oh God, provide me with more knowledge"); past the fruit and vegetable markets that Major Gavrilis had helped restock with the loan of his SAT phone and the bank he bombed to chase out the Fedayeen.[6] We slowed and turned left into the driveway and parking lot of a broad complex. Across the street was a multistory sand-brown building with a large sign in Arabic and English: "Mayor of Rutba." Beside us was the rebuilt Rutba General Hospital. The Chevy's siren shrieked again, as if to announce us.

So much for traveling incognito.

By the time we arrived at Rutba General it looked as if the town's elders had responded to an urgent call to meet in the hospital director's office. A room intended for no more than six or eight people was crowded with twice as many. Iraqi men stood quietly in the corners, along the walls, in the doorway, and they sat or stood up front. Looking around at the serious faces, I wasn't sure if we'd parachuted into a party, a meeting, or an interrogation. Armed or unarmed, military or civilian, no matter. We needed to explain ourselves.

Cliff cleared his throat and offered to go first; Sami interpreted during his pauses.

"It is an honor to be back in the city of Rutba. A memorable time for us is when we were here at the end of March 2003."

At the desk seated at the head of the room was a thirty-something Iraqi man, clean cut with a goatee, blue jeans, pullover, and brown leather coat with fur-lined collar. Inexplicably, he wore a solid metal bracelet imprinted with the Nike swoosh.[7] As Cliff and Sami volleyed English and Arabic, he stared straight ahead, like he was looking through Cliff, or he stared down at the desk. I noticed his jaw muscles clenching, the same way my father's would when, as a child, I needed scolding. I figured he had lost a loved one in the war. Or, I guessed, he might be irritated. We had barged into town unannounced and hijacked Rutba's one day of rest. It was a Friday, Islam's Sabbath.

"We had been ordered out of Baghdad, left in a three-car caravan, and the trailing car had an accident just west of Rutba," Cliff (and Sami) continued. "An eastbound Iraqi driver stopped and welcomed us. We got into his vehicle, and another vehicle, and we were brought into Rutba. Medical personnel opened their doors and said it doesn't matter if you're Iraqi or American, it doesn't matter whether you're Muslim or Christian, we will take care of you."

Eventually, we each introduced ourselves and added a little something to the story or explained how we were involved in helping to retell it. Weldon said his life was probably saved in Rutba and that "ever since that day, March 29 of 2003, I have looked forward to the day that we could come back to Rutba to see you and to thank you. . . . So this is a very special day and I am grateful." Shane echoed the sentiment and told of how Jonathan and Leah were so moved by the kindness they'd witnessed in Rutba that when they founded a charity in the summer of 2003 in Durham, North Carolina, a community project where Christians live, eat, pray, and work together to reduce violence and foster reconciliation and peace, they recalled the actions of Iraqis. Of Rutba. Their Christian charity is an inspiration drawn from the humanitarianism of Muslims. Named for Muslims, too. They called it "Rutba House," Shane announced proudly.

During Sami's interpretation and explanation of Rutba House, you could feel the mood of the room lift. The men jamming the doorway, the men against the wall, the men up front and, even, the clenched-jaw guy staring from behind the desk, they seemed to relax. We exhaled, also.

The story of Rutba "is so powerful," Shane said excitedly, his enthusiasm and Southern accent filling the room, "not because it is exceptional or extraordinary, but because it exemplifies what we've experienced from the Iraqi people. But it's not what many people in the U.S. see on the news."

Peggy then explained how the story resonated with her not only because of the help that Iraqis gave to the peacemakers, but because of *when* they gave it. Rutba was being attacked by American-made bombs fired by American-made jets. "It shows that human love can go from one person to another and, in spite of the label 'enemy,' we are still able to be kind and loving to each other," she said.

As Sami interpreted, another middle-aged Iraqi man strolled authoritatively into the room; he was sharply dressed in dark dress slacks, sport coat, and collared shirt; several Iraqis stood to offer him their seats. The man sitting at the desk scooted over to make room at the head of the room. Sami continued uninterrupted, and, in Arabic, he told the two men at the desk of how we had chosen to enter Iraq that day without armed protection despite repeated warnings from the militaries of Jordan and the United States. "We told the soldiers and the militaries, 'We don't need guns to protect us. The only thing we need to protect us is the love and the recognition of one another,'" he said, referring to Iraqis and Americans. "That is the only means that will guarantee safety and peace."

The two men nodded in agreement, and then they began whispering to each other. After a couple of minutes, others joined in. Finally, the man whose jaw muscles had been clenched, spoke.

"Welcome here. Welcome in Iraq," he said in English.

He introduced himself as Dr. Nizar Jameel Yaseen, originally from Baghdad. This was the first he had heard about the taxi accident and Rutba's rescue of injured Americans. When Dr. Farouq Al-Dulaimi[8] left for Ramadi in 2004, Dr. Yaseen replaced him as the director of Rutba General Hospital. "I was not here in 2003, so I did not see you and you did not see me," he said slowly, speaking English with a thick Arabic accent. "We want to offer you the best that we have at the hospital and in the city. . . . For the Iraqi people, I say to you, 'Welcome.'"

The man seated next to Dr. Yaseen introduced himself as Rutba's mayor, Qasim Al-Mar'ai, a former pilot in the Iraqi military. During the previous year he had traveled to several American cities as part of a delegation of Iraqi politicians visiting Washington, New York, Philadelphia, Raleigh, North Carolina, etc. While on the tour he had shopped for a sister city to join with Rutba in helping it to grow and prosper in postwar Iraq.

That same year, Sami, in his work with Muslim Peacemaker Teams and the nonprofit Iraqi & American Reconciliation Project, had helped pair his hometown, Najaf, with his adopted home, Minneapolis. When Al-Mar'ai mentioned his visit to Raleigh and his wish for Rutba to have a sister city, Sami and Shane looked at each other and shifted in their seats. Raleigh is in an area of North Carolina known as "Research Triangle," a trifecta that includes Durham. Having arrived at the meeting after Shane introduced himself, Al-Mar'ai missed the story about Durham's Rutba House. Shane retold it, and as Sami interpreted, Al-Mar'ai shifted in his seat too. He knew where Shane was headed with the story and began saying *na'am, na'am* ("yes, yes"), even before Shane finished. Rutba partnered with Durham? *Na'am.* The following day, the fervor for a Rutba-Durham marriage would build into a formal request asking Durham, home to the Rutba House, to partner with Rutba, home to Sunni Muslims in western Iraq. [9] It was composed by hand in Arabic and English, first on a legal pad and then on white construction board as large as a street sign. The mayor, the doctor, the peacemakers, several locals, and even an Iraqi war veteran who had introduced himself to the room in Arabic—*Ismee Logan, ana talib waa ana adrs a salaam* ("My name is Logan, I am a student and I study peace")—all gathered around the sign with cameras rolling and clicking. Everyone posed for the universal grin-and-grip photo. Clearly, democracy was blooming in the Anbar desert.

A l-Mar'ai offered to put us up in the staff quarters of Rutba General Hospital. He offered to feed us breakfast, lunch, and dinner, too—to have it brought to us right there in the hospital. He offered to have anyone we wanted to meet and interview brought to us in the staff quarters of the hospital, for example, some of the medical staff from 2003, a local sheikh, teacher, whoever. There would be no need for us to, say, wander around Rutba in need of anything. He made sure of this. He offered to bring everything to us right there behind the concrete walls of the rebuilt Rutba General compound. It wasn't just an offer. He insisted.

Located in a vast and rural stretch of the Syrian desert near Iraq's borders with Syria, Jordan, and Saudi Arabia, Al Anbar and Rutba have a long history of exceptional hospitality, Al-Mar'ai explained. "This is how Rutba historically is known. Any guest visiting Rutba . . . this guest of ours would never have to go to a restaurant or a place outside (such as a hotel). But they would move from home to home being fed and taken care of. This is what the Iraqi people are known by. But, again, the province of Anbar is unique with this attitude."

Two months earlier in New York City, Iraqi Ambassador to the United Nations Hamid Al-Bayati had recalled for me how Iraqi families in small desert towns like Rutba used to burn fires outside at night to serve as a kind of lighthouse for foreign travelers. If someone needed water or food or a bed, locals would assist them. Insist, even. Although that was many generations ago, before cars raced through Al Anbar on the desert autobahn, Al-Bayati explained that hospitality is rooted deeply in Islam and in Iraqi culture, and that even today Iraqis will provide for a guest indefinitely.

I told the ambassador the story of how Shane had asked for a ride back to the wrecked taxi in 2003, but the locals in Rutba responded, *La, la, la*. "No, no, no." They were afraid of the U.S. jets overhead. But they offered to host the injured peacemakers, and Shane got the sense that the invitation was open ended. They could have stayed in Rutba indefinitely.

Al-Bayati smiled knowingly. "Part of our [religious] tradition is that having a guest is a *privilege*. When you feed somebody and take care of somebody, it's an honor . . . it's like a gift given from God."

But for Al-Mar'ai, the offer to accommodate us in a guarded compound across the street from his office was also about security. Like Captain Foster and Major Nedal, he was concerned for our safety. Rutba's unique position as a desert thoroughfare makes it readily accessible to travelers, traders, importers, exporters—and to foreign fighters. Al-Mar'ai knows this well. Two years earlier, on November 2, 2007, two suicide bombers wearing explosive belts had attempted to kill him and his security guards outside his house.[10] During the next six months he said there were fifteen separate attempts made by insurgents to kill him.[11] These assassination attempts occurred during the "Anbar Awakening," a period beginning in 2006 when Anbar locals, led by tribal sheikhs, began cooperating more with American troops and resisted the foreign fighters who were driving Anbar's insurgency.[12]

Before we left the meeting, Al-Mar'ai offered us one more thing. Or several, actually. Like parting gifts, we left the office flanked by members of the mayor's security detail.

"I'm sure the area of Rutba is safe for you, but we need to do extra measures," he said at sunset on Islam's Sabbath. "We are approaching elections, and there are some political struggles, so we don't want anybody to take advantage of your presence and do harm to you"

The next morning I woke up long before the desert's 7:20 sunrise. The streets, the hospital, our rooms on the second floor of the three-story living quarters were middle-of-the-night quiet. The day's high temperature would reach the low forties, but barefoot and predawn on the stone floor, it felt below freezing. Similar to the facilities at the Iraqi border crossing, our rooms had three beds or cots each. It's where the cleaning crew normally slept and what Dr. Yaseen called home. He was thirty-three, single, childless, and somewhere on the same floor he had his own room.[13]

On the first floor of the living quarters, where we were fed like presidents or dictators (chicken, lamb, vegetables, eggs, kabobs, fresh pita bread the size of hub caps), there was a living area with couches, chairs, and a twenty-six-inch flat-screen LG television. Turning it on the first time, Fox television's teen drama, "The O.C.," played, subtitled in Arabic. At dinner the first night Dr. Yaseen explained to us the difference between a genuine hospital and a medical clinic posing as one. Reliable electricity. Without it, doctors cannot store blood and perform major surgery. As he spoke the lights went out. If it hadn't been so common it might have seemed ironic, even funny, but we had already seen how the electricity in Rutba ebbed and flowed. Ten minutes, thirty minutes, an hour; you never knew when lights, the television, wall clocks, whatever, would turn off or back on.

On Saturday morning, January 16, I went toward the light. From the stairs I could see it behind the closed door of the living area; so, in sweatpants, sweatshirt, and carrying my laptop and work satchel, I made my way there. The second I opened the door and stepped inside—*boom!* A fuse box, gun or something, like a car backfiring. The room fell pitch black. All I could see was the last flash of image imprinted on my retina. Guns. AK-47s, I thought. As many as a half dozen, maybe; each propped against a wall, a chair, the TV stand. Probably one for each shadow I'd seen lounging on couches or chairs; the strangers now in the dark with me.

A light bulb came on. It was attached to the headband of a young police officer in the dark camouflage of the Ministry of Interior. He wore one star on the shoulder of his uniform and a miner's hands-free headlamp. At dinner Logan had pulled out something exactly like it when we had to eat in the dark. Seems the military guys are always prepared. This one introduced himself as "Marc"— Lieutenant Marcus Amar, I wrote in my notebook.[14] He said he and the other Iraqis playing cards in the dark and napping on a couch had been there all night.[15] They'd been sent to the hospital to protect us. By order of the mayor, he said.

Like the first two guards at the entrance to Rutba, Lieutenant Amar had been trained by the U.S. military. His English was fluent. Two years earlier, before "the people in Baghdad they go nuts and they starting killing people who are Sunni," he said, he was an engineering student attending college in Baghdad. Similar to classes in Iraq's medical schools, most of his engineering courses were taught in English. But at age nineteen, as a Sunni living in the new post-Saddam, Shia-dominant capital of Iraq, he didn't feel safe, even though he and the Sunni-led Ba'ath Party had never been friends.[16] He returned to Rutba after his freshman year. A couple of months later, two guys he knew hid an Improvised Explosive Device (IED)—the insurgents' weapon of choice—on the road directly in front of his house. It was rigged with a cell phone remote. To protect himself and his family from arrest and/or injury, he told American soldiers about it. Soon afterward, Uncle Sam came calling for him. Would he like to be all that he could be? The engineer decided to be a cop. He was sent to Mosul for two months of training with the American military.

In his stories, in his eyes, and in the way he chain-smoked a favorite brand of French cigarette, he looked and sounded far older than his twenty-one years. After Major Gavrilis's Special Forces had driven out the Fedayeen and disbanded the Ba'ath Party, Lieutenant Amar said life was "going well" in Rutba, especially if your family had always been on the wrong side of the Ba'athists. But beginning in the fall of 2004, he said an influx of foreign fighters into Rutba from Jordan, Syria, and, especially, Saudi Arabia, where Sunni Muslims are a vast majority, ignited a holy war. He was in high school at the time, and teenage friends of his who prayed five times a day and went to mosque could earn large sums of money to kill "the enemies" of Sunni Islam. And the prey wasn't only the occupying U.S. and British forces, but Iraq's Shia Muslims. If you killed Shia (Iraq's new political majority), you were paid. Even if you killed randomly and for no reason. "Some of my friends, they join with these guys," he said. "They train [them] on the snipers and the guns."

The recruits were only about ages sixteen and seventeen, he said, too young to understand fully what they were getting into. But, he added, "If you have a gun at that time, it means you've got the power."

He's seen a young Shia boy[17] murdered by insurgents just for being Shia, he says, and a friend who says he was forced to murder Shia after he witnessed insurgents killing them. The friend said they told him to try killing a Shia, too—do it once or they would kill him. Just try it, they insisted, like it was a sport. They promised it would be easy. "And when he did, he said it was easy— it was too easy," Lieutenant Amar recalled. His friend had come to him crying. But not crying about the murder, per se. He was crying about his lack of remorse. "I should feel bad," he told Lieutenant Amar, who wasn't a policeman yet. The friend confessed to his Sunni sheikh, told him how the worst part was the lack of remorse. Lieutenant Amar said the sheikh responded, "No, that is not what you should feel. You did the right thing."

When he'd returned to Rutba from Mosul to work as an interior ministry policeman, Lieutenant Amar says his circle of friends changed. Had to. Some of the guys he'd been running with were now "bad guys" to anyone sworn to uphold the law. And the friend who lacked remorse, he'd become "a really bad guy," Lieutenant Amar said. Outside of town and on the side of the highway one night, that friend asked him what he would do if he found him in Rutba illegally with a weapon. "I would shoot you," he told him. Two weeks later, he and another officer responded to a call about two men with weapons outside of Rutba's only hotel, a mud-brick mom-and-pop on the main drag near Rutba General. Police and the bad guys ended up in a gunfight, and the bad guys lost. When Lieutenant Amar went closer to see who they had shot and to get their weapons, he recognized one of the dead.

"He's the same one," Lieutenant Amar said, playing cards many months later near the end of a midnight shift in Rutba General. "He's my friend."

As usual, the electricity had gone off in the hospital when he recalled this story. It was cold, dark. Lieutenant Amar looked away for a second, sniffed, studied his fanned-out hand of cards.

"So," he finished, looking up and forcing a smile, "it's the life."[18]

The brief time we were in Rutba we were holed up in the living quarters of Rutba General protected by shifts of police and AK-47s—flanked by the same whenever we dared to venture off the property. Or when we stepped outside. And, especially, when we walked across the main street to the mayor's office or across the compound to the main hospital. For us to go anywhere in Rutba seemed to require logistics and security akin to President Obama and Vice President Biden going out for noontime hamburgers.

Maybe Rutba just didn't know what to make of us. In a meeting in the mayor's office the morning after we arrived, Al-Mar'ai said we were the first American civilians to visit postwar Rutba. The last time had been March 29, 2003. And like the care given that day to Cliff, Weldon, and Shane, Al-Mar'ai said the rooms, the feasts, the VIP security, all of it was "a normal and regular reaction" for Rutba when it hosts visitors.

"As you may know, terrorism is not an Islamic behavior," he had assured us the previous evening, just before surrounding us with an army of security. "It's something that came [from] outside of Islam. . . . The outsiders, they did this and tried to distort the real image of Iraq or Muslims in Iraq. And the extremism is not only in our society, but it's in Christianity and Judaism too."

The head of our hastily assembled security team was a wiry and gravely serious man with a graying mustache and deep lines creasing his face. Hafedh Jum'ma wore the same style dark leather coat worn by the four Ba'athist security guards who trailed me, Kathy Kelly, and others through Basra in February 2003. But where they lightly and incessantly rubbed prayer beads, Jum'ma was more likely to grip and squeeze. He looked tense. All the more with us in his care. If he'd had his way we would have never left the living quarters of Rutba General.

During the next three days he would hurry us through visits in the main hospital; herd us in and out of the Health Care Center in Rutba; [19] keep lookout while we photographed a game of sandlot soccer from the cover of an idling car; cancel our visit to a private residence; and, pretty much, maintain a mantra of *yalla, yalla* (rough translation: "C'mon, hurry, let's go") the entire time we were in Rutba. In other words, he kept us safe. On Sunday, after we visited Rutba's all-boy Horan Primary School and mingled with an assembly of students that performed the Iraqi national anthem[20] and presented us with a gilded copy of the Qur'an, which sits today on the top shelf of Logan's favorite bookcase, Jum'ma had seen enough. Even if we hadn't. The school's principal said he had been the next door neighbor of the father and son killed in the 2003 bombing of Rutba General, and he invited us to his house for dinner, dessert, tea, whatever we had time to do. We had nothing but time. We eagerly accepted. Sami said we only had time for tea because he feared the principal would spend a fortune if we visited his house for dinner. However, several hours later, Sami told us there would be no tea or dinner or visit of any kind at the principal's house. He and Jum'ma cancelled it. They feared that a visit to a private residence endangered not only our lives, but it put the principal and his family at risk. Evidently, just hosting an American in your home was enough to get an Iraqi killed.

After two wars and twelve years of economic sanctions, Iraqis didn't need to hate us or blame us to be motivated to kill us. A good payday might suffice. Lieutenant Amar said insurgents were paying Rutba's teenagers U.S. $4,000 in 2004 when his friends accepted offers to kill occupiers and Shia. Back then that many American dollars converted to nearly six million of Iraq's new dinar. That's 1,500 dinar for every dollar. Today, you need only 1,170 Iraqi dinar to buy one (weakened) U.S. dollar, but that still reflects the stuff of Dickens novels. Iraqis were so poor in the years leading up to the war and afterward that they would sell, literally, their kitchen sink. The depreciation of the Iraqi dinar in the 1990s caused Iraq's banking system to collapse, taking with it the savings of Iraqi families.[21] As recently as 2008, nearly 80 percent of Anbar's families still had no savings or bank account,[22] and one in five children had been left fatherless by age eight from either the 2003 invasion or the fighting that followed it.[23]

As a sign of Al Anbar's improving middle class, a RAND Corporation study seemed to grasp for threads. It found hope in this: "Most [Anbari] households say they can afford to eat a protein-rich meal every other day. . . ."

Before the first Gulf War the Iraqi dinar traded at a value more than three times greater than the U.S. dollar.[24] At one point during the sanctions era the American dollar was equal to 4,000 Iraqi dinar, then stabilized at 3,100 dinar per dollar. The gutting of Iraq, encouraged and directed by three U.S. administrations (presidents George H. W. Bush, Bill Clinton, and George W. Bush), had been fast and methodical. By the time the Americans and Brits invaded, Iraq was already emaciated.

Kill an American in Iraq for U.S. $4,000? You bet.

Lieutenant Amar said he had been tempted to take the offer himself.

For those reasons and others, Jum'ma looked worried, even angry, whenever we poked a camera outside the car's window or let the *kaffiyehs* fall loose to our shoulders—more shawl than headdress. Anglo-Americans might still fetch a pretty price on the Rutba market. A carload of us could draw a small fortune. And even in the new economy with a relatively healthier dinar, every surge in electricity, every C-section rushed to Ramadi, served to remind Rutba of the things the Ba'athists did well, such as maintaining the electrical grids.

In the marketplace and on the walls of homes, you still see portraits of Saddam. Even Sami's good friend, a kindly grandfather, reserved and observant, the man who sent his son and a neighbor to retrieve us at the Iraqi border, says of the dead dictator, "Despite the cruelty of Saddam we lived with dignity . . . and we loved him. We still love him."

So when the hospital falls dark it doesn't seem to matter where the fault lies: domestic or foreign. Rutba General needs a new $20,000 diesel-fueled generator that no one is buying. It also needs to double the size of its staff of ten doctors. Dr. Yaseen doesn't have hope for either of these occurring. Shane asked how long it would take for Rutba General to become a fully functioning hospital again, and Dr. Yaseen shrugged off the question.

Shane pressed. "Ten years? Fifty years?"

"No," the doctor said. "I think it is not functional here. Forever."

He waved his hands like a ref over an unconscious fighter.

The medical staff, teachers, a sheikh, the mayor, almost anyone you ask about the spotty electricity, assigns blame to the war. Viewed chronologically, that's a reasonable conclusion: Rutba had reliable electricity before the United States invaded in 2003; Rutba's electricity has been maddeningly unreliable ever since. American-grade, Raytheon-made bombs knocked out Rutba's lights. Shock and Awe made sure of it. But the ongoing surges and power outages are a consequence of something far more complicated. Sadiq Majed Mubarak, the head of Rutba's Department of Electricity, says the city's consumption of electricity has quadrupled since 2003. Beginning around 2006, Rutba's electrical grid became increasingly overloaded and unreliable, even as its gigawatts capacity doubled. Today, the capacity covers only half the demand. But Mubarak doesn't place the blame on Raytheon and the Pentagon. Not entirely. He blames postwar expansions of houses and the construction of newer, larger, and more energy-demanding homes. He points a finger at consumption.[25]

As a Middle East thoroughfare Rutba is a hub of trade, importer and exporter; and in the post-Saddam era some of Rutba's families are living large. At least larger than before. This new housing has brought with it modern energy-consuming appliances—air conditioners, water pumps, washers, dryers, dishwashers, all the bells and whistles that draw a larger-than-fair share from Rutba's finite electric supply.[26] When the grid overloads, it buckles. *Boom!* Lights go out. Blood can't be refrigerated. C-sections and major surgeries are routed two hundred miles away to Ramadi. A hospital functions more like a clinic.

Coming and going from Rutba you can see one of these new housing developments on the outskirts of downtown, near a dusty soccer (football) field where kids kick up and inhale clouds of sand and dirt. This juxtaposition of the classes is so very American of Iraq. The neighborhood next to the neglected field could be a suburb of Nevada or Arizona. Large Syrian desert lots hold immaculate looking $100,000 houses (equal to 11.7 million Iraqi dinar), each with four or five bedrooms, two or three baths, water pump, air conditioner, dishwasher, and with a satellite dish on the roof.

So, in that way, the faulty electricity is an indirect casualty of war. Of Iraq's new democracy. Of humankind's innate selfishness. Simply, capitalism loosed a greater freedom to consume.

And with freedom, we have the birth of Rutba's One Percent.[27]

After the tea was cancelled, Logan's enthusiasm waned. Five days before he'd boarded Air France for Amman, he'd written in his journal how he was trying "to get my heart right" for the return to Iraq. It was a paraphrase of what the "1-14 Golden Dragons" had been told in Iraq each time they prepared to go off-base (or "outside the wire").

"Get your head straight," officers told soldiers.

This was different. It was outside the wire, for sure, but the risks were for peace instead of war. In his journal he wrote, "I am focusing on maximizing this experience for the positive."

But Logan was traveling with us undercover. Sami didn't believe Iraqis were ready in 2010 to host an American soldier. Rutba's wounds were too raw. To advertise Logan's military past would have increased the risk both for us and for our Iraqi hosts, Sami explained. So he had asked Logan not to identify himself as an Iraq war veteran.

Logan struggled with Sami's request, especially at the primary school where we met young boys whose fathers were killed in the war. Earlier that day, Sami suggested that it might be okay for Logan to discuss the war from a soldier's perspective if he distanced himself from the war by phrasing comments and questions in the third person (e.g., "I work with guys in the military who fought in Iraq . . ."). When we were invited to the principal's house, Logan had hoped Sami would free him up to talk about the regret and grief that some American soldiers felt. At Horan Primary School he'd met a redheaded child whom the principal introduced as a war orphan, and as Logan made his way through a courtyard filled with students, textbooks, book bags, and teachers, his frustration at remaining silent grew. His parents are school teachers, and he's considered becoming one himself. In an environment that felt so intimately familiar, he wanted to be himself; fully present and genuine. Anything less felt fake.

After leaving the school, he wrote in his journal: "I would really enjoy the opportunity to express my 'vicarious' grief on behalf of 'those soldiers I work with' to the redheaded boy through the principal. Lots of proxies involved and only a slim chance of doing it, but I know it would be very powerful for 'the soldiers I work with.'"

Of course he was referring to himself and the pressing need to vent whatever it was that he couldn't release unless he was fully present. He needed his identity back. When the principal's tea was cancelled, Logan retreated to Rutba General's flat roof, and with a dramatic view that counts eight minarets and stretches to the desert highway, he resigned himself to an experience that would not be personally maximized. "Pains me that the folks we've spoken to think that atrocities are the only stories soldiers have to share," he wrote later in his journal. "Maybe this is a bridge I'm not allowed to help build."

So we'd spent a year coordinating the trip with everyone's schedules (twice, if you count the 2009 postponement), flown thousands of miles to the Middle East, spent four days in Amman lobbying for visas, and we'd ridden nearly three hundred miles across the Syrian desert in taxis, pickups, and Opels, only to come to Rutba and ask Rutba to come to us.

Not my best work.

Thank God and a Hail Mary, the Good Samaritan Muslims of Rutba showed up on the Christian Sabbath. Allah is good.

The nurse arrived first. Tarik Ali Marzouq walked unannounced into Rutba General's living quarters a few minutes after ten o'clock on Sunday morning, January 17. It was as if he'd been waiting backstage since March 29, 2003. His smile was large and missing a front tooth; his beard leprechaun thick, and he wore a skull cap, or *kufi*, matching his white lab coat. The peacemakers had not been expecting him; it was as if he just magically appeared. For a second, maybe less, they weren't sure who he was. Then a smile shot across Cliff's face. His hand went over his heart in greeting, gratitude, love, peace, respect. (Like saying "aloha" to someone, the hand over the heart means many things—all of them good.) Then Shane's face lit up. Then Weldon's and Peggy's, and just as recognition of Tarik brought everyone to their feet, there was another grand entrance.

On Tarik's heels strode the debonair medical assistant, the tall, classically handsome Jassim Muhammad Jamil in dress slacks and a tan jacket. Perhaps it was the view he'd had from the ceiling, but Cliff immediately recognized the man who had pulled his scalp back together and threaded him with the final stitches.

Everyone began pointing fingers. Cliff at Tarik, asking if he'd helped sew his head. Jassim at Weldon saying *na'am, na'am*, "yes, yes," I remember you. Cliff and Tarik at each other, laughing and comparing their beards. Shane at his glasses, goatee, and long dreads, explaining to Tarik that in 2003 his glasses had come off in the car accident, and that his hair had been short and his chin a little bit smoother. "I look different now," he laughed.

Nothing choreographed, nothing meticulously planned, the reunion fell into place like an old episode of television's "This Is Your Life."

Cliff told the story about his near-death experience at the clinic, and as Sami interpreted Jassim nodded knowingly. "I am impressed that you believe in this. This is part of our belief too," he said in Arabic. "We have it in Islam."

Weldon explained that he had felt immediate relief in 2003 when Tarik and Jassim began to help him despite the fact he had multiple fractures and Rutba had no anesthesia to offer. "I knew my life was in your hands," Weldon said, "and that you would take care of us."

Logan, Jamie and I remained in the background—filming, taking notes, observing, enjoying. Writing in his journal later that day, Logan sounded reenergized. "Big moment. Two of the same (staff) from 2003 just appeared and the awaited moment just kind of happened. Shane got teary-eyed, and I know Weldon was very happy to finally meet someone from that day. . . . Some of the things said back and forth were just the epitome of humanity. Real powerful. *Hum dil Allah:* Grace be to God."

Minutes into the conversations and interpretations—a flurry of English and Arabic sent back and forth through Sami—there was a familiar loud sound.

Boom! A fuse box, a gun, a car backfiring. No one paid it much attention. The room was generating its own energy.

Jassim and Tarik had shown up that day for their morning shifts at the hospital when people told them the Americans they had treated seven years earlier had returned to Rutba. Jassim said he was at first confused. "I thought you lost something or you left something and you came back to take it. I never thought that you came back to say Thank you," he said. "Is it *possible* that you came back for a simple service [we] provided?"

He said that after the hospital was bombed a staff of sixty became a staff of five. Since most of the employees lived outside of Rutba, and since there was no hospital in which to work, they went home to ride out the war. The four or five employees who were at the clinic on March 29, 2003, were the hospital's local staff.

"Thank God that with our least [number of] staffers, we could do the job," Jassim said.

Shane explained why he thought it was important to keep Rutba's story alive and to continue to do what was asked of him seven years earlier. To tell the story of Rutba. "So many other people's hearts are brought to life by this story, which we know is not exceptional to Iraqi culture. But, when people hear it, the power of it to transform hearts is unbelievable."

Jassim and Tarik looked at each other, momentarily speechless. "You came a long distance from where you live, thousands of miles. I am so impressed that you did not forget this," Jassim said. "I assume that you are so well educated [to be] driven by this noble motive to come and say thank you. I wish the rest of humanity . . . was just like you."

Seconds later, Shane wiped at a tear. Jassim looked to Sami, who nodded as if to say, *na'am*, "yes, it's okay." Jassim stepped across the room and gave Shane a hug. Then he hugged Cliff. And then Weldon.

"We have not forgotten and we will never forget," Weldon told them.

Jassim pointed toward the sky and said *na'am*, "the gospel is written."

In his thirty years of nursing, Tarik said, it is in "this very moment I feel like I have been doing really good. Your presence here is my reward."

His left hand was injured and lightly bandaged, and when Sami leaned in to look at it and ask about it, Tarik kissed him on the cheek. Then he kissed Weldon, Cliff, and Shane.

Cliff emphasized the seriousness of his and Weldon's injuries, telling Tarik and Jassim, "I think two of us are alive today because of [you]."

"So," Tarik replied, a huge smile spreading across his face, "you are satisfied with the service we provided?"

Like at Major Gavrilis's dinner with Rutba's town leaders in 2003, where Americans ate with their hands and the Iraqis with forks and spoons, the living quarters at Rutba General erupted in our universal tongue. Everyone was laughing.

"At this very moment," Jassim said, "as much as you are happy to see us, and to come and say thank you, we are more so than you. We are even happier."

That evening, Shane, Cliff, and Weldon were in the living area still glowing from the afternoon reunion when an Iraqi grandfather with forearms as thick as cordwood cleared security and stood in the doorway.

The ambulance driver.

Sa'ady Mesha'al Rasheed pointed to Shane. Then to Cliff. Then to Weldon.

Anna ata thak arak. Anna ata thak arak. Anna ata thak arak.

"I remember you. I remember you. I remember you."

He looked again at Weldon, like he was adjusting his focus.

Anna ham elt ak.

"I carried you."

Until that moment Weldon had not recalled being lifted out of the bed of the station wagon, cradled in the arms of a former Iraqi soldier, and then carried into the Health Care Center in Rutba. But as Sami was interpreting Sa'ady's pointed introduction, Weldon recognized the gentle, weathered face. In that flash of memory it all came rushing back.

"That's right! You did."

Weldon's eyes filled with tears. He placed a hand over his heart.

Sa'ady described how a bad bout with asthma nearly crippled him that day, but when he saw Weldon bloodied, prone, and nearly unconscious, "I couldn't stop myself." He had to help. "This is what we have been taught by our religion, our culture, our tradition."

Earlier that day, Tarik and Jassim had walked the group across the packed dirt compound to the main area of Rutba General Hospital. They led them down hallways crowded with families, past a waiting area with patients smoking, and into an exam room filled with supplies and a bed unearthed from the charred rubble of the bombed hospital. The hallway outside of the room, the doorway, the room itself had become crowded with Iraqis and Americans and the lone Iraqi-American (Sami) among us, when Tarik made a promise. As he began to speak a respectful hush spread from the room to the hallway.

"As you do when you go back and you tell your people about Rutba," he said, "we also are committed to tell our people about your visit and your noble mission."

Jassim touched his heart and said he respected the honesty and the work of the peacemakers, and he wished he could join them. Also, he wished he had more time to tell them about the true nature of Islam. He hoped that one day they might return to Rutba so that they could resume the conversation.

Insha'allah, Cliff said.

Insha'allah, Jassim replied.

11

HOME OF THE BRAVE?

*There's another question people ask a lot: Did it bother you
killing so many people in Iraq? I tell them, "No." And I mean it.
The first time you shoot someone, you get a little nervous.
You think, can I really shoot this guy? Is it really okay?
But after you kill your enemy, you see it's okay. You say, Great.*
—Chris Kyle in *American Sniper*[1]

*Walking toward Rutba General from the living quarters, L to R: Jamie, Ali (son of
Sami's friend and our driver from the border crossing), Shane, Jassim, Sami, Peggy,
Tarik, Weldon, Cliff, two locals.* Photo credit: Greg Barrett

2003

As fast and smooth as the ride from the Health Care Center in Rutba to the Jordanian border was for Weldon, the two-hundred-mile ride from Al Karama to Amman was slow and torturous. It took three ambulances and all night to transport him and his broken body from the Ruweished refugee camp near No Man's Land to the emergency room at Arab Medical Center in Amman. With a doctor and Jonathan at his side, holding his hand and steadying the IV drip, the first ambulance blew its engine about an hour into the race.

Weldon is a car buff and lying in the back he heard the breakdown coming miles earlier. The engine bearings were straining to turn the motor. "I knew there was no way we were going to make it to Amman in that ambulance," he recalls.

But in the cold and the dark of Jordan's East-West Highway 10, the driver kept attempting to restart it. He turned the ignition key again and again, the engine coughing, grinding, growling, until, finally, with Weldon shivering and looking pale, he radioed for another ambulance crew.

A hundred miles or so closer to Amman, a tire blew out on the second ambulance. Left rear. The same as the Iraqi taxi. Without stray ordnance to give it a shove and a lift, the ambulance limped slowly to the highway's shoulder. The driver jacked up the car, jerking Weldon around in the process, but the flat tire wouldn't come off.

He radioed for another ambulance. This one arrived from Amman at 4 a.m.

It was "beginning to feel like a dark, dark comedy," Jonathan said. But "crazy as it was, it just wasn't funny. Weldon, I began to worry, might not make it."[2]

By the time the third ambulance delivered him to the emergency room at Arab Medical Center, the sun was beginning to rise on Sunday, March 30, 2003. He was treated, stabilized, admitted to intensive care, but doctors told Jonathan to relax. Weldon would live to fight (against) another war.

Shane, Cliff, Weldon, Peggy, and Leah had ridden through the night on a bus from the border to Amman and regrouped at another of the peacemakers' mom-and-pop one-star hotels: Al Monzer, a downtown Arabic school converted into a dusky hostel (now closed). Shane worried about Cliff's head, which was caked in blood and ruining breakfast for everyone. So after changing into a pair of white bell-bottom jeans loaned to him by Shane, and rolling up the legs (Shane is a half foot taller than Cliff), Jonathan and Shane convinced Cliff to go with them to Arab Medical, a four-mile taxi ride from Al Monzer.

The doctors, the nurses, the techs, everyone at Arab Medical was curious about what terrible event the Americans had endured. Weldon arrived broken and as pale as chalk; Cliff looked like he was wearing a bloody Halloween costume; Shane's left arm hung in a pale blue sling.

The story of the Iraq Peace Team and Rutba's Good Samaritans circulated through the ultramodern rooms and halls of Arab Medical. A doctor added two stitches to Cliff's head, but didn't bill him. Same with Shane's new sling. As they were leaving, a Palestinian nurse offered to come by Cliff's room at the Al Monzer after work. He said the wound would need to be cleaned and rebandaged. Cliff figured the guy needed extra money, so he agreed.

Shane, Cliff, Jonathan, and Leah were booked on flights to JFK the following day. Weldon would remain in Arab Medical for two more days with members of CPT keeping him company.

That Sunday evening, March 30, 2003, Shane, Jonathan, and Leah went to an Arabic church service not far from the Al Monzer. The sanctuary of The Heart of the Holiest Jesus Christ was filled with hundreds of Catholics, Protestants, and Orthodox Christians singing familiar songs like "Amazing Grace," and they recited the Lord's Prayer in different languages. Together, the congregation read a statement declaring their Christian love for the Muslim community and reaffirming the belief that we are all created in the image of God.[3]

After the service a Chaldean Catholic bishop told Shane that the church in the Middle East is concerned about the church in the United States. The news that day was about the 101st Airborne securing an airfield outside of Sami's hometown of Najaf, the continued U.S. bombings of Baghdad, and B-52 bombers attacking the northern cities of Kirkuk and Mosul. All this violence and bombing being orchestrated under the pretense of peace.

"Many Americans are for this war," the bishop said, sounding puzzled that U.S. clergy had not prevailed in leading the Americans in a more peaceful direction. To him it seemed like the American church had lost its influence— any ability to shepherd the Americans by the teachings of Christ.

Shane didn't say it, but he thought the American church had lost more than its influence. It had lost its bearings. Or, as Jonathan says, "Operation Iraqi Freedom had laid bare a frightening lack of moral vision in our churches."[4]

Looking for a glimmer of good news, or maybe because he could feel Shane's discomfort, the bishop switched to a gentler topic, a more friendly demographic.

"What are the Christians saying?" he asked.[5]

At the time a lot of Christians back home were singing "Amazing Grace" and "God Bless America" as if church and state walked hand-in-glove. Some churches, where iconic crosses had been removed for fear of scaring off new worshipers, displayed the American flag prominently in the sanctuary.

"My heart sank," Shane recalled later. "I tried to explain to him that many of the Christians in the U.S. are confused and [they] hope that this is a way God could liberate the Iraqi people."[6]

The bishop shook his head and said humbly, "But we Christians do not believe that. We believe 'Blessed are the peacemakers.' We believe if you pick up the sword, you die by the sword. We believe in the cross."

Tears welled up in Shane's eyes.

"We will be praying for you," the bishop said. "We will be praying for the church in the U.S. . . . to be the church."[7]

The nurse came to Al Monzer that night and gently cleaned Cliff's wound. He washed gently around the stitches and over them, patting them dry and applying ointment or cream. When he was finished Cliff wondered if he had enough money to pay. The nurse had spent between one and two hours caring for him.

Shokran, Cliff said. "Thank you."

"How much do I owe you?"

It was if he had slapped the nurse.

"What do you owe me?" he asked loudly. "You don't owe me anything. But I owe you everything."[8]

He was referring to the work of CPT and the Iraq Peace Team.

Two days later, on April 1, 2003, Weldon was discharged from Arab Medical. As he was packing to leave the hospital his primary nurse walked in.

"Can I talk with you?" Hisham asked.

Weldon knew Hisham to be gentle, competent, and very quiet. Something in his tone sounded different, serious. He sensed that Hisham wanted to discuss a personal matter.

"Yes, Hisham. What would you like to talk about?"

"Where will you go now?" Hisham asked. "Back to Baghdad or to America?"

Weldon said he was returning to his family in the United States.

Hisham hesitated for a second, as if he was building up courage.

"Will you take a message back to America for us?"

Weldon nodded. "Yes, yes, of course."

"Please tell America that we love Americans . . ."

His voice was gentle—and resolute.

"But we hate American aggression."[9]

RUTBA'S REFLECTION

Shane Claiborne

Rutba General, 2010: Front row, Weldon, Cliff, Shane. Back row, Tarik Ali Marzouq, Jassim Muhammad Jamil, and, fourth from left, Sami Rasouli.
Photo credit: Jamie Moffett

There are some stories that you wish had never happened. And there are other stories that you hope you never forget. The story of Rutba is a story that the world cannot afford to forget.

Rutba is a mirror to the world. It is a story full of violence, anger, blood, bombs, and bitterness. And it is a story full of grace, love, hospitality, community, and courage. It simultaneously shows us some of the best that humanity is

139

capable of . . . and some of the worst. The world has much to learn from Rutba—both her scars and her hope.

In spite of what you may have heard from a lot of "gospel preachers" and televangelists, the word "gospel" actually does mean "good news." And Rutba is a good news story—in a world where there is lots of bad news. While I'm not about to fight for Greg's book here to be added to the New Testament canon, I do love the title.

The Gospel of Rutba is good news.

In the belly of the most troubled region of the world, Rutba has the potential to fascinate the world with the power of love—again. Headlines of hatred have hijacked the airwaves for far too long. The story of Rutba is not about extremists for hatred, but extremists for love. It's about the triumph of love.

Rutba is not a fairy tale—it's filled with gut-wrenching pain that still haunts me to this day. But some of the most beautiful stories—like the original gospel of Jesus itself—start in the all-too-familiar human pain and death before there is resurrection. Even though the people of Rutba have suffered some of the most horrific stuff humans can do to one another, there is this constant, steady, almost instinctive, witness of goodness and grace. It does make you curious if, in all our talk of original sin, have we forgotten the truth of original innocence?

As a Christian, I am captivated by the biblical Gospels—so captivated in fact that I have formed my whole life around them and in relationship to the Christ at the heart of them (at least on good days). One of the things that strikes me as I read the biblical Gospels after the experiences in Rutba is that they are filled with story after story of interruptions and surprises. Jesus is on his way somewhere and he is interrupted—by suffering, by sickness, by hunger, even by a party where folks have run out of wine. Amid the interruptions, you find story after story of grace and generosity and healing. It reminds me that we need to allow ourselves to be interrupted more often—especially by the pain and suffering of others.

Another thing that strikes me about the Gospel stories in the Bible is how many of them are hubbed out of little towns like Capernaum, where scholars say only a few hundred people lived. And yet, what happens in these little no-name towns begins to change the world. God is there, even in the unlikely places—especially in the most unlikely places. It reminds us that history is often made through little people, in little towns, through little acts of compassion. Mother Teresa once said, "We can do no great things, but only small things with great love. What's important is not how much we do, but how much love we put into doing it."

One of Jesus's most scandalous stories is the story of the Good Samaritan. As sentimental as we may have made it, the original story was about a man who gets beat up and left on the side of the road. A priest passes by. A Levite, the quintessential religious guy, also passes by on the other side (perhaps late for a meeting at church). And then comes the Samaritan . . . you can almost imagine a snicker in the Jewish crowd. Jews did not talk to Samaritans, or even walk through Samaria. But the Samaritan stops and takes care of the guy in the ditch and is lifted up as the hero of the story. I'm sure some of the listeners were ticked. According to the religious elite, Samaritans did not keep the right rules, and they did not have sound doctrine . . . but Jesus shows that true faith has to work itself out in a way that is Good News to the most bruised and broken person lying in the ditch.

Apparently God likes to bust open every closed mind and create a little hiccup in the chest of every cold heart.

Now we are the ones who see that story from the ditch. We are the ones who were left to die but were surprised by grace.

Even though many of my friends in Iraq are Muslim, I feel like I am a better Christian from knowing them. I can only hope that they are a little closer to God from knowing us. I am as passionate and as in love with Jesus as I was ten years ago. We did not see all of Rutba get "born again." In fact, my friend Jonathan who's a Baptist pastor said he's the one who got "born again . . . again"—in Iraq.

Now that the war in Iraq is over, history will tell how we remember it. I'm sure there will be all sorts of books on the Iraq war—some claiming victory, some calling it the terrible mistake that it was. Political pundits will defend their parties and candidates. But in the end, I hope that history will also remember the story of this little town called Rutba.

Thank you, Greg Barrett, for your contribution.

There is a verse in the New Testament that speaks of being "living epistles."

Another way of saying it might be, "Make the Scripture come to life by the way you live." Preach the gospel with your life. May *The Gospel of Rutba* invite us to do something today that people might want to write about tomorrow.

ACKNOWLEDGMENTS

Following a talk in Chicago for my last book I went for coffee with three-time Nobel Peace Prize nominee Kathy Kelly. Six years earlier, in January 2003, Kathy had brought me, a wire reporter, into prewar Iraq with her band of courageous peacemakers. Traveling from Amman to Baghdad and from Baghdad to Basra, I would see how Kathy's stubborn strain of activism was matched only by the subject of my first book, Father Joe Maier, a Catholic priest firing a social revolution in the slums of Bangkok. On the night of my Chicago book reading, July 10, 2008, I asked Kathy to let me write a book about her and her peacemaking. She's modest. She put me off by asking that I first write about an up-and-coming social revolutionary from Philadelphia, Pennsylvania, a Tennessean named Shane Claiborne. I knew of him. In response to a question during my talk earlier that night I had quoted from his bestselling 2006 book *The Irresistible Revolution: Living as an Ordinary Radical*. In it Shane summarizes the story of Rutba, Iraq (pp. 213-16) in a way that invites readers to learn more. That particular anecdote resonated with me because the Iraqis he described in Rutba sounded like the same generous and kind Sunni and Shia that I had met in Baghdad and Basra. Kathy's push to get to know Shane was all the encouragement I needed to go deeper into that story. For that, and many other things that Kathy has helped me with during the research of this book (e.g., introducing me to Muslim Peacemaker Teams co-founder Sami Rasouli), I am eternally grateful.

I'm also very grateful to Sami. Without him the return to Rutba in 2010 would not have been possible. He not only helped plan our trip into Iraq twice (the first one scheduled for 2009 was canceled), but he served us as an interpreter, translator, and overall fact-checker, returning to Rutba to double-check finer points and then making numerous phone calls to triple-check things that had been double-checked. As we were leaving Iraq in January 2010, Shane and I attempted to pay Sami for his expenses and many services. He accepted our offer and told us to donate it to Rutba General Hospital.

Also, this book was made possible only by the participation of its numerous subjects, Shane, Cliff Kindy, Rev. Weldon Nisly, Peggy Gish, Logan Mehl-Laituri, Jonathan and Leah Wilson-Hartgrove, and retired Lieutenant Colonel James Gavrilis of Army Special Forces. The enduring patience and understanding of Orbis Books publisher Robert Ellsberg cannot be overstated. Ditto for the Orbis production and marketing crew whom I handicapped with insanely tight deadlines. Thanks to literary agent, Carol Mann, and her ace staff, namely Eliza Drier. Thanks to Jamie Moffett for taking the journey with us and documenting its magic.

Last but never least, thanks to my first line of editing (Mom) and to my wife. The two of you always have my back, especially when I'm locked away in my office for weeks and months at a time. Fortunately, in the quiet and loneliness of that solitude, I was blessed with the companionship and soulful wisdom of two peace-loving musicians, Joel and Thomas West. Thank you for your music and the wakeup your lyrics provided whenever I felt too tired to keep writing and fighting for a more sane and humane world, for example:

> Come on everybody rise up like Lazarus;
>   wake up from the dream that is not reality.
> Those who are deceived stay inside the nightmare
>   that they believe, and they will never be free.
>   —*Lazar* from the album
>   *Chants, Woes & Lamentations*

NOTES

Foreword

1. Scene begins 44:53; ends 45:17. The 2010 Oscar-nominated DreamWorks Animation film *How to Train Your Dragon*, written by Will Davies, Dean DeBlois, and Chris Sanders. The screenplay is based on English author Cressida Cowell's children's book *Hiccup: How to Train Your Dragon* (London: Hodder Children's Books, 2003). That book is now one in a series of How to Train Your Dragon books written by Cowell and published by Little, Brown Books for Young Readers.

2. Ibid. Scene begins 36:10; ends 41:00.

3. From the U2 song "I'll Go Crazy if I Don't Go Crazy Tonight," No Line on the Horizon, 2009.

Chapter 1
No Place to Hide

1. This Chinese proverb is prominently displayed on a wall at the Marines' sniper school, Camp Pendleton, California. The lesson being taught by the U.S. military? Killing an enemy combatant in full view of his or her fellow soldiers is powerfully influential. Combatants, townspeople, family members, etc., whoever is witness to the shooting, will feel the terror of it. If the killing is particularly gruesome, all the better. For example, U.S. Marine sniper John Ethan described the strategy like this: "Sometimes a guy will go down, and I'll let him scream a bit to destroy the morale of his buddies. Then I'll use a second shot." See Tony Perry, "Marine Corps Snipers Aim to Strike Fear," *Los Angeles Times*, April 17, 2004, p. 8A.

2. This figure is pulled from my own calculations based on an unclassified U.S. Air Force tally about the first month of the war on Iraq. Between March 20, 2003, Baghdad time and April 19, 2003, Baghdad time, some 29,199 ordnance (19,948 "guided munitions," or smart bombs; 9,251 "unguided munitions," or dumb bombs) were dropped using 41,404 "sorties," or military aircraft. That is an average of 941 bombs per day (just from the air). "Munitions employment for OIF (Operation Iraqi Freedom) reached across the entire spectrum of the U.S. weapons inventory," the report read. However, it did not count the various munitions fired by ground troops and from battleships. For more, see T. Michael Moseley, Lieutenant General, USAF Commander, "Operation Iraqi Freedom: By the Numbers," Munitions Expended, pp. 7-11, April 30, 2003, CENTAF Assessment and Analysis Division, Prince Sultan Air Base, Saudi Arabia; available at http://www.globalsecurity.org/military/library/report/2003/uscentaf_oif_report_30apr2003.pdf.

3. Paul Wiseman, "Special Report: Cluster Bombs Kill in Iraq, Even after Shelling Ends," *USA Today*, December 11, 2003, p. 1A. Wiseman's investigation concluded that the Pentagon "defied international criticism and used nearly 10,800 cluster weapons; their British allies used almost 2,200." Wiseman wrote that "the attacks also left behind thousands of unexploded bomblets, known as duds, that continued to kill and injure Iraqi civilians weeks after the fighting stopped." The Air Force began working on safer cluster bombs with self-destruct fuses in the mid-1990s, and started using them in Afghanistan, *USA Today* reported. However, during the war in Iraq, U.S. ground forces dipped into stockpiles of more than 740 million cluster bomblets, all with a history of high dud rates. As recently as April 2011, the United Nations reported that between 48,000 and 68,000 Iraqis have undergone amputations due to leftover landmines and unexploded ordnance (or UXO). In 2009, on average two Iraqis were killed or injured every week. In Rutba's Al Anbar province during the first week of May 2003, Christian relief agency World Vision International reported twenty cases of Iraqi children being injured by landmines and unexploded ordnances.

4. Hawaii was only a U.S. territory when Japan preemptively attacked the United States by bombing Pearl Harbor on December 7, 1941. Hawaii would not vote to accept statehood for another eighteen years, August 21, 1959.

Chapter 2
Prayer for a New Dawning

1. Captain Todd Brown was speaking to *New York Times* reporter Dexter Filkins outside an Iraqi farming village named Abu Hishma (pop. 7,000), about fifty miles north of Baghdad. After a rocket-propelled grenade had pierced a Bradley Fighting Vehicle near Abu Hishma on November 17, 2003, and killed Dale Panchot, a twenty-six-year-old staff sergeant from Northome, Minnesota, Army commanders called in bombing strikes on nearby homes "suspected" of housing Iraqi fighters; other homes of suspects and their families were bulldozed, similar to tactics used by the Israeli Defense Forces (IDF) in occupied areas of the West Bank and Gaza. Article 33 of the Fourth Geneva Convention Relative to the Protection of Civilian Persons in Time of War reads, "No protected person may be punished for an offense he or she has not personally committed. Collective penalties and likewise all measures of intimidation or of terrorism are prohibited. . . . Reprisals against protected persons and their property are prohibited." In my reading of this, and in the reading of the International Court of Justice and the UN General Assembly, collective punishment such as the house demolitions of "suspects" and/or the homes of their families is a blatant violation of international law.

In other tactics mirroring the IDF, the Army imposed a curfew on Abu Hishma, encased the town in razor wire, and issued mug-shot ID cards to all of its male residents. Any man entering or exiting had to show the English-language ID card and pass through a single checkpoint manned by U.S. soldiers. The fifteen-hour curfew—from 5 p.m. to 8 a.m.—prevented Abu Hishma's Muslim men from attending their mosque's morning and evening prayers. See Dexter Filkins, "Tough New Tactics by

U.S. Tighten Grip on Iraq Towns," *New York Times*, December 7, 2003. Also, Dexter Filkins, *The Forever War* (New York: Knopf, 2008), pp. 156-63 (Kindle edition).

As for Panchot, he was a churchgoing Lutheran from a small town 200 miles north of Minnesota's Twin Cities. He had grown up eager to join the military and be like his grandfather, who fought in the South Pacific during World War II. One week before the attack in Iraq nearly severed him in half, killing him instantly while 6,500 miles from home, Panchot phoned to tell his parents that he had reenlisted for three more years of active duty. Like other enlisted soldiers, he needed the military to pay for college. Afterward, he planned to leave the military. He wanted to teach history and raise a family away from the rigors of Army life. See Bob von Sternberg, "3rd Minnesota Soldier Dies in Iaq," *Star-Tribune* (Minneapolis, MN), November 19, 2003, p. 1A.

2. During the first days of Shock and Awe in March 2003, an overpass near the highway interchange to Rutba was bombed and collapsed onto the Amman-to-Baghdad highway, blocking eastbound traffic. On March 25, 2003, two vanloads of North American peacemakers veered off the highway and detoured through Rutba, and back out to the highway. They drove quickly.

3. This perspective of Rutba comes from an American peacemaker who traveled the Amman-to-Baghdad highway more than a dozen times between the first Gulf War and the 2003 U.S. invasion.

4. According to Rutba's mayor, its hospital director, and several other locals.

5. This American fear of Islam cuts deeper than 9/11. In August 2011 the Center for American Progress, a "progressive" (read: liberal) political think tank in Washington, DC, released a 138-page report titled, "Fear, Inc.: The Roots of the Islamophobia Network in America" (http://www.americanprogress.org/). In a year-long investigation of what it defined as the "exaggerated threat of Islam" and the fear of some Americans that Muslims want to spread Sharia (or Islamic law) across the United States, the report's six investigators stole a page from Journalism 101: They followed the money.

According to the report, after the terrorism of 9/11, more than $42 million flowed into a well-organized campaign of anti-Muslim propaganda funded by ten politically conservative foundations using five "misinformation" experts: Frank Gaffney of the Center for Security Policy; David Yerushalmi at the Society of Americans for National Existence; Daniel Pipes at the Middle East Forum; Robert Spencer of the Jihad Watch and Stop Islamization of Americas; and Steven Emerson of the Investigative Project on Terrorism. One level below the ten foundations and their five experts is a close-knit genealogy of pundits, politicians, and grassroots political organizers. By using inflammatory language and isolated anecdotes to depict all Muslims as inherently homicidal, the report described how an irrational fear of Islam moved from the American fringe into its mainstream. In effect, it circulated via a network of influential blogs (e.g., Atlas Shrugs [http://atlasshrugs2000.typepad.com/]), political heavyweights (e.g., the Tea Party), and news media (e.g., Fox News; Glenn Beck; Rush Limbaugh, etc.).

"Due in part to the relentless efforts of this small group of individuals and organizations, Islam is now the most negatively viewed religion in America," the report concluded. "Only 37 percent of Americans have a favorable opinion of Islam: the lowest favorability rating since 2001, according to a 2010 ABC News/*Washington Post* poll."

Also, the report quoted from a 2010 *Time* magazine poll showing that 28 percent of voters do not believe Muslims should be eligible to sit on the U.S. Supreme Court, and nearly one-third of the country thinks followers of Islam should be barred from running for president.

So, why slander Islam? Who benefits? A closer reading of the contributors to Islamophobia and their political and business connections provide clues: The fanning of public fears helps justify fat defense budgets, military spending, and overseas deployments, and it vindicates Washington's hawkish posture toward Muslim countries and anything or anyone that confronts Israel's occupation of the West Bank and Gaza. It also fits with the rugged, no-nonsense image worn by the GOP, and swells political coffers and the chests of nationalism.

In the end, however, it keeps the Crusades alive by pitting Christianity and Judaism (Judeo-Christians) against Islam. The world's three Abrahamic faiths locked in a civil war. To read more, see the Center for American Progress report at http://www.americanprogress.org/issues/2011/08/islamophobia.html.

6. For example, UN Security Council Resolution 661. Nearly thirteen years before the Pentagon unleashed Shock and Awe, the UN Security Council, led by the U.S. government, used strict economic sanctions in an attempt to break the grip that Iraqi President Saddam Hussein had on Iraq. But to have any effect on the dictator the sanctions had to first affect the lives of millions of everyday Iraqis. To various degrees, the sanctions remained in place until President George W. Bush heralded the end of "major combat operations" in the second Gulf War and declared "mission accomplished" on May 1, 2003. By then the sanctions had gutted Iraq's middle class and were blamed for hundreds of thousands of deaths caused by malnutrition, poor water quality, and a lack of proper healthcare.

In the first Gulf War more than seven hundred Iraqi targets had been bombed, including bridges, roads, and the electrical grids that powered 1,410 water-treatment plants. Coupled with economic sanctions that blocked or rationed dual-use imports such as water pumps, electric generators, and chlorine (which, the United States and the United Nations said, could also be used in making mustard gas) epidemics ensued. Worse, the United States had predicted the epidemics. In a January 1991 document titled "Iraq Water Treatment Vulnerabilities," the U.S. Defense Intelligence Agency stated that the bombing of Iraq combined with an embargo of chemicals and supplies could fully degrade Iraq's civilian water supply. "Unless the water is purified with chlorine, epidemics of such diseases as cholera, hepatitis, and typhoid could occur," read declassified portions of the report. The subject line of the Pentagon paper read: "Effects of Bombing on Disease Occurrence in Baghdad." Ignoring these consequences for everyday Iraqis, Washington followed the plan like a blueprint. See Thomas J. Nagy, "The Secret Behind the Sanctions," *The Progressive,* September 2001, p. 22. Read the full story at http://goo.gl/0IiEN.

By some estimates, even those of UN organizations, the bombing of Iraq's infrastructure and the sanctions resulted in the deaths of more than one million Iraqis, half of whom were children under age five, according to reports from the United Nations Children's Fund (UNICEF) and the World Health Organization. In an independent study published nineteen months after the end of the 1991 Gulf War, the *New England*

Journal of Medicine reported a trend that foretold Iraq's sorry future: During the first eight months of 1991, nearly 47,000 more children than normal died in Iraq, and the country's infant- and child-mortality rates more than doubled, to 92.7 and 128.5 per 1,000 live births respectively. During more than twelve years of UN sanctions and an international trade embargo Iraqi children died at abnormally high rates from dehydration and waterborne illnesses such as cholera, diarrhea, and other intestinal diseases. National surveys of Iraq conducted by UNICEF reported that sanctions greatly contributed to Iraq's degraded water supply. The daily per capita share of drinkable water produced for Iraqis in Baghdad was reduced from 330 liters per day in 1990 to 150 liters in 2000. In other urban areas of Iraq it was less than 110 liters, and in rural areas less than sixty-five liters. In May 2000, UNICEF reported that close to half of Iraqi children under age five suffered from diarrhea, and more than one-third suffered from acute respiratory infections. Meanwhile, per-capita income in Iraq dropped from $3,510 in 1989 to $450 in 1996, attributable in large part to the loss of jobs and decline in value of the Iraqi dinar. By the mid-1990s, unemployment and under-employment exceeded 50 percent. Iraq's gross domestic product, which peaked in 1990 at $74.9 billion, fell to $10 billion and remained under $20 billion throughout most of the 1990s. In 1995, the United Nations attempted to fix some of these consequences with its Oil-for-Food Program. But seven years later the UN Security Council was still withholding more than 1,450 import contracts worth $4.6 billion in humanitarian supplies for Iraq. The United States, concerned with Saddam's potential for developing weapons of mass destruction, had initiated nearly 90 percent of the blocks on humanitarian supplies.

About one month before the war in 2003 I interviewed Iraqi pediatrician Dr. Qusay Al Rahim at Baghdad's Al Mansour Children's Hospital. It was a filthy place that was open-air and fly-infested. But Al Rahim said he had seen several improvements at the hospital under the Oil-for-Food Program. For example, electricity that had been intermittent for years was again reliable; more than half of the pharmaceutical drugs his patients needed were again available, and hospital elevators that had long been grounded because Iraq could not import the parts needed to repair them were working again. Best of all, he said, colostomy bags no longer had to be washed and reused. Yes, that's correct: at one point during sanctions, the Al Mansour Hospital was washing and reusing colostomy bags. There had been a critical shortage caused by the embargo. As the United States and Britain prepared to bomb Iraq again in 2003, there were still unmet critical needs at Al Mansour Children's Hospital. "For example," Al Rahim said, "we have a shortage of Vitamin K." The fat soluble vitamin is a blood coagulant commonly used to prevent hemorrhaging in newborns.

So, yes, as an American in Iraq you don't expect to be received very well.

7. On April 25, 2011, eight years into the reconstruction of Iraq, Stuart W. Bowen, Jr., Special Inspector General for Iraq Reconstruction (SIGIR), testified to Congress about a myriad of ongoing problems plaguing American efforts to rebuild Iraq. The U.S. government was spending approximately $17 million per day of taxpayer money just on Iraq's reconstruction. If you also counted the actual military operation itself—for example, all of the F-16 jets, Apache helicopters, Abrams tanks, and the necessary fuel; the widely varied arsenal of guided and unguided bombs; automatic rifles and grenade launchers; military salaries and life insurance policies—the U.S. tab for the Iraq

war climbed to an estimated $300 million per day, Washington economist Scott Wall-sten told the *New York Times* in 2007. But if you consider only the money being spent to rebuild what was broken, not counting the priceless commodity of life, the cost to U.S. taxpayers totaled $58 billion in 2011, making Iraq the most expensive overseas rebuilding program in U.S. history. Of that amount, at least $1.7 million per day ("a reasonably prudent estimate," Bowen said) was being lost to mismanagement and waste, a hemorrhaging that had been steady from the outset and totaled between $5 to $6 billion. "Six billion [dollars] in waste is a disturbing figure, needless to say," Bowen told Congress in 2011. "But the number may in fact be much higher if the Iraqis do not sustain what we have provided." Bowen, a Bush appointee and former Deputy General Counsel on the staff of Texas Governor George W. Bush, said the reconstruction of Iraq was cursed from the beginning because "the US government failed to anticipate fully or plan effectively for working in the unstable security environment that existed when reconstruction began." Much-publicized (and apparently padded) estimates on the total costs of the war, including medical care for the war's wounded veterans, dis-ability payments and benefits, the war's ongoing effect on oil prices, etc., totaled $200 billion per year, according to a *New York Times* report and comparative graphic pub-lished in 2007. Even if the estimate were only half that amount, it would amount to enough federal tax money to pay for universal healthcare for all U.S. citizens lacking medical insurance ($100 billion); and it would be more than enough federal money to provide free universal preschool education each year for all of the nation's three- and four-year-old children ($35 billion) plus immunize all of the world's children against measles, diphtheria, polio, tuberculosis, tetanus, and whooping cough ($600 million), according to the *Times* analysis. View the comparative graphic on Iraq war costs at https://acrobat.com/app.html#d=BvXFrhBDnD*KHRgPIF04sw.

8. Author notes from interviews conducted January 15-18, 2010, and interviews conducted in July 2009 by Iraqi translator Sami Rasouli, founder of the Iraq Peace-maker Teams.

9. Ibid.

10. It doesn't seem to matter to Rutba's locals that the general demise of their hos-pital can only be partially traced to its destruction in 2003. The hospital's problems in 2010 are far-reaching, and traceable to things other than the U.S. bombing of it in 2003. But for people who need major surgery or intensive care, and have to drive 195 miles one-way to Ramadi, the problem began with the bombing of March 26, 2003. More on that in a later chapter.

11. Ibid.

12. Author interviews with former Special Forces Major James Gavrilis, August and October of 2011.

13. Of course, oxygen tanks and fertilizer also could have caused the secondary explosions that swept across the hospital compound. According to local sources, both were stored on hospital grounds. Ammonium nitrate is a chemical compound com-monly used as a high-nitrogen fertilizer. It's also popular as an oxidizing agent in high explosives. It is the main component of ammonium nitrate/fuel oil (or ANFO), the most widely used explosive in the United States for construction, coal mining, metal mining, and quarrying. It is also a key ingredient in improvised explosive devices

(IEDs), such as car bombs and fertilizer bombs. Ammonium nitrate was an integral ingredient used in the second most destructive terrorist attack in the United States— the 1995 Oklahoma City bombing.

14. Author notes from interviews January 15-18, 2010. Also, follow-up interviews in Rutba through Iraqi interpreter Sami Rasouli in October 2011.

15. Charles J. Hanley, AP special correspondent, "Anti-war Group Finds Bombed-out Hospital," *The Gazette* (Montreal, Quebec), March 31, 2003, p. A14.

Chapter 3
Onward Christian Soldiers

1. "Islam is as Islam does," read a bumper sticker I saw on a family van with Pennsylvania plates driving south on I-77 in North Carolina on August 12, 2010. Next to that bumper sticker was another: "Peace through Whoop-Ass." And next to that one, same van, a third: "Look busy, Jesus is coming."

2. That is Shane's description of his former professor and mentor from *The Irresistible Revolution: Living as an Ordinary Radical* (Grand Rapids, MI: Zondervan, 2006). There's plenty of evidence to support it. I've never met Dr. Anthony Campolo or heard him speak, but when I read in *Christianity Today* how he used to begin many of his talks at universities, churches, and such, I knew he was my kind of Baptist: "I have three things I'd like to say today. First, while you were sleeping last night, thirty thousand kids died of starvation or diseases related to malnutrition. Second, most of you don't give a shit. What's worse is that you're more upset with the fact that I said 'shit' than the fact that thirty thousand kids died last night." See Ted Olsen, "The Positive Prophet," *Christianity Today*, January 2003 (http://www.christianitytoday.com/ct/2003/january/1.32.html).

3. The 2005 feature film *Lord of War* is the somewhat fictional story of Yuri Orlov, whose character is said to be a composite of real-life alleged Russian arms trafficker Viktor Bout and the late Oleg Orlo, a Russian businessman who allegedly smuggled missiles to Iran. Yuri Orlov (played by Nicolas Cage) is the film's narrator, and he begins the movie by explaining, "There are over 550 million firearms in worldwide circulation. That's one firearm for every twelve people on the planet. The only question is [dramatic pause, a drag on his cigarette], How do we arm the other eleven?" In a scene toward the film's end, Orlov and his brother Vitaly (played by Jared Leto) are in Sierra Leone trading weapons to the rebels of the Revolutionary United Front. When Vitaly realizes the guns and grenades they are selling will be used to massacre innocent people he is killed in a bold attempt to destroy the weapons cache. That's when Orlov turns philosophical. "They say, 'Evil prevails when good men fail to act,'" he says, repeating a famous quote often (though errantly) attributed to British statesman-author-philosopher Edmund Burke, the eighteenth-century founder of modern conservatism. (In 1770 Burke wrote, "When bad men combine, the good must associate; else they will fall, one by one, an unpitied sacrifice in a contemptible struggle.") Similarly, agnostic scientist Albert Einstein contended that the world is dangerous not because of evil but because of people too scared, too selfish, too comfortable, too

apathetic, too *something* to act against it. In *Lord of War,* Orlov finishes the thought with an ominous flourish: "What they ought to say is, 'Evil prevails.'"

The film's postscript reads: "While private gunrunners continue to thrive, the world's biggest arms suppliers are the U.S., U.K., Russia, France and China. They are also the five permanent members of the UN Security Council."

Fade to black.

4. For example, "You have heard that it was said, 'Eye for eye, and tooth for tooth.' But I tell you, do not resist an evil person. If anyone slaps you on the right cheek, turn to them the other cheek also" (Matthew 5:38-39). "You have heard that it was said, 'Love your neighbor and hate your enemy.' But I tell you, love your enemies and pray for those who persecute you" (Matthew 5:43-44). "Blessed are the merciful, for they will be shown mercy" (Matthew 5:7). "Blessed are the peacemakers, for they will be called children of God" (Matthew 5:9). And when the disciple Peter raises his sword to defend Jesus he is rebuked by his savior: "Put your sword back in its place, for all who draw the sword will die by the sword" (Matthew 26:52). Of course pacifists, peacemakers, and non-pacifist journalist-authors who write about them are also accused of cherry picking Scripture—and not only because the chosen Scripture is cherry colored.

But when a Christian pastor such as Reverend Rick Warren of the mega-church Saddleback enthusiastically justifies warfare, and then cherry picks Scripture from the Old Testament (aka the Hebrew Bible) to explain his revered perspective, there aren't any red letters. His argument even makes it sound like defense contractors might be counted among Saddleback's faithful tithers.

Is it ever right to fight? Warren is asked in an undated blog and sermon. He responds, "Yes! There are times when it's the lesser of two evils. There are times when it is appropriate and there are times when it is inappropriate. Ecclesiastes 3:8 says, 'There is a time for war and a time for peace.' The Bible is very realistic. Sometimes war is the right thing."

Asked if Jesus was a pacifist, Warren depicts Christ like a UFC (Ultimate Fighting Championship) fighter painted in tattoos. "I DON'T think He was!" he explained in the blog (see http://www.saddleback.com/story/5581.html), repeated on the Christian Broadcasting Network as recently as February 19, 2011 (http://www.cbn.com/spirituallife/BibleStudyAndTheology/Discipleship/Warren_RighttoFighta.aspx). "Twice in the New Testament, He cleansed the temple by force. The Bible says He made a whip, and He went in and cleansed the temple. He didn't politely ask them, 'Would you guys, pretty please, get out of here?' He forced them out." To support his version of the brawny Prince of Peace, Warren resorts to what Jesus did *not* say rather than what is attributed verbatim to Christ in the red-lettered Sermon on the Mount. Warren argues, "He never told Roman soldiers to leave the army. If Jesus had been a total pacifist, every time he saw a soldier, He would have said, 'Leave your army! Come follow Me.' But He never once said it was morally wrong for them to be in the service. In fact, in Matthew 24:6, He said there will always be wars in the world until the Prince of Peace comes back."

Keep in mind, this is the California minister who wrote the "Blueprint for Christian Living" (40 Days of Purpose), selling seven million copies the same year Washington invaded Iraq, with the vast majority of Americans supporting the preemptive war.

Read in its fuller context, in Matthew 24 Jesus is talking to his disciples at the Mount of Olives when he describes for them the hardheaded foolishness that humanity must endure before the world finds peace. Without some serious cherry picking I don't see how those red letters line up to favor war:

"Don't let anyone mislead you, for many will come in my name, claiming, 'I am the Messiah.' They will deceive many. And you will hear of wars and threats of wars, but don't panic. Yes, these things must take place, but the end won't follow immediately. Nation will go to war against nation, and kingdom against kingdom. There will be famines and earthquakes in many parts of the world. But all this is only the first of the birth pains, with more to come" (Matthew 24:4-8).

5. This counts only the first month of the air assault on Iraq, totaling 29,199 guided and unguided bombs delivered by more than 40,000 sorties. See T. Michael Moseley, "Operation Iraqi Freedom: By the Numbers," April 30, 2003, CENTAF Assessment and Analysis Division, Prince Sultan Air Base, Saudi Arabia (http://www.global security.org/military/library/report/2003/uscentaf_oif_report_30apr2003.pdf).

6. Other than Cliff, Weldon, Peggy, Leah, and Jonathan, the deported CPT members included Betty Scholten of Mt. Rainer, MD, Kara Speltz of Oakland, CA, and Michael Birmingham of Dublin, Ireland. With phone lines still down in downtown Baghdad and their communication back home and to news organizations greatly limited, three days later many more IPT and CPT peacemakers left Baghdad for Amman.

7. Jonathan Wilson-Hartgrove, *To Baghdad and Beyond: How I Got Born Again in Babylon* (Eugene, OR: Cascade, 2005), p. 62.

8. Ibid., p. 63.

9. The Iraq Peace Team (aka Voices in the Wilderness) had seventeen peacemakers in Baghdad at this time; Christian Peacemaker Teams had fifteen.

10. Wilson-Hartgrove, *To Baghdad and Beyond*, p. 72.

11. Beth Alderman, *Lay Saints* documentary film (Seattle, WA: Multifaith Witness Films & Books LLC, 2009).

12. Wilson-Hartgrove, *To Baghdad and Beyond*, p. 76.

13. Dated September 18, 2001, Deputy Prime Minister Tariq Aziz's letter to Kathy read, "I express to you and your comrades in Voices in the Wilderness [VITW, also founded by Kathy, preceded IPT] as friends and honest American citizens who stood by the Iraqi people. . . . Through you, I address my condolences to the families of the victims, notably the noble American citizens who have expressed their solidarity with the Iraqi people in their plight [referring to the UN economic sanctions]."

14. Aziz was one of Saddam Hussein's closest advisers. He was also the only Christian in Saddam's regime, which was comprised primarily of Sunni Muslims. As a member of the Revolutionary Command Council (Iraq's executive and legislative bodies during Saddam's rule) Aziz was sentenced in 2010 to hang for his role in the regime's murderous crackdown on Shiite opposition parties. At this writing (October 2011) Aziz is in an Iraqi prison awaiting execution. The European Union, several Western governments (not including the United States) and the Vatican have asked Iraqi officials to show Aziz clemency and spare his life. Iraqi President Jalal Talabani, who by law would have to approve the execution order, said he will never sign it. However,

Reuters reported in August 2011 that Aziz, age 74, has asked Iraqi Prime Minister Nuri al-Maliki to expedite his execution because of chronic health problems. Aziz's lawyer said he is suffering from diabetes, high blood pressure, heart problems, prostate problems, and ulcers. One way or another, Aziz has said, he expects to die in prison.

15. Wilson-Hartgrove, *To Baghdad and Beyond*, p. 76.

16. Ibid.

17. Ibid., p. 79.

18. Jordan was the first neighboring country to open its borders to refugees from Iraq. The Ruweished camp served humanitarian needs, for sure, but it also served as a net to catch the war's runoff before Iraq's refugees flooded Jordan like Palestinian refugees from the West Bank and Gaza areas had in previous decades. Jordanian authorities were blunt in their insistence that Iraq's refugees would not be allowed to remain permanently. Initially they agreed to keep Ruweished open for three months, but as the lawless aftermath and insurgent fighting continued to rage in Iraq they relented. The camp remained open until the last refugee was resettled in 2007. The majority were resettled in Canada, New Zealand, Australia, Sweden, Brazil. and the United States.

19. Wilson-Hartgrove, *To Baghdad and Beyond*, pp. 44-45.

20. Descriptions gleaned from Weldon's journal entries and CPT members' video of the drive that day. Video was used in the documentary film *Lay Saints*, directed by Beth Alderman (Seattle, WA: Multifaith Witness Films & Books LLC, 2009).

21. Wendell Berry, *In the Presence of Fear* (Great Barrington, MA: Orion Society, 2001).

22. Ibid.

23. Despite pleas of leniency from international humanitarian organizations such as Human Rights Watch, beginning in the mid-1990s Saddam's regime maintained order with brutal penalties for relatively minor crimes and nonviolent offenses. For example, convictions for theft, military desertion, draft dodging, forgery, and currency speculation were punishable by amputation of ears or hands. To distinguish criminals from war veterans maimed in combat, the Ba'athist regime branded the foreheads of criminal amputees with the figure of a cross. Convictions of offenses considered more serious by the regime, for example, armed robbery, smuggling antiquities, sex trafficking and prostitution, were punishable by death.

Chapter 4
Boys and Their Guns

1. Corporal Ryan Jeschke, a native son of northern Virginia, was attempting to comfort twenty-six-year-old Marine Sergeant Charles Graves at a roadblock they were manning on the night of March 31, 2003. Their Charlie Company in the Marine First Reconnaissance Battalion was assigned to block traffic on the main road and bridge leading out of Al Hayy, Iraq, a Shia Muslim city, 135 miles south of Baghdad. Two primary problems with the task: the coiled concertina wire stretched across the road as a blockade was barely visible at night, and the U.S. military was told to shoot approaching drivers if they didn't stop after one warning shot. There was legitimate fear that the cars or trucks could be wired with bombs. But warning shots fired at cars will alarm

drivers, especially at night and especially in a war zone. Confused and/or frightened, Iraqi drivers would sometimes accelerate in a rush to escape harm.

In this tragic story in Al Hayy, recounted first in *Rolling Stone* magazine by embedded journalist Evan Wright (see "From Hell to Baghdad," *Rolling Stone*, July 10, 2003, p. 57), Jeschke, Graves and some other Marines are manning a nighttime roadblock when a four-door sedan approaches and accelerates at the first crack of a warning shot. The Marines, perhaps skittish and trigger happy from firefights earlier that day, riddle the sedan with dozens of rounds from high-caliber rifles. The car screeches to a stop. Surprisingly, two civilian-looking Iraqi men emerge uninjured, their arms raised in surrender. The driver appears confused, and he is soon apologizing. *Asif, asif, asif,* "Sorry, sorry, sorry." Checking the vehicle for weapons (there are none) Jeschke and Graves see a small girl lying in the backseat, eyes open, looking frightened. She looks to be cowering. Graves guesses she is about three years old, same age as his daughter. He notices blood on the upholstery and picks her up thinking about what medical supplies the Marines will need to treat her.

Wright describes what happens next with visceral details (*too* visceral if you are one who prefers not to know the everyday realities of warfare—in which case you will not want to read beyond this parenthetical):

"The top of her head slides off and her brains fall out. When Graves steps back, he nearly falls over when his boot slips in the girl's brains."

The apologetic father meekly asks the Marines for permission to retrieve his daughter's body. He leaves his wasted, bullet-riddled sedan behind and is last seen walking the dark road carrying the corpse of his daughter. Jeschke, who is haunted by the sight of the father carrying his headless daughter, later recalls for Graves what the company's Arabic interpreter (a Kuwaiti civilian) told him. He said, "Arabs don't grieve as hard as we do. I don't really believe him. I can't see how it would be any different for them." Also, see Evan Wright, *Generation Kill* (New York: Putnam), pp. 218-19 (Kindle edition).

2. James A. Gavrilis, "The Mayor of Ar Rutbah," *Foreign Policy*, November-December 2005. Also, author notes from interviews with Gavrilis in Arlington, Virginia, August 5, 2011, and by phone, October 7, 2011.

3. Gavrilis and much of the U.S. military would no doubt take issue with this statement: ". . . the mess that he and his soldiers created." In earlier drafts of this chapter I wrote, "the mess that he and his soldiers helped to create." Gavrilis would have disagreed with that also. In our interviews he never suggested that the war in Iraq was anything less than a righteous sacrifice made by the U.S. military and its allies to liberate an oppressed people. If there was a mess created in Rutba it was only because the "Saddamists"—the Fedayeen, the Ba'athists, the Republican Guard, and anyone who resisted the foreign militaries—fought back. My final edit to the chapter reflects the objective fact that the United States invaded a sovereign nation without provocation.

4. Linda Robinson, *Masters of Chaos: The Secret History of the Special Forces* (New York: PublicAffairs, 2004), p. 10 (Kindle edition).

5. In *One Bullet Away: The Making of a Marine Officer,* author and former Marine Captain Nathaniel Fick uses the analogy of a slingshot to explain the preparedness of the U.S. military on the eve of the 2003 invasion of Iraq. Fick led the Second Platoon,

Bravo Company, of the First Reconnaissance Battalion, and as his platoon drove north from Kuwait to the Iraqi border they passed Army camps named for the terrorism of 9/11—Camp Virginia, Camp New York, Camp Pennsylvania. Deceptive illusions about the reason for invading Iraq, but effective. Fick describes how months of training followed by a month of living on edge in the desert had everyone juiced for combat. "We were ready. The platoon was physically and psychologically primed," Fick writes. No one wanted to turn back and have to wait longer. At that point they wanted only to put their training to the test and see the war finished. "We weren't a gun to be cocked and put on the table. More like a slingshot. Load a stone, pull it back, and wait. Wait too long and the elastic goes slack, leaving you standing there with only a rock." See Nathaniel Fick, *One Bullet Away: The Making of a Marine Officer* (New York: Houghton Mifflin, 2006), p. 188 (Kindle edition).

6. James Hagengruber, "Marines Face Last Insurgent Stronghold in Iraq's Anbar Province," *Christian Science Monitor*, April 8, 2008, World, p. 1.

7. Early into the Iraqi insurgency Washington began grouping all foreign fighters who aided in Iraq's resistance as "Al Qaeda in Iraq" or "Al Qaeda operatives" or "insurgents tied to Al Qaeda," etc. I don't know if this was an effort to drum up public support by linking the ongoing war in Iraq to the terrorists of 9/11 or if it was political shorthand intended to reflect the seriousness of the threat, but either way it was misleading. The Iraqi tie-in to Al Qaeda comes from Jordanian Abu Musab al-Zarqawi, a militant Islamist whose paramilitary group Jama'at al-Tawhid wal-Jihad (Group of Monotheism and Jihad) had been around since the 1990s. Neither Zarqawi nor his terrorist group (estimated by BBC News to have only a few hundred members) were members of Al Qaeda per se. The most you can say is that Zarqawi, an extreme fundamentalist Sunni, pledged loyalty to Osama Bin Laden, a Shia, and his Al Qaeda network beginning in 2004. He changed the name of his terrorist group to Tanzim Qaidat al-Jihad fi Bilad al-Rafidayn (Organization of Jihad's Base in the Country of the Two Rivers) and waged a bloody campaign in Iraq of kidnappings, beheadings, and suicide bombings. By the time U.S. forces killed him in June 2006 he was considered by U.S. officials to be the most wanted terrorist in Iraq. But from the start the wholesale connection that Washington made between Zarqawi, an extreme fundamentalist Sunni, and Osama Bin Laden, an extreme fundamentalist Shia, was a suspicious stretch. Even more of a stretch was the easy classification of all foreign fighters as Al Qaeda.

8. Thomas P. Daly, *Rage Company: A Marine's Baptism by Fire* (Hoboken, NJ: Wiley Books, 2010), p. 348.

9. Nir Rosen, "Every Time the Wind Blows: 'This Is the Wild, Wild West,'" *Asia Times,* October 24, 2003 (http://newamerica.net/publications/articles/2003/every_time_the_wind_blows_this_is_the_wild_wild_west).

10. Our guardian angel was none other than Ali Shalal Al Qaissi, an Abu Ghraib detainee tortured for six months in 2003-2004. After the *New York Times* published a front page story about Ali in March 2006 (see "Symbol of Abu Ghraib Seeks to Spare Others His Nightmare"), he became an international symbol for the abuse suffered by Iraqi detainees (http://www.nytimes.com/2006/03/11/international/middleeast/11ghraib.html?_r=3). It was believed that Ali was the lone man photographed in one of the most circulated images of the prison scandal: standing atop a

box wearing only a hood and a blanket fashioned into a poncho, arms outstretched, electrical wires clasped to his middle fingers. Although Ali is not the detainee in that specific iconic photo, he was detained by the U.S. military at Abu Ghraib, and he says he was photographed while being tortured in the exact same manner. Oddly, it is this tortured Iraqi who wanted to protect us. Sami explained that Al Qaissi knew members of the Christian Peacemaker Teams, and he didn't want to see any of them harmed.

11. Jonathan was unable to accompany us on the rescheduled trip because his wife, Leah, was due to give birth.

12. John Keay, *Sowing the Wind: The Seeds of Conflict in the Middle East* (New York: W.W. Norton, 2003), p. 240.

13. There is an exception to this Anglo perception of Rutba: British explorer and famed travel writer Freya Stark. She immersed herself in British colonialized Iraq twice, beginning seven years after the signing of the British Mandate of Mesopotamia, and again in the 1940s, before and after the Royal Air Force bombed Rutba. She learned Arabic and Persian and preferred to stay in local communities when she traveled, shunning the Western expatriate crowd. In her writings from Al Anbar in 1931 she spoke of Rutba as if it were a jewel planted in the desert by Walt Disney—a place of destination rather than a town to escape. At the time Rutba's British Imperial Airways landing strip (built by the Royal Air Force) and its barren blockhouses hosted oil contractors, pipeline workers, and transport companies ferrying foreigners between Amman and Baghdad. It was a far cry from the Iraq that most of the modern world came to know under the dictates of Saddam Hussein's regime.

"Rutba is the palace planted in the wilderness when Aladdin's uncle rubbed the lamp; how else can it have got there? It is 200 miles from anywhere. It has beds to sleep in and waiters who spontaneously think of hot water. You walk into a room and dine on salmon mayonnaise and other refinements and read notices on walls like those of an English club house in the country. . . . I had not felt so near home since the day when, coming down upon Jordan from Hauran (in Syria), we discovered marmalade in Jericho." See Freya Stark, *Baghdad Sketches: Journeys through Iraq* (London: John Murray, 1937), p. 4.

As tenacious as she was as a travel writer, Stark was just as relentless in her rose-colored advocacy for liberty, democracy, and an overall westernization of Iraq. She served the British government in its Middle East Propaganda Section of the Ministry of Information. This conflict of interest seemed to affect the objectivity of her work in ways that history would later mock. For example, on the first page of "Baghdad Sketches" she boldly predicts: "In a very short time a railway will link Baghdad with Europe." And as John Keay recounts in "Sowing the Wind," after the Royal Air Force bombed Rutba into oblivion in the Second World War, Stark returned to the place she called Rutba Wells to preach about the seeds of homegrown democracy. Standing amidst the charred blockhouses and a howling Syrian desert, she made her rose-colored case:

"Democracy, as she informed a cell of her 'brothers' gathered amid the bombed-out remains of Rutba Wells, must grow from the grass roots upwards. 'It is men like yourselves who carry the seed of the little plant,' she told her audience of assorted police and tribesmen; Baghdad would yet have its own 'Mother of Parliaments,' just like London's; they had only to tend the seedling so that it took root and became 'a part of your land'; it was a living thing, not a theory; 'that is the meaning of Democracy.'"

14. Keay, *Sowing the Wind*, p. 271.

15. The 70-ton, $2 million "tow truck" is the M88 Recovery Vehicle (aka HER-CULES—Heavy Equipment Recovery Combat Utility Evacuation System). Imagine a tank with a winch. Manufactured today by British defense contractor BAE Systems Inc., the HERCULES represents a reversal of conventional thought—if not reversal of fortune. It has, in effect, been outsourced to the United States. BAE provides a hefty lift to the local economy of West Manchester Township, Pennsylvania, home to the BAE factory that makes the vast majority of the M88s. The tow tank might be only a speck in the Pentagon's large inventory of stock and supply, but it is a giant in any rural American town with fewer than eight thousand households. The BAE Systems Ground Systems factory in West Manchester Township employs about 1,600 locals from York County, Pennsylvania. About half are hourly wage earners with a United Steelworkers of America union; the rest are salaried employees.

West Manchester's benefactor, the London-based BAE corporation, paid $4.2 billion cash in 2005 to buy HERCULES-maker United Defense Industries. The deal reflected the world's—or at least Europe's—faith in the American war culture. BAE was banking on the Pentagon's ongoing War on Terrorism. And rightly so.

From the start the defense contractor from Tony Blair's London was a magnet for U.S. government contracts. In June 2005, the Department of Defense awarded BAE a no-bid contract worth $143 million to remanufacture and upgrade fifty-nine M88s. Eighteen months later, BAE received another $251 million contract for the modification and production of an unspecified number of M88s. Eight months later, in July 2006, the Pentagon gave BAE another contract totaling $55 million for manufacturing and modifying an unspecified number of M88s. In March 2008, it added $185 million for ninety M88s with an option for sixty more at a cost of $163 million. Pennsylvania Gov. Ed Rendell was so pleased with his new British neighbor he awarded it a $2.5 million grant and $1.8 million in tax credits in March 2008. Exactly one year later, March 2009, another no-bid Pentagon contract for thirty-nine M88s costing $81 million was given to BAE. Like clockwork, or annual dividends, one year later BAE received another Defense Department contract worth $70 million for thirty M88s. On March 3, 2011, the Defense Department gave BAE a $7 million contract "for work" on M88 vehicles. A two-sentence news brief in the *York Dispatch* made the contract look like loose change. Then, in July 2011, the Pentagon awarded BAE another contract totaling $165 million for forty-three M88s and their associated parts. One month later, in August, the Pentagon added a contract for $108 million to modify forty-five M88s using remanufactured hulls supplied by the U.S. government. About 90 percent of the work was to be routed to the BAE factory in West Manchester Township's 143-acre factory; the rest went to a BAE plant in Aiken, South Carolina.

To date, the HERCULES contracts given to BAE total $1.4 billion. As of this writing the work was expected to keep the West Manchester Township factory busy making, remaking and modifying the M88 tow tank through December 2013.

It's no wonder that in August 2011, when a Congressional Super Committee comprised of twelve lawmakers began deliberating on ways to carve more than $1 billion from the federal budget over the next decade, the local *York Daily Record* sounded alarms. "If they can't agree by Thanksgiving, budgets will be cut across-the-board by a set percentage, authorizing a $500 billion hit for defense spending for multibillion-dollar weapons programs," the newspaper reported, alluding to the effect this could have on defense contractors such as BAE. Then, like a sigh of relief, reporter Lauren Boyer told *Daily Record* readers, "Members of the committee, six Republicans and six Democrats, represent states where the country's largest military contractors employ thousands of workers."

16. An ABC News/*Washington Post* poll of 509 American adults conducted on April 9, 2003, reported that 77 percent approved of Bush's job as president; 80 percent supported the war; and 90 percent of those supporting the war would remain in favor of it even if the United States never found Iraq's alleged Weapons of Mass Destruction (WMD). During this heady week when Saddam Hussein's Firdos Square statue toppled and Marines paraded into Baghdad, Pew Research Center and Gallup/CNN/ *USA Today* polls of 809 and 495 American adults, respectively, reported similar support for the U.S.-led invasion of Iraq.

17. Bush's undersecretary of state for arms control and international security was John Bolton. The day that U.S. Marines planted the American flag in Baghdad and, momentarily, draped it over the face of the giant statue of Saddam Hussein in Baghdad's Firdos Square, Bolton was in Rome meeting with Vatican officials about proposals for Iraq's humanitarian assistance and postwar reconstruction. Leaving the meeting, Bolton, a native of Baltimore, Maryland, who two years later served briefly as the U.S. ambassador to the United Nations (he was never confirmed by the Senate) met with reporters. It was April 9, 2003, a heady day for the American military might. TV news around the world focused on the triumphant and mostly uncontested arrival of Marines into Baghdad, and the subsequent defacing and crumbling of Saddam's statue. According to the Associated Press, Bolton was asked if Syria and Iran (like Iraq, nations that Washington believed were in pursuit of weapons of mass destruction) could be the next targets of U.S. military invasion. Although Bolton said Washington had designs only on peaceful resolutions, he added wryly, "We are hopeful that a number of regimes will draw the appropriate lesson from Iraq—that the pursuit of weapons of mass destruction is not in their national interest."

18. What? *Redneck* is offensive? It takes one to know one—and I am. Not a hee-haw, Confederate-flag-waving redneck. Or its wealthy first cousin, the tweed-coat-wearing, mint-julep-sipping redneck. Just redneck, like the majority of blue-collar Southern whites. If Merriam-Webster's is correct in its definition—"*sometimes disparaging*: a white member of the Southern rural laboring class"—then I don't feel disparaged by noun or adjective. In that regard, the folk around Fort Campbell and I are close kin. I was born and raised in working-class Bristol, VA-TN, and, like a majority of today's enlisted soldiers, I graduated from high school with no money saved and no immediate options for college tuition. That made me the ideal Army recruit, if you believe military recruiters and economic studies by think tanks like the RAND Corporation. The Army's FAQ section on soldier recruitment (http://www.2k.army.mil/ faqs.htm#economy) describes the fallout from the current economic recession and relatively high national unemployment as an opportunity for the military. To fill its

boots, to stock the War on Terrorism's frontlines, a poor economy is a rich environment for military recruitment. Of course, the Army doesn't say it exactly that way, but you can read between the lines for yourself:

Question: "Has the economic downturn affected recruiting?"

Answer: "While competitive forces remain difficult, the impact of a recession, growing unemployment, and improving attitudes towards military service present a favorable recruiting environment. Attitudes toward overseas contingency operations have improved. Propensity to enlist has increased nationally."

After I graduated high school in 1980 I accepted a recruiter's offer of a Greyhound ticket to travel to an Army physical in Knoxville, Tennessee. But several months earlier I had dislocated my right shoulder twice, once in a parking lot dustup and again in a boxing ring. An Army doctor in Knoxville examined it, read the X-ray, and then put me on the Greyhound home. He said to get the shoulder repaired and come back. Instead, I took a job working swing shifts and graveyard shifts in a Burlington Industries factory on the Tennessee–Virginia state line. Living on my own with no dependents it took only two years before I had enough money saved to attend an in-state university. The cost of my room, board, and tuition at Virginia Commonwealth University in Richmond, Virginia, was less than $2,000 per semester. If I entered VCU today on the same room-board-tuition plan, it would cost me $9,018 per semester. That's another six years or so on the swing and graveyard shifts—assuming that factory or any other weaving mill were open and hiring. Burlington Industries closed its mill in Bristol, TN-VA in December 1984. The factory where my father had worked since he was a teenager paid well above minimum wage and helped me and my brother pay for college. But that factory, like so many others affected by the 1994 North American Free Trade Agreement, went further south. Not NASCAR, blue-grass south, either. *Hablo del uso de sombrero, Sur que bebe tequila.* In other words, south-of-the-border south. So, like today's enlisted military, the kids who go overseas to fight in Afghanistan, Iraq, Horn of Africa, etc., if I were graduating from high school today I would either go headstrong into the military with a wrenched shoulder because Uncle Sam would be desperate enough or I'd return home and let a surgeon repair the torn ligaments in my shoulder. Then I'd climb onto the next Greyhound to Knoxville. What choice would I have? Slinging grease at McDonalds?

Just because the United States hasn't used a military draft since 1973 doesn't mean that boots are filled by an all-volunteer system. That's as much a euphemism as "defense" department. Economic conscription is alive and well. It feeds on the greed of corrupt bankers, mortgage failures, economic recession, the rising costs of college, and the fact that factories long ago moved their jobs to South America or Asia, anywhere but in the United States. Unless, of course, it's a factory that makes our weapons of war.

19. Linda Robinson, *Masters of Chaos: The Secret History of the Special Forces* (New York: PublicAffairs, 2004), p. 219 (Kindle edition).

20. Even before the war in Iraq the $380 billion annual defense budget for fiscal 2002-2003 was about ten times what Britain or France spent on defense and twice as much as the combined defense budgets of eighteen other NATO countries. (See Vernon Loeb, "As Military Spending Booms, Budget Debate Looms," *Washington Post*, February 16, 2003, p. A19.) One month before commencing with Shock and Awe, the

Defense Department said Washington's War on Terrorism was costing $1.6 billion per month. From September 11, 2001, to September 30, 2002 (the year's fiscal end), the "global fight on terror" had cost American taxpayers $28 billion, reported Defense Department spokesman Lieutenant Colonel Gary Keck. This did not include preparations for war with Iraq, such as $2.3 billion just to deploy troops and equipment to the Middle East. At the time, these figures were reported by the Western media with sticker-shock alarm, as if defense spending was out of control. Now, fast forward to September 30, 2011, the end of the latest fiscal year (as of this writing): The Pentagon's baseline budget of $549 billion with $159 billion added for fighting terror in Iraq and Afghanistan equals $708 billion. That total figure drops slightly to $670 billion in the 2012 budget proposal. From October 7, 2001, when the War on Terrorism began with U.S. bombs dropped on Afghanistan, through April 2011, the cost of fighting in just Afghanistan and Iraq—everything from ordnance dropped to personnel and equipment and the training of local security forces—cost American taxpayers an average of $9.7 billion per month. But this doesn't include the expenses in Pakistan and the long-term care of war veterans, and it doesn't begin to calculate the cost of human lives and suffering. See Nancy A. Youssef, "True cost of Afghan, Iraq wars is anyone's guess," McClatchy Newspapers, August 15, 2011.

21. Robinson, *Masters of Chaos*, p. 219 (Kindle edition).

22. Ibid., p. 190.

23. Jordanians were overwhelmingly opposed to the U.S.-led war in 2003, but King Abdullah II allowed the U.S. military to use Jordan's land and air space before, during, and after the invasion of Iraq. In the 1991 Gulf War Abdullah's father, King Hussein of Jordan, had refused to cooperate with the American military or assist in its military plans. He referred to Saddam as a friend and asked the United States to let Arab leaders mediate Saddam's invasion of Kuwait. In the new war against Saddam and with a new king, there was no such sentiment.

Five months before the March 2003 invasion of Iraq, government-made posters around Amman read, "Jordan First." It was the Jordanian government's attempt to placate the population and convince five million residents (60 percent of whom were Palestinian) that the survival of their country comes before solidarity with Iraqis. In September 2002, Jordan's foreign minister, Marwan Muasher, told an audience at the Council on Foreign Relations in Washington: "If it comes down to war, we are not going to allow our strategic friendship with the United States to be jeopardized."

Following the war, Jordan's decision to side with the Bush administration was handsomely rewarded. In the Emergency Wartime Supplemental Act passed by Congress in April 2003, Jordan was a significant beneficiary. All told, Jordan received more than $1 billion ($406 million to buy and refurbish a new set of F-16 jets and $700 million in funds from the U.S. Agency for International Development) to supplement budget shortfalls stemming from the war. Combined with previous military and aid grants totaling $400 million, Jordan received promises from Washington for $1.5 billion in 2003, making it Washington's third-largest recipient of aid behind Egypt and Israel. Washington described the aid as an investment in Jordan's continued stability. Jordanian officials said it was in recognition of Jordan's important role in the Middle East region.

However, many Jordanians read beyond the political jargon. Four months into the war, Laith Shubeilat, a conservative member of Jordan's Islamic party, told the *Los Angeles Times*, "What name can you give this but prostitution? Our sovereignty boiled down to how many millions of dollars? It's like 'Indecent Proposal.' How much will you sell yourself for?" See Jane Perlez, "Threats and Responses: Iraq's Neighbors," *New York Times*, October 8, 2002, p. 13; and T. Christian Miller, staff writer, "Jordan Tastes Fruits of U.S. Friendship," *Los Angeles Times*, July 14, 2003, p. 3.

24. King Abdullah II began his education at the Islamic Educational College in Amman. He later attended St. Edmund's School in Surrey, England, and concluded his high school education in the United States. He graduated in 1980 from Deerfield Academy, a private boarding school in Deerfield, Massachusetts. In 1982 he took an advanced course in Middle Eastern studies at Pembroke College in Oxford, England; five years later he attended the Edmund A. Walsh School of Foreign Service at Georgetown University in Washington, DC.

25. On March 20, 2003, the Iraqi military accused Jordan of assisting U.S. forces by allowing them to cross into Iraq's Al Anbar province. Jordan's Information Minister, Mohammad Affash Adwan, acted aghast. In remarks to the Jordan News Agency (PETRA), Adwan maintained Jordan's highly sensitive antiwar posture: "Such information is utterly lies, baseless and aimed at harming Jordan and its firm and public position" against the war on Iraq. "Jordan has said time and again that it will not be a launching pad for an attack on Iraq." A week later, as the U.S. media began reporting that thousands of allied soldiers invaded Iraq via Jordan (e.g., E. A. Torrreiro, *Tribune* staff reporter, "Allied Troops Wage Quiet Battle in the West," *Chicago Tribune*, March 26, 2003, p. C-4), Adwan maintained the obvious charade: "I can tell you categorically they did not come from Jordan."

26. Robinson, *Masters of Chaos*, p. 192.

27. Manufactured by AM General LLC, primarily in a factory in Mishawaka, Indiana, just six miles east of basketball-loving South Bend, Indiana. Two notable headlines in the Indiana press around the time of the ten-year anniversary of 9/11: "More than 140 Hoosiers Killed in War on Terror," a September 11, 2011, story in the *Fort Wayne Journal Gazette* listing the state's military killed in the Middle East since February 2003. Ages of the dead ranged from 19 to 41, but the majority were in their twenties. Four were killed when the Humvees they were riding in overturned or crashed. "AM General to Lay Off 350, Cut Humvee Production" reported the Associated Press on September 29, 2011. Company officials blamed the layoffs on "defense budget cuts and the drawdown of U.S. troops in Iraq and Afghanistan."

28. Manufactured en masse in a nondescript factory tucked behind a Regal Cinemas 16, World Market, and Home Depot in Columbia, South Carolina, gun-maker FN Manufacturing is a subsidiary of FN Herstal of Belgium. Since October 2001, when Washington began its War on Terrorism, FN Manufacturing has doubled its workforce to more than seven hundred employees in Columbia. Factory laborers earn between $12 to $17 per hour. This one factory will crank out some ten thousand military weapons per month. Among the arsenal: MK240 machine guns, M-16 rifles, MAG58 machine guns and—for when antiwar protestors get too loud, angry, aggressive, impatient—the FN 303. The FN 303 is a semi-automatic rifle that looks like a sawed-off shotgun, but

it fires rubber balls filled with paint and bismuth, a hard, brittle chemical. It's used by police for riot control. See Noelle Phillips, "Gunmaker Prospers as Warfare Continues," McClatchy Newspapers, June 22, 2008. In April 2010, the well-guarded factory next to Columbia's upscale Village at Sandhill shopping mall received more good news: the Department of Defense awarded FN Manufacturing an "indefinite-delivery/indefinite-quantity contract for [the] refurbishing and overhauling of machine guns in support of multiple military agencies." What economic recession?

29. Manufactured in a General Dynamics Armament Systems factory in coastal Saco, Maine, three miles from a popular waterslide and thrill-ride park. Funtown Splashtown USA bills itself as the place "Where the Great American Family Comes to Play." The Mk 19 is an automatic grenade launcher with a rapid firing rate of sixty rounds per minute, and it is trafficked around the world; used by the militaries of more than thirty nations. The General Dynamics plant in Saco also makes the M-2 50-caliber machine gun.

In the late 1990s, the factory ceased production on the Mk 19 and the M-2 because the Pentagon said its stock of both was full. But the War on Terrorism changed that assessment. As recently as 2007, the factory in Saco was turning out ten Mk 19s and ten M-2s every day. See Katheryn Skelton, "The business of war: Maine companies are active in Iraq in the air, on land and on the sea, developing products that protect the troops and keep equipment working," *Sun Journal* (Lewiston, Maine), October 28, 2007, p. A-1.

30. Notes from author interview of Gavrilis, August 5, 2011. Also, Robinson, *Masters of Chaos*, p. 211.

31. Article 18 of the Fourth Geneva Convention appears to state clearly that Rutba Hospital, which housed civilian patients and staff on the night it burned, was off-limits to the U.S. attack: "Civilian hospitals organized to give care to the wounded and sick, the infirm and maternity cases, may in *no circumstances* [emphasis added by author] be the object of attack but shall at all times be respected and protected by the Parties to the conflict."

However, Article 19 of the Fourth Geneva Convention appears to put it back into play: "The protection to which civilian hospitals are entitled shall not cease unless they are used to commit, outside their humanitarian duties, acts harmful to the enemy. Protection may, however, cease only after due warning has been given, naming, in all appropriate cases, a reasonable time limit and after such warning has remained unheeded."

Regardless, Special Forces Major James Gavrilis says Rutba General was not targeted. It was a victim of collateral damage.

32. For example, see Charles Duhigg, "Enemy Contact 'Kill 'em, Kill 'em': U.S. Troops Are Trained to Respond Instinctively during Combat," *Los Angeles Times*, July 18, 2004, p. A-1. Also see Rye Barcott, *It Happened on the Way to War* (New York: Bloomsbury USA, 2011), p. 84 (Kindle edition); and Nathaniel Vick, *One Bullet Away: The Making of a Marine Officer* (New York: Houghton Mifflin, 2006), p. 18 (Kindle edition).

33. U.S. Department of Defense budget request for fiscal 2012 submitted in February 2011 (http://comptroller.defense.gov/budget.html).

34. Defined by federal money received annually on U.S. contracts and tracked by

the Federal Procurement Data System. The top five annually are defense contractors. See "Top 100 Contractors Report Fiscal Year 2010" (https://www.fpds.gov/fpdsng_cms/index.php/reports/62-top-100-contractors-report).

35. For example, if you just track the stock dividends of the perennial top five defense contractors based on the New York Stock Exchange (NYSE) you chart a swelling of percentage increases in the decade that followed September 11, 2011: Lockheed Martin (LMT) equals 680 percent increase in per-share stock dividends or 161 percent increase in Earnings Per Share (EPS); Boeing (BA) +250 percent or +635 percent EPS; Northrop Grumman (NOC) +250 percent or +187 percent EPS; General Dynamics (GD) +336 percent or +191 percent EPS; Raytheon (RTN) +190 percent or +400 percent EPS.

36. Robinson, *Masters of Chaos*, p. 200.

37. B-1 price tag: $283 million. In case you were wondering.

38. Robinson, *Masters of Chaos*, p. 203.

39. Ibid., p. 205.

40. Defined without my literary license, *namaste* is a composite of two Sanskrit words that together mean, basically, "the light of God in me recognizes the light of God in you." It's a salutation common for Yogis and Hindus, as well as many other spiritual practices that emphasize the sacred oneness of all humanity. It is frequently accompanied with the *mudra*, a slight bow with prayerful hands raised in front of your chest. The mudra is exactly like the Buddhist *wai*, a gesture frequently followed by the Thai word *sawasdee*, derived from the word *svasti*—Sanskrit for living in a purified state of health, happiness, and wholeness. Similar to my favorite Hawaiian word, *pono*, meaning, roughly, to live divinely empowered second-by-second, minute-by-minute, day-to-day by your righteous actions, thoughts, and words. To me, it all sounds like the fruits of the Spirit described by the Apostle Paul in the New Testament (Galatians 5:22-23).

Seems like every time I go down one of these etymological rabbit holes in pursuit of philosophical/religious meaning and origin I tug on a root connected to most other philosophies and religions. One big circle of life and afterlife. I could argue that a lot of our religious quarreling is over semantics (not to be confused with Semitics).

In his book *The Irresistible Revolution: Living as an Ordinary Radical* (Grand Rapids, MI: Zondervan, 2006), Shane tells of how he began to understand the full meaning of *namaste* while volunteering at Mother Teresa's leper colony in Calcutta. Dabbing and cleaning the residents' skin lesions sparked in him the sort of kinetic connection generated in selfless service. In these moments of active worship, God goes from a noun that's worshiped from a hard pew to a verb that is electric, alive. and expressed through us. The first patient Shane treated at the leprosy colony stared at him gently as Shane cleaned the man's skin lesions. Eventually they locked eyes. Shane writes, "He stared at me with such intensity that it felt like he was looking into my soul. Every once in a while he would slowly close his eyes. When I was finished, he said to me that sacred word I had come to love: 'Namaste.' I smiled with tears in my eyes and whispered, 'Jesus.' He saw Jesus in me. And I saw Jesus in him. I remember thinking back to the stained-glass window my United Methodist church bought for over $100,000. I saw a clearer glimpse of Jesus in this leper's eyes than any stained-glass window could ever give me."

Much later in *The Irresistible Revolution,* Shane quotes the late Jewish philosopher Martin Buber, who in 1938 moved from Germany to live with Palestinians in Jerusalem, the designated capital of the League of Nations 1923 Palestine Mandate. Buber, a cultural Zionist who valued the Jewish traditions, not its politics, argued for an Arab-Jewish bi-national Zionist governorate rather than a Jewish-only Zionist state. In the book *Ich-Du* or *I and Thou* (New York: Scribner, 1958) some of Buber's letters are translated from German to English. In them he expounds on the mutually holistic existence of all humans. In effect, *namaste.* When Shane writes of Buber you can hear the lessons he gleaned among the Hindu dying in Calcutta and the Muslims he met in Baghdad and Rutba, Iraq. He writes, Buber "speaks of how we can see a person as simply a material object, something you look at, an 'it,' or we can look into a person and enter the sacredness of their humanity so that they become a 'Thou.' (And as a Jewish philosopher who immigrated to Palestine to advocate for Arab-Jewish cooperation, Buber knew all too well how easily we objectify and demonize others.)"

41. Manufactured by Colt Defense LLC in a gun factory across New Park Avenue from the Home Depot in West Hartford, CT, voted by *Kiplinger's Personal Finance Magazine* in 2010 as one of the nation's "10 Great Cities for Raising Families" and one of the "10 Best Cities for the Next Decade." As recently as 2008 the Army was purchasing more than 100,000 M4 carbines per year from Colt LLC at a cost of $178 million. As of 2011 the Defense Department had bought more than 700,000 M4 carbines from Colt LLC, which had sold more than 100,000 M4s overseas. See Adam Verwymeren, "Army seeks to replace M4 and M16," United Press International, October 30, 2008; and Richard Lardner, "Influence Game: Colt Aiming to Keep Rifle Business," Associated Press, May 25, 2011.

42. Ibid. Gavrilis was writing his own copy, and it was repeated almost verbatim in books and news media. Don't get me wrong; compared to much of the other arrogance, civilian bloodshed, and mass killing of conscripts inspired by Washington and the Pentagon, Gavrilis behaved like a prince. But let's keep it in perspective. His Bravo Company came to Rutba uninvited, with strict orders to do what they were highly trained to do: kill anyone who defends their homeland against a foreign invasion. Conscript or civilian, no matter. If they pick up a gun and aim toward you, dead. No headcounts. No casualty report. Gavrilis never had orders to keep count. War is messy. "Kill, kill, kill." That is the literal mantra of military boot camps. The end objective of the Army is ultimately no different than that of the Marines when defined by ground combat. Kill, kill, kill. See Greg Barrett, "Marine's Memoir Commands Our Attention—And Personal Investment," Huffington Post, July 5, 2011, http://goo.gl/zPgOv.

43. For example: Mark Moyar, *A Question of Command: Counterinsurgency from the Civil War to Iraq* (New Haven: Yale University Press, 2009); Linda Robinson, *Masters of Chaos: The Secret History of the Special Forces* (New York: PublicAffairs, 2004); Thomas E. Ricks, *Fiasco: The American Military Adventure in Iraq* (New York: Penguin, 2006). I'm not saying the recollection of early success in Rutba is inaccurate. But it's all relative. Anything positive in Rutba has to be seen in its full light and con-

text: The town was part of a sovereign country and province being occupied by foreign military forces. By all accounts Gavrilis and the First Battalion of the Fifth Special Forces Group treated Rutba leaders and everyday citizens with more respect than, say, the Army outfit that preceded them (Lightning Troop of the 3rd Armored Cavalry Regiment), but Rutba was still a city bombed, invaded, and occupied.

44. Ibid. Not only does Gavrilis describe initial success working with Rutba officials and the town as a whole in his *Foreign Policy* article dated November-December 2005, but town elders, for example, the mayor of Rutba in 2010, a former Iraqi fighter pilot named Qasim Mar'ai; Rutba General Hospital director Dr. Nizar Jameel Yaseen and others refer to the relatively "good treatment" and respect shown by the Special Forces soldiers—"the older guys," as Dr. Yaseen said—who occupied Rutba. Some of their assessment is taken secondhand from things they heard other locals describe, and some, like that of Rutba General ambulance driver Sa'ady Mesha'al Rasheed, is first-hand. Author notes from interviews conducted in Rutba in January 2010.

45. Dick Foster, "Fort Carson officer guilty of assaults; captain convicted on three charges while serving in Iraq," *Rocky Mountain News* (Denver, Colorado), March 17, 2005, p. A16.

46. Tom Roeder, "Captain Gets Fine, 45 Days for Abuse; Jury Allows Fort Carson Officer to Remain in Army," *The Gazette* (Colorado Springs, CO), March 18, 2005, front page Metro section.

47. Ibid. Also, Tom Roeder, "Defense: Carson GI Kept Order Captain Accused of Forging 'Reign of Terror' in Iraqi City," *The Gazette* (Colorado Springs, CO), March 15, 2005, front page Metro section.

48. Dick Foster, "Officer Denies Accusations; Fellow Soldiers Tell of Brutal Behavior by Captain in Iraq," *Rocky Mountain News* (Denver, Colorado), March 16, 2005, p. A27.

49. Robert Weller, "Army Captain Convicted of Assaults on Iraqis; Acquitted on Other Charges," Associated Press, March 17, 2005.

50. For the record, prosecutor Major Tiernan Dolan's comparison of Martin to Buford Pusser was not fair to the real-life Tennessee sheriff portrayed by actor Joe Don Baker in the original *Walking Tall* movie. The late six-foot-six Pusser only swung his bat or fired his gun at lawbreakers, which, during his six-year reign as sheriff of McNairy County (1964-1970) in western Tennessee, included the extremely violent Dixie Mafia and State Line Mob. Both ran gambling dens, prostitutes, and moonshine from bases sitting on the Mississippi–Tennessee state line. Their crimes frequently bled (literally and figuratively) into Pusser's McNairy County.

Chapter 5
Bombs Away

1. Then-Lieutenant Nathaniel Fick said this while going over the Rules of Engagement (ROE) with his Marines on the eve of the 2003 invasion of Iraq. A native of Baltimore, Maryland, an altar-boy son of an attorney and a social worker, Fick was twenty-five-years old when he led First Recon Bravo Company Second Platoon Marines through the scrappy towns of southern Iraq. In Evan Wright's 2003 *Rolling*

Stones series on the Second Platoon he describes an update that Fick gave his Marines a few days after he had reminded them of the ROE. It was March 24, 2003, and the Second Platoon was in a hot-zone resistance in southern Iraq; they had just been ordered to help secure the town of Nasiriya and the bridge leading away from it toward central Iraq. "Change in the ROE," Fick said, huddled with his Marines around the platoon's Humvees. "Anyone with a weapon is declared hostile. If it's a woman walking away from you with a weapon on her back, shoot her. If there is an armed Iraqi [civilian] out there, shoot him. I don't care if you hit them with a forty-millimeter grenade in the chest." In other words, they no longer had to wait until fired upon or threatened. If a civilian, woman or man, had a gun or rifle for their own safety, pull the trigger. In the back or chest, no matter. Also, see Evan Wright, *Generation Kill* (New York: Putnam, 2004), pp. 33 and 84 (Kindle edition).

2. Layla Al-Attar was a famous Iraqi painter, whose fame in the Middle East has been compared to Norman Rockwell's in the West. In June 1993, under order from President Clinton, twenty-three cruise missiles exploded into a Baghdad residential neighborhood. The target was the headquarters for the Mukhabarat, Iraq's intelligence agency. Clinton said the strike was in retaliation for an alleged plan to assassinate former President George H. W. Bush (an allegation now believed to be false) when he was visiting Kuwait in April 1993. Sixteen of the twenty-three missiles struck the target; at least three hit homes in the Al Mansour neighborhood. Eight civilians were killed, including Layla Al-Attar, the director of the Iraqi National Art Museum. Her husband and housekeeper also died in the attack. Heading into a church the following day, a Sunday morning, reporters asked President Clinton about the attack and the resulting civilian casualties. Clinton said he regretted the death of civilians, but the attack had been successful because "we sent the message we needed to send."

3. Classes in Iraq's medical schools are taught only in English. Every medical doctor licensed in Iraq speaks English. Various interviews between the author and Iraqi medical staff.

4. "U.S. Navy Ships Fire Tomahawks in Gulf," March 19, 2003, U.S. Navy. The USS *Donald Cook* and USS *Cowpens* fired from the Red Sea; USS *Millius* and USS *Bunker Hill* fired from the Persian Gulf; submarines USS *Cheyenne* and USS *Montpelier* were also involved (http://www.navy.mil/Search/display.asp?story_id=6395).

5. The Pentagon and White House routinely described the invading armies as a "coalition of forces" and/or "allied troops," as if the United States were just one of many nations so eager to unseat Iraqi President Saddam Hussein that they were willing to put their soldiers and economies in harm's way. But Washington's talk of a coalition was grossly misleading. The war never resembled a partnership, much less an investment of equals. For example, of the 29,199 bombs fired on Iraq from March 19, 2003, to April 18, 2003, we now know that U.S. forces launched 28,396. Of the 466,985 military personnel deployed during the month-long opening phase of the war, the United States supplied 423,998 of the troops. See T. Michael Moseley, "Operation Iraqi Freedom: By the Numbers," pp. 3 and 11, April 30, 2003, CENTAF Assessment and Analysis Division, Prince Sultan Air Base, Saudi Arabia (http://www.globalsecurity.org/military/library/report/2003/uscentaf_oif_report_30apr2003.pdf).

6. "Department of Civilian Defense Public Shelter Number 25," read a sign

written in English and Arabic outside a multilevel air-raid shelter in the affluent Sunni neighborhood of Amiriyah in Baghdad. It had steel doors, ten-foot-thick reinforced concrete, generators, televisions, hot water heaters, and its doors would shut and lock automatically in the event of air-raid warnings. The Pentagon claimed that the shelter was a communications center for the Iraqi military. Military sources quoted by various reporters, including Robert Fisk of London's *The Independent*, said that the Pentagon suspected that Ba'ath Party leaders and their families were using the shelter, and that civilian deaths were considered a necessary consequence of targeting the shelter. Neighborhood residents and Iraqi officials say that during the first Gulf War the shelter was packed every night with civilians, primarily women and children. At about 4:30 on the morning of February 13, 1991, when two F-117A stealth bombers dropped 2,000-pound bunker busters on it, hundreds of people were asleep inside it. On the shelter's bottom floor were large water heaters that broke open when the GBU-27 bombs hit. With the shelter's doors locked and melting shut, there was no escape. Incineration and boiling water would be blamed for the deaths of 408 civilian Iraqis. See D. Robert McFadden, "Iraqis Assail US as Rescue Goes On," *New York Times*, February 15, 1991 (http://www.nytimes.com/1991/02/15/world/war-in-the-gulf-iraq-iraqis-assail-us-as-rescue-goes-on.html?scp=6&sq=%22Air-raid+Shelter%22+Iraq&st=nyt); Scott Petersen, "Smarter bombs still hit civilians," *Christian Science Monitor,* October 22, 2002 (http://al-amiriyashelterfilm.com/Domains/al-amiriya/assets/download/Smarter_bombs_still_hit_civilians.pdf); Robert Fisk, *The Great War for Civilization: The Conquest of the Middle East* (New York: Knopf, 2005), p. 627.

7. In the "Mitigation Assessment Team Report: Oklahoma City Bombing," FEMA concluded that the bomb used to attack the Alfred P. Murrah Federal Building in Oklahoma City on April 19, 1995, was equivalent to the blast delivered by roughly 4,000 pounds of TNT (http://www.fema.gov/rebuild/mat/mat_fema277.shtm). The 1,000-pound warheads on Tomahawk Cruise Missiles, those delivered on land by conventional means, such as fighter jets, and those delivered long-range by warships and submarines, each carry a blast equivalent of up to 4,200 pounds of TNT.

8. Lieutenant Colonel David F. Toomey III of Haworth, New Jersey (pop. 3,390), and Major Mark Hoehn (now Lieutenant Colonel) of Ohiopyle, Pennsylvania (pop. 77), serving with the U.S. Air Force's 379th Air Expeditionary Wing, attacked Al Dora in single-pilot F-117A Nighthawk stealth jets that allowed them to switch flight controls onto autopilot and focus solely on the target, Saddam Hussein's Dora Farms palace and compound. Four months later, CBS Evening News told Americans what Iraqis and most of the Middle East already knew. Toomey and Hoehn missed. One bomb fell on a neighborhood home, and three fell just outside the compound's walls. Also, after further investigation, the Army reported that there were no bunkers at Saddam's palace—and therefore no need for a 2,000-pound bunker-busting bomb, much less four of them.

9. Bradford W. Parkinson and James J. Spilker, Jr., *The Global Positioning System: Theory and Applications*, American Institute of Aeronautics and Astronautics, Inc., 1996, "GPS Error Analysis," pp. 473-485 (http://books.google.com/books?id=lvI1a5J_4ewC&pg=PA475&lpg=PA475&dq=satellite+constellation+geometry+GDOP&source=bl&ots=k5thSoKYHv&sig=L5P9dqGAN-UJFIBisveq6muujl8&hl=en&

ei=2lYrTJqtK8WqlAfpneDUAw&sa=X&oi=book_result&ct=result&resnum=2&
ved=0CBYQ6AEwAQ#v=onepage&q=satellite%20constellation%20geometry%20
GDOP&f=false).

10. Author interviews with peacemakers in Iraq during Shock and Awe, including
Voices in the Wilderness founder Kathy Kelly. See also Kathy Kelly, *Other Lands Have
Dreams* (Oakland, CA: CounterPunch and AK Press, 2005), p. 62.

11. Nicknamed "Commando Solo," the PSYOP operation is run by the 193rd Special Operations Wing of the Pennsylvania Air National Guard. That particular unit is
based out of Harrisburg International Airport in Middletown, Pennsylvania. Middletown is a borough in Dauphin County, the northernmost area of Pennsylvania Dutch
country, known for its peaceful, nonresistant, and pacifist Amish and Mennonite communities.

12. Shown in the 2005 documentary film directed by Eugene Jarecki, *Why We
Fight* (scene beginning at 1:21:20 of film; ending at 1:21:24) (http://www.sonyclassics
.com/whywefight/).

13. U.S. Navy, "Coalition Forces Continue Tomahawk Launches," March 21,
2003. Thirty U.S. Navy and coalition warships currently assigned to Naval Forces
Central Command launched Tomahawk Land Attack missiles (TLAMs) March 20
during military operations "to disarm Iraq." The U.S. ships which launched Toma-
hawks were USS *Bunker Hill* (CG 52), USS *Mobile Bay* (CG 53), USS *San Jacinto*
(CG 56), USS *Cowpens* (CG 63), USS *Shiloh* (CG 67), USS *Briscoe* (DD 977), USS
Deyo (DD 989), USS *Fletcher* (DD 992), USS *Arleigh Burke* (DDG 51), USS *John S.
McCain* (DDG 56), USS *Paul Hamilton* (DDG 60), USS *Milius* (DDG 69), USS *Hig-
gins* (DDG 76), USS *Donald Cook* (DDG 75), USS *O'Kane* (DDG 77), USS *Porter*
(DDG 78), USS *Oscar Austin* (DDG 79), USS *Augusta* (SSN 710), USS *Providence*
(SSN 719), USS *Pittsburgh* (SSN 720), USS *Key West* (SSN 722), USS *Louisville* (SSN
724), USS *Newport News* (SSN 750), USS *San Juan* (SSN 751), USS *Montpelier* (SSN
765), USS *Toledo* (SSN 769), USS *Columbia* (SSN 771), USS *Cheyenne* (SSN 773) and
two Royal Navy submarines, HMS *Splendid* and HMS *Turbulent* (http://www.navy
.mil/search/display.asp?story_id=6466).

14. For example, the town of Ur in southern Iraq is believed by many historians
and theologians to be the birthplace of Abraham (or Ibrahim), a prophet and/or father
of the world's three major monotheistic religions—Judaism, Christianity, and Islam,
in that order. Iraq's two great rivers, the Tigris and Euphrates, are believed to be two
of the four rivers branching off from the Garden of Eden, the mythical (or literal) site
of humanity's original sin, which separated humankind from God (or Allah). En route
to Basra from Baghdad in February 2003 I flew over the presumed site of the Garden
of Eden (or Garden *in* Eden, if read literally from the transcription of the book of
Genesis) on Iraqi Airways, a commercial airline that resembled any American commercial airline, for example, U.S. Airways. Iraq is also home to the ancient site called
the Tower of Babel in the city of Babylon, located about an hour's drive south of Baghdad. According to the Scriptures, the Tower of Babel (or "the city and its tower," as
recorded in Genesis) is where humankind regrouped after the Great Flood that made
Noah famous. It is in Babylon that humankind managed to mess things up yet again,
if you believe Scripture. In the Torah, the Old Testament, and the Qur'an, after the

masses built the Tower of Babel to honor themselves, God shooed them from Babylon and scattered humankind around Earth, a four-corner timeout of sorts. To add insult to injury, God confounded them by giving each tribe its own distinctive language. Of note, after the invasion of Iraq in 2003, the First Marine Expeditionary Force based out of Camp Pendleton, California, occupied Babylon and did irreparable damage to archaeological sites there when it dug into ancient ruins to construct helicopter pads, fuel stations, and to fill barrier sandbags.

15. Moseley, "Operation Iraqi Freedom," p. 11.

16. That's how military analyst Willie Arkin described the bombs dropped on Baghdad during six weeks in 1991. Writing in the U.S. Air Force quarterly magazine *Airpower Journal,* now called *Air and Space Power Journal,* Arkin, a former Army intelligence officer and military affairs columnist for the *Los Angeles Times* and *Washington Post,* disputed General Colin Powell's concern that the Pentagon's use of 287 tons of bombs on Baghdad during the first Gulf War could indicate a new and dangerous lust for bombing. "In 43 days of war," Arkin wrote, "a mere 330 weapons (244 laser-guided bombs and 86 Tomahawk cruise missiles) were delivered on Baghdad targets (a mere three percent of the total of all *smart weapons* expended)." Now, reread that sentence and replace Baghdad with a U.S. metropolis of similar population size, for example, Washington, DC. Those mere smart bombs of the first Gulf War resulted in a significant loss of Iraq's water and sewer plants, electrical grids, communication grids, and more than three thousand civilian lives. See William Arkin, "Baghdad: The Urban Sanctuary in Desert Storm?" *Airpower Journal,* Spring 1997, http://goo.gl/NHiCx.

17. To be fair, scenes of Baghdad burning did nothing to dampen Burns's hawkish enthusiasm. Even five years later when he reminisced on the invasion in a *New York Times* essay, "War Torn," the two-time Pulitzer Prize–winning Burns wrote glowingly of A-Day, as if he'd been front-row at a U2 concert: "Five years on, it seems positively surreal. On the evening of March 19, 2003 [*sic*], a small group of Western journalists had grandstand seats for the big event in Baghdad, the start of the full-scale American bombing of strategic targets in the Iraqi capital." See John F. Burns, "A Staggering Blow to the Heart of the Iraqi Capital," *New York Times,* March 22, 2003 (http://www .nytimes.com/2003/03/22/international/worldspecial/22BAGH.html?ex=1205726 400&en=9dcd9273f0cbf31b&ei=5070); "War Torn," John F. Burns, *New York Times,* March 16, 2008 (http://www.nytimes.com/2008/03/16/weekinreview/16jburns .html?scp=5&sq=John%20F.%20Burns&st=cse).

18. One month after the invasion, CNN chief news executive Eason Jordan told Howard Kurtz on CNN's Reliable Sources: "I went to the Pentagon myself several times before the war started and met with important people there and said, for instance—at CNN, 'Here are the generals we're thinking of retaining to advise us on the air and off about the war'—and we got a big thumbs-up on all of them. That was important." This is documented in the book and film *War Made Easy: How Presidents & Pundits Keep Spinning Us to Death* (scene beginning at 0:21:38 of film; ending at 0:21:53) (http://www.warmadeeasythemovie.org/). The inherent conflict of interest generated in such an arrangement hinders objectivity from a news analyst presented to the viewing public as a credible, unbiased source.

19. See "How Tomahawk cruise missile works," USAToday.com (http://www .usatoday.com/graphics/news/gra/gcruisemissile/frame.htm).

20. Sales for Raytheon finished with an increase of 18 percent for the first quarter of fiscal year 2003. In fiscal 2004, the U.S. Navy awarded Raytheon a contract worth $287 million to build as many as 2,200 more satellite-guided Tomahawk Cruise Missiles. The value of the overall contract included as much as $1.6 billion over five years if all orders were placed. See Theo Emery, "Tomahawks Performance Bolsters Raytheon," March 25, 2003, Associated Press; Thomas Stauffer, "Raytheon Wins Contract to Build Latest Version of Navy Cruise Missile," *Arizona Daily Star,* August 19, 2004.

21. One could argue that the latter should be counted with the former. Soldiers ordered by a ruthless dictator and regime to defend their homeland against foreign invaders are doubly victimized. First, by the dictator who conscribes them to a poorly equipped military; second, by the super-sized superpower that plows through them with modern weapons.

22. Al Dora, a market and farming suburb in southern Baghdad, was home to Sunni, Shia, and Christian residents. Most of the Christians were congregants of the Chaldean Catholic Church, an autonomous Eastern branch of Roman Catholicism. Former Iraqi Deputy Prime Minister Tariq Aziz is a Chaldean Catholic. By most accounts, before the war of 2003 encouraged a vast exodus of Christians, the Muslim-majority of Iraq (pop. 30 million in 2003) lived peacefully with its Christian minority population of 800,000. In Dora, Muslims and Christians continued to live harmoniously until May 2007 when Muslim extremists issued a *fatwa,* or religious edict. It gave Christians a choice: convert to Islam or leave Iraq and forfeit all property. If Christians didn't convert or leave, they faced death. Today, there are few if any Christians living in Dora.

23. As described by Jon Lee Anderson in "War Wounds: Bombs Fall and the Lights Go Out," *New Yorker,* April 13, 2003 (http://www.usatoday.com/graphics/news/gra/ gcruisemissile/frame.htm).

24. Author interviews with U.S. peacemakers Shane Claiborne and Kathy Kelly, both present on March 24, 2003, in Al Kindi General Hospital.

25. By mandate of the UN Security Council, the Austria-based IAEA inspected Iraq for the possibility of weapons of mass destruction. Right up until the start of war, IAEA officials insisted there was no evidence to warrant an invasion of sovereign Iraq. They requested more time to complete its inspections to the satisfaction of the Bush administration. The White House ignored IAEA and proceeded with Shock and Awe. See reports from the disbanded IAEA Iraq Nuclear Verification Office (http://www .iaea.org/OurWork/SV/Invo/index.html).

26. It was only after the American peacemakers were treated in Rutba on March 29, 2003, and continued on to Jordan that news of the hospital's bombing, several days after the fact, began to circulate in the international media. The story never gained traction, in part because it came to light amid the media storm surrounding the April 1, 2003, rescue of Army private Jessica Lynch.

27. The closest that Washington or the Pentagon has come to an apology for any of these errant bombings was following the Amiriyah shelter massacre in 1991.

In reference to the incineration of Amiriyah's 408 Iraqi civilians, Lieutenant General Thomas Kelly, the director of operations for the Joint Chiefs of Staff during the first Gulf War, offered this statement the following day: "We were as careful as we possibly could be. We didn't know civilians were in there. We struck it. We suffer remorse as a result of that." With that, the Pentagon said the investigation into the accident was closed. See Patrick E. Tyler, "U.S. Stands Firm on Bomb Attack and Says Investigation Is Closed," *New York Times*, February 15, 1991 (http://www.nytimes.com/1991/02/15/world/war-gulf-strategy-us-stands-firm-bomb-attack-says-investigation-closed.html?scp=8&sq=The+Amiriya+Shelter&st=nyt).

28. On the night of March 26, 2003, Robert Fisk of Britain's *The Independent* wrote in his notes, "I'll bet we are told that Saddam is ultimately responsible for [the day's civilian] deaths. . . . Faulty Iraqi anti-aircraft missiles—the same old excuse—had probably killed them all, the Americans said. It was not possible. The two missiles had exploded equidistant from each other on both [Abu Taleb Street] carriageways. No guidance system could fail on two anti-aircraft missiles at exactly the same time, causing them to land so neatly on the same road" (Robert Fisk, *The Great War for Civilization: The Conquest of the Middle East* [New York: Random House, 2005], p. 951).

29. Robert Fisk, "Final proof that war is about the failure of the human spirit," *The Independent*, April 10, 2003 (http://www.independent.co.uk/opinion/commentators/fisk/robert-fisk-final-proof-that-war-is-about-the-failure-of-the-human-spirit-593978.html).

30. Two hours after President Bush's declaration-of-war speech on March 20, 2003, Saddam Hussein was on Iraqi TV with a declaration of his own. He attempted to rally the Arab world, which for decades has condemned Israel's treatment of the Palestinians, by linking the war to the Israeli-Palestinian conflict. The invaders "will lose any hope in accomplishing what they were driven to by the criminal Zionists and those who have agendas," Saddam told his country. "Let Iraq live. Long live Jihad and long live Palestine."

31. "Baghdad Shops Attack Kills 14," BBC News, March 26, 2003 (http://news.bbc.co.uk/2/hi/middle_east/2887555.stm); "Eyewitness: Shock and Anger," BBC News, March 26, 2003 (http://news.bbc.co.uk/2/hi/middle_east/2888429.stm).

32. Paul Wiseman, "Cluster Bombs Kill in Iraq, Even after Shooting Ends," *USA Today,* December 16, 2003 (http://www.usatoday.com/news/world/iraq/2003-12-10-cluster-bomb-cover_x.htm). Moseley, "Operation Iraqi Freedom," p. 11.

33. Textron Defense Systems data sheet, p. 2, https://acrobat.com/#d=M3A0wfJItApLjCbgKuw5Uw.

34. Information gleaned by author from calculations of the declassified report by Moseley, "Operation Iraqi Freedom."

35. His name, Ali Abdulrazek, age 40. He was walking to a family member's house in the Sha'ab neighborhood of Baghdad on the morning of April 6. It was the only way he could talk to them because the telephone lines were dead. He told Fisk that he heard a jet roar overhead, and then there was a "terrible noise" and flash of light. "There was a family, a husband and wife and kids, in front of me. . . . I went to try and help the family . . . but they were all gone, in pieces. Then I realized I couldn't see properly." Shrap-

nel from a missile had cut out Abdulrazek's left eye, explained Dr. Osama Al-Rahimi. See Robert Fisk, "Amid Allied jubilation a child lies in agony, his clothes soaked in blood," April 8, 2003, *The Independent* (http://www.independent.co.uk/opinion/commentators/fisk/amid-allied-jubilation-a-child-lies-in-agony-clothes-soaked-in-blood-593791.html).

36. Mohammed Abdullah Alwani was traveling home on his motorcycle from the Rashid Hotel when he passed a road where an American armored vehicle was parked. He told Fisk that he didn't see the armored vehicle until the last moment. "They opened fire and hit me and I managed to stay on the cycle. Then their second shot sent bits of shrapnel into the bike and I fell off." At the hospital blood continued to run down his leg, and near his liver there was a bloody gash one-half inch deep. Ibid.

37. Saadia Hussein al-Shomari worked for the Iraqi Ministry of Trade. She lived in the eastern Baghdad district of al-Jadida. As she was leaving home one day in the first week of April a cluster bomb dropped in her neighborhood, a relative told Fisk. She is "pin-cushioned with bloody holes," Fisk wrote in the April 8, 2003, edition of *The Independent*. As Fisk spoke to Saadia's relative, a doctor was swiping flies off her wounds with a piece of cardboard. Ibid.

38. Jon Lee Anderson, *The Fall of Baghdad* (New York: Penguin, 2004), p. 243.

Chapter 6
At War with War

1. George W. Bush, *Decision Points* (New York: Crown, 2010), p. 255. To justify his characterization of the bombing of Baghdad as "precise," Bush juxtaposed Shock and Awe with the American and British firebombing of Dresden, Germany, in World War II (fifteen square kilometers of the city burned, including 24,866 houses, 72 schools, 22 hospitals, 18 churches; 20,000 to 25,000 residents died), the atomic bombing of Hiroshima (80,000 to 166,000 killed from the explosion, subsequent fires, falling debris and radiation exposure), and Nagasaki (60,000 to 80,000 killed similarly); and with the use of about 400,000 tons of napalm on Vietnam. Compared to such carnage and collateral damage the bombardment of Iraq could be seen as relatively precise. I guess. We'll never know for sure. Collecting precise data on the number of Iraqis killed in the 2003 invasion and the ongoing war was evidently not part of the Pentagon's war plan. However, according to numbers gleaned from some 52,000 U.S. military field reports that had been kept secret until WikiLeaks published 391,832 classified Pentagon documents in 2010, American soldiers reported 109,032 Iraqi deaths between the years 2004 and 2009. These field reports do not appear to be a coordinated effort to track the consequences of war in Iraq. Rather, they were just part of the daily grind—soldier emails, reports, and records passed from Iraq to the Pentagon. Of the dead Iraqis counted in these war logs more than half (66,081) were listed as civilian. The dead do not include Iraqis killed during the war's heaviest fighting of 2003 or by most coalition forces other than the U.S. military. Iraq Body Count, the British-based nongovernment project that began tracking Iraqi deaths in March 2003, estimates that between

106,000 and 115,000 civilians in Iraq have been killed since the U.S.-led invasion in March 2003. A database of those killed in the ongoing violence is available at http://www.iraqbodycount.org/database/.

2. It's the same Christ quoted in Christian Scripture saying, "Blessed are the merciful, for they shall obtain mercy" (Matthew 5:7); "Blessed are the peacemakers, for they shall be called the children of God" (Matthew 5:9); "All they that draw the sword shall perish with the sword" (Matthew 26:52); "My kingdom is not of this world. If it were my servants would fight" (John 18:36).

3. Five hundred thousand tons is wildly conservative and represents only the total ordnance through 2004 by one California-based aviation unit for the Marine Corps. As reported by Seymour Hersh of the *New Yorker,* during the height of firefights in and around Falluja in the fall of 2004, the Marines issued a press release that gave an indication of the heavy bombardment used in U.S. aggression. "With a massive Marine air and ground offensive under way," the press release read, "Marine close air support continues to put high-tech steel on target. . . . Flying missions day and night for weeks, the fixed wing aircraft of the 3rd Marine Aircraft Wing are ensuring battlefield success on the front line." Since the beginning of the war, the press release continued, the 3rd Marine Aircraft Wing alone had dropped more than *five hundred thousand tons of ordnance.* "This number is likely to be much higher by the end of operations," Marine Major Mike Sexton said. In the battle for the city, more than seven hundred Americans were killed or wounded. Hersh writes, "U.S. officials did not release estimates of civilian dead, but press reports at the time told of women and children killed in the bombardments." See Seymour M. Hersh, "Up in the Air: Where is the Iraq War Headed to Next," *New Yorker,* December 5, 2005 (http://www.newyorker.com/archive/2005/12/05/051205fa_fact).

4. As a registered and active U.S. voter, a baptized Christian, and a longtime member of the U.S. print media, you can certainly include me on any and all apologies stemming from the 2003 invasion of Iraq.

5. After much controversy and debate, the Maryville school board officially declared in 1999 that the Confederate flag was not an official school symbol and ordered it removed from all school facilities, property, and uniforms. Six years later, the school board banned all flags, banners, stickers, and various other items from home football games.

6. Of note, Lamar Alexander, the senior U.S. Senator from Tennessee and Conference Chair of the Republican Party, is a proud Red Rebel alum.

7. Separated shoulder, torn ligaments, Army doc said it required surgery. See endnote 18 in chapter 4.

8. Pat Lafon worked at William Blount High School until she retired in 2005. She also taught various family and consumer science classes, for example, sewing, home economics, etc.

9. After all, his mom was always expert with thread and needle, even taught Shane how to sew his own clothes and helped him make the three-piece gray tuxedo he wore at his May 7, 2011, wedding to the Simple Way's Katie Jo Brotherton. Their wedding-day "stretch limo" was a loaner—a two-seater bicycle strung with cans, streamers,

and a "Just Married" sign. You can see them leaving their downtown Philly wedding reception on it at http://www.flickr.com/photos/jamiemoffett/5697347519/in/photostream.

10. The original three, Shane, Weldon, and Cliff; CPT veteran Peggy Gish; Muslim Peacemaker Teams co-founder Sami Rasouli, who served as our guide and interpreter; former Iraq war veteran and conscientious objector, Logan Mehl-Laituri, who at this writing (November 2011) is a student at Duke Divinity School.

11. This changing of euphemisms was approved by President Obama in February 2010 and went into effect on September 1, 2010, just as Obama was drawing down U.S. troops in Iraq to 50,000. Sounding more like his predecessor than the political change he had promised, during a national TV address on August 31, 2010, Obama explained the change in names: "Through this remarkable chapter in the history of the United States and Iraq, we have met our responsibility. Now, it is time to turn the page."

12. First Letter of John 4:18 (KJV): "There is no fear in love; but perfect love casteth out fear: because fear hath torment. He that feareth is not made perfect in love." Biblical scholars, such as Stephen L. Harris, author of *Understanding the Bible* (New York: McGraw-Hill, 2010), generally believe the epistle was written by the Apostle John and was his attempt, as an eyewitness to the life of Jesus, to assure doubters that Christ was incarnated in the flesh rather than just as a spirit. In this letter to his "dear children," John presents God as light, love, and life, and he describes how people can join in fellowship with God by putting into practice the lessons and example of Jesus's life—as opposed to just worship and study.

In the U2 song "I'll Go Crazy if I Don't Go Crazy Tonight," quoted in this book's foreword by Reverend Desmond Tutu, Bono is pulling from 1 John 4:18 when he sings "Is it true that perfect love drives out all fear."

13. At the time Shane didn't know that Eastern University students Jonathan and Leah Wilson-Hartgrove were scheduled to travel to Baghdad with the Christian Peacemaker Teams, which worked in close proximity with Kathy's Iraq Peace Team aka Voices in the Wilderness.

14. Berrigan also went to post-war Iraq in January 2004 with outspoken peace activist Bishop Thomas Gumbleton, a Roman Catholic priest (now retired) with the Archdiocese of Detroit. Along with Canadian singer and songwriter Bruce Cockburn and photojournalist Linda Panetta, Gumbleton and Berrigan wanted to see how Iraqis were adjusting to Operation Iraqi Freedom. After visiting a squatters camp in Baghdad that housed more than a thousand people displaced by the war, Berrigan described Dickens-like conditions in a bombed-out building that lacked water and electricity: "We stepped around and over raw sewage as we entered this building to see where the people were squatting. All around the outside of the building was debris from the bombs. The children were running over these piles as if it were a playground. . . . One little girl held my hand the entire time I was there. I was able to communicate with her through an interpreter. She was 10 years old and had dreams of being a doctor when she grew up. Her mom is a homeless widow with four children. I don't know how her dream can possibly be realized." See Kim Mulford, "Love Motivates Mom, Activist to Oppose Iraq War," *Courier-Post* (Cherry Hill, NJ), February 4, 2006, p. G-1;

and see Eils Lotozo, "Haunting Images: Philadelphia Peace Activists Who Traveled to Baghdad Recently Found Iraqis without the Basics and Fearing for Their Safety," *Philadelphia Inquirer*, February 3, 2004, p. E-1.

15. After a book talk I gave in Chicago a few years ago Kathy and I went out for coffee with some of her friends. During the conversation I explained to Kathy how I wanted to write a book about her and her tireless social activism. Typical of Kathy, she thought there was someone more worthy (or maybe she just didn't want me hanging around). In Iraq she had been so impressed by the "young man who made his own clothes from burlap, lived simply, loved being of service to neighbors, and cut quite a figure in dreads" that she insisted I first write a book about his work. "Shane is the one you should be writing about," she said modestly, "not *me*."

16. John Powers, "Shock and Awe," *LA Weekly*, February 28, 2003, p. 13.

17. William Bundh, "U.S. Plan for Saddam: Shock and Awe," *Philadelphia Daily News*, February 26, 2003, p. 6.

18. Read the letter in its entirety at https://acrobat.com/app.html#d=x1eXUmey dcs2gwDiItBhOw.

19. On the war's first full day, Thursday, March 20, 2003, CNN drew an average audience of 3.7 million viewers compared with 4.1 million for Fox News. During the first five days of the war, the viewership for CNN rose 439 percent compared to the first quarter, and Fox News enjoyed gains of 309 percent.

20. After the *Washington Post* tracked the partial remains of one soldier to a landfill in King George County, Virginia, the Dover Air Force Base mortuary, the main port of entry for American war dead, admitted that between 2004 and 2008 the incinerated remains of at least 274 American soldiers had followed the same route as household trash. As of this writing, December 29, 2011, the Pentagon and Congress were investigating how the lapse occurred and how many more remains might have been treated similarly. A full investigation would require examining the records of about 6,300 dead soldiers whose remains had passed through the Dover mortuary since 2001. The practice of dumping remains in a landfill was concealed from families who had authorized the military to dispose of the remains in a dignified and respectful manner, Air Force officials said. See Craig Whitlock and Mary Pat Flaherty, "Hundreds of Troops' Ashes Put in Landfill," *Washington Post*, December 8, 2011, p. A1 (https://acrobat.com/app.html#d=0bW9gP4gbbx4y5m02cC55w).

21. Or, rather, we apologize for publicly counting our dead and lying about counting yours. Turns out the Pentagon was counting dead Iraqis—insurgents and civilians—even as it told the news media it wasn't. In the 391,832 classified Pentagon documents released in October 2010 by WikiLeaks were war logs that included field reports by the U.S. military. These reports from 2004 to 2009 attempted to track the deaths in Iraq resulting from the U.S. military, insurgents, and/or sectarian violence related to the ongoing war and occupation. Although the logs are not a definitive recording of the deaths (e.g., the first year of the war, including the bombing of Rutba General Hospital, was not included in the drove of data), they did have the details of more than 100,000 Iraqis killed after the U.S.-led invasion, including more than 15,000 deaths that were previously unrecorded. In a painstaking analysis of the data,

London's *Guardian* newspaper plotted every death recorded in the war logs and created a map with data for each incident. You can view *The Guardian*'s detailed Map of Death at http://www.guardian.co.uk/world/datablog/interactive/2010/oct/23/wikileaks-iraq-deaths-map. You can see an interactive map that follows a day of Iraq events (bombings, kidnappings, firefights, an American death, etc.) as they are being recorded in the U.S. war logs at http://www.guardian.co.uk/world/interactive/2010/aug/13/iraq-war-logs.

22. From 1789 until 1947 there was no Department of Defense. Washington kept it real, called it like it was. The department that ran Army operations was called, simply, the U.S. Department of War or the War Department. And there was no Secretary of Defense, only the Secretary of War.

23. The same day that Soviet President Leonid Brezhnev wrote to President Reagan to protest U.S. economic sanctions against Poland for the martial law imposed by the repressive and authoritarian People's Republic of Poland. In the Christmas day letter to Reagan, Brezhnev, sounding like any other politician, communist or freely elected (i.e., wildly hypocritical), was "calling upon you and the government of the USA to end at last the interference in the internal affairs of a sovereign state . . . This manipulation in the most diverse forms—overt and covert—has been underway for a long time, already." Read the full and declassified letter at https://acrobat.com/app.html#d=GMY4BcqicEOjPdz-NQX1XQ.

24. During the peacemaker trip into Iraq, January 2010, Logan was a senior at Hawaii Pacific University. As of this writing, November 2011, he is a student at Duke Divinity School in Durham, North Carolina, and the soon-to-be author of a book scheduled for release in July 2012: *Reborn on the Fourth of July: The Challenge of Faith, Patriotism & Conscience* (Westmont, IL: InterVarsity Press).

25. For more, see http://www.centurionsguild.org.

26. Joe Bageant, *Deer Hunting with Jesus: Dispatches from America's Class War* (New York: Crown, 2007), p. 200.

27. Ephesians 6:12 (KJV).

28. Acts 5:29 (KJV).

29. Romans 13:1 (KJV).

30. Romans 13:1 (NIV).

31. Romans 13:9 (KJV): "Thou shalt not commit adultery, Thou shalt not kill, Thou shalt not steal, Thou shalt not bear false witness, Thou shalt not covet; and if there be any other commandment, it is briefly comprehended in this saying, namely, Thou shalt love thy neighbor as thyself."

32. Romans 13:9 (NIV): "The commandments, 'You shall not commit adultery,' 'You shall not murder,' 'You shall not steal,' 'You shall not covet,' and whatever other command there may be, are summed up in this one command: 'Love your neighbor as yourself.'"

33. During the ninety-minute variety show/peace rally the ever-persistent Ben Cohen provided an illustration that he's been presenting to audiences since at least August 19, 1999, when he was the guest speaker at a National Press Club luncheon in Washington, DC. He uses 10,000 BB pellets as a prop. Each BB is supposed to

represent a nuclear weapon in the possession of the United States. (The current size of the inventory is actually about half that number, not counting 3,500 "retired" nuclear weapons that await disassembling—a testament, perhaps, to Cohen's persistent nuclear-reduction campaign.) Each of the Pentagon's estimated 2,150 "operational" nuclear weapons packs the explosive power of fifteen "Little Boys," the atomic bomb dropped in 1945 on Hiroshima. More than 100,000 deaths resulted from Little Boy, the first incident of nuclear energy used as a weapon. The U.S. Department of Energy estimated that Little Boy's radioactive fallout and other effects on health increased its death toll to 200,000 or more by 1950. Little Boy had the lethality of only one-fifteenth of one of Cohen's BBs. At the National Press Club in 1999 and in Philadelphia in 2011, and in many places and videos in-between, Cohen explains that it takes just six of these nuclear weapons to wipe out all of Russia. But the United States keeps thousands stockpiled and ready—enough nuclear warheads to incinerate the world many times over, as if that were possible. To maintain and secure this stockpile, American taxpayers spend more than $17 billion annually. At events like Jesus, Bombs and Ice Cream and the Veterans for Peace annual conference, Cohen concludes his BBs illustration with this message: "Our country, the last remaining superpower on Earth, needs to learn how to measure its strength not in terms of how many people we can kill, but in terms of how many people we can feed, clothe, house, and care for." To see a video of Cohen giving his BBs presentation at the 25th annual conference for Veterans for Peace in 2010, see http://www.youtube.com/watch?v=2FvfKM9j61c&feature=youtu.be.

34. The fuller context of Logan's quotes at "Jesus, Bombs and Ice Cream," a peace rally held in Philadelphia on the eve of the 10th anniversary of 9/11, were: "Wandering the Mesopotamian wilderness like Cain before me, I saw things nobody should ever have to see." And, later, "By trading my humanity for nationalism, I had begun down the descending spiral of violence, which threatened to corrode the very fabric of my moral character. The things I did and failed to do were nearly my undoing...." You can watch a video of Logan's full testimony at http://vimeo.com/31963960.

35. See http://co.mcc.org/veteran/logan.

36. By the time the U.S. military officially pulled out of Iraq on December 15, 2011, McConnell's name was buried in a long list of seventy-eight Minnesotans killed in Iraq (another nineteen Minnesotans had died in Afghanistan), and his death was listed as just one of 4,487 Americans killed in Iraq since the 2003 invasion. The *Military Times*, a newspaper owned by my former longtime employer, Gannett Company, Inc., maintains an online database of Americans who have died in Operation Enduring Freedom (Afghanistan), Operation Iraqi Freedom, and Operation New Dawn. To see McConnell's photo and story, or to see the faces of any of the thousands of other soldiers killed in Afghanistan and Iraq, go to the Gannett-run website at http://www.militarytimes.com/valor/search?conflict=3.

37. Like every other soldier Logan knew, McConnell, a native of Duluth, Minnesota, who had lost his mother to cancer when he was fifteen-years-old, joined the Army for financial reasons. His sister, Becky McConnell, said her brother was "terrified" of going to Iraq, but after working odd jobs without much success he signed up in 2002

"to become more responsible to his daughters financially." See Larry Oakes, "Duluth Soldier Found Pride and Purpose," *Star-Tribune* (Minneapolis, MN), February 19, 2004, p. 1B.

38. Descriptions of the funeral and burial come from McConnell's hometown newspaper. In his military death he was given something he never received in his life: a story on the front page of the Duluth newspaper. See Chuck Frederick, "'He Represented Our Army and Our Nation with Spirit'—More than 100 Mourners Remember Daniel James McConnell, a Duluth Soldier Killed in Iraq," *Duluth News-Tribune*, November 24, 2004, p. 1A.

39. Oakes, "Duluth Soldier Found Pride and Purpose," p. 1B.

40. These are not your granddaddy's gunships, that is, Vietnam-era cargo planes with mounted machine guns firing 7.62mm rounds from two rear windows and a side door. The modern-day AC-130H/U gunships are turboprop planes tricked out like tanks. They're armed with 40mm and 105mm cannons with newer models (the AC-130U "Spooky") adding a 25mm Gatling gun capable of firing 1,800 rounds per minute. For comparison, the main armament of the M1 Abrams tank is a 105mm cannon. Each AC-130H/U costs roughly $190 million to $210 million to manufacture and arm. Lockheed-Martin and Boeing share the wealth in an arrangement common in the trickle-down economics of military spending. Lockheed designs and builds most or all of the airframes at its factory twenty miles north of the Six Flags over Georgia amusement park in Marietta, GA, a plant adjacent to Dobbins Air Reserve Base and Southern Polytechnic State University; Boeing converts the airframes into gunships through its 16,000-employee Defense, Space & Security division headquartered in St. Louis (Missouri's largest manufacturer and second-largest employer), and outfits it in part with Raytheon-made products; for example, the APQ-180 fire control radar system in the AC130U integrates with the 40mm and 105mm cannons to help locate and track the target. The AC-130 "is an excellent candidate for the world's deadliest aircraft," boasts Discovery TV on its Military Channel.

But a ten-year-old could have told you most of this. Our kids are indoctrinated (conditioned?) to the military industry's deadliest weapons via popular video games on Xbox and PlayStation, and even the apps for their iPods. In bestselling first-person shooter games such as Modern Warfare II and III they "earn" the right to fly an AC-130 gunship and rake the enemy with Gatling gunfire by first going on a tear of killing at ground-level. In Modern Warfare II you need eleven successive kills to earn your AC-130 wings; Modern Warfare III requires thirteen.

The iPod app "AC-130 Spectre," named for the AC-130H and rated for children age nine and above, offers this adventure from the Apple iTunes website: "CLIMB ABOARD an AC-130 GUNSHIP and RAIN DEATH from the SKY in this VISUALLY STUNNING take on MODERN WARFARE." The app costs $1.99, and as of December 4, 2011, it had been downloaded two million times.

41. As are mine, the hands of a law-abiding American taxpayer whose money supports the military industrial complex directly and indirectly. Also, as a modern-day American with a modern-day stock portfolio (read: relatively dense) my wife and I may be profiting from the vast military industrial complex. We keep meaning to go

through our stock portfolios with investigative eyes to make double and triple sure we're not complete hypocrites. There are so many companies, monopolies, and consolidations involved directly and indirectly in war-making that it requires more than a quick check. By the time you read this I promise that we will have completely itemized our stock portfolios. Send me an email at greg@gregbarrett.org if you want to know what we found and from what companies (if any) we divested our investments. You could argue that in my previous profession, as a newspaper and wire reporter for twenty years, I profited from the military industrial complex even as I reported stories from prewar Iraq that attempted to draw attention to the people most likely to be killed in war—everyday Iraqis who posed no danger to the United States or Israel. At the time I owned stock in Gannett (NYSE: GC) and, later, I owned stock in the Tribune Company (NYSE: TRB), back when Tribune stock was still traded publicly. Bottom line: War sells newspapers.

42. Erin Thompson, "Free-Fire Fallout Vets Grapple with Atrocities: Interview with an Iraqi War Vet," *The Independent,* March 14, 2008. See full interview at http://www.indypendent.org/2008/03/14/free-fire-fallout-vets-grapple-atrocities-interview-iraqi-war-vet.

43. The mosque is built over the silver-covered tomb of the Shia Islam's most revered saint, Imam Ali Ibn Abu Talib, the Prophet Muhammad's cousin and son-in-law. In rank of holiness and reverence in the Shia branch of Islam, it is behind only Mecca and Medina in Saudi Arabia.

44. From Logan's videotaped testimony at "Winter Soldier: Iraq & Afghanistan—Eyewitness Accounts of the Occupations," a four-day event in March 2008 sponsored by Iraq Veterans Against the War.

45. Major General John R.S. Batiste and Lieutenant Colonel Paul R. Daniels, "The Fight for Samarra: Full-Spectrum Operations in Modern Warfare," *Military Review*, May-June 2005, p. 15, https://acrobat.com/#d=xi8RuBoGBFKcBelTbqkOfQ.

46. Batiste and Daniels, "The Fight for Samarra," p. 13. Return Samarra's government to "competent civilian control" was the Pentagon's goal? That stopped me mid-sentence. I had never known that competence was a prerequisite of democratic rule. If this is something new added to the Iraqi model of democracy I'd love to see it applied in U.S. elections.

47. This is from testimony Logan gave in March 2008 at an event in Silver Spring, Maryland, called "Winter Soldier Iraq and Afghanistan: Eyewitness Accounts of the Occupations." Former U.S. soldiers and members of Iraq Veterans Against the War gathered at Winter Soldier to give eyewitness accounts of things they witnessed and experienced during combat in Afghanistan and Iraq. See video excerpts of Logan's testimony at http://youtu.be/GR8PolIfP-8.

In testimony given in 2008 at Winter Soldier, and later to Congress, American combat veterans described inconsistent Rules of Engagement that were routinely downgraded. For example, Jason Lemieux, a former Marine sergeant from upstate New York who served three combat tours in Iraq from 2003 to 2006, told of how the ROE for his infantry unit when it crossed from Kuwait into Iraq in March 2003 followed Geneva Convention guidelines, for example, soldiers were authorized to shoot anyone wearing a military uniform (except medical and religious personnel) unless they surrendered. But with so many Iraqi soldiers wearing civilian clothes, by the time his unit arrived in Baghdad, "I was explicitly told by my chain of command that I could shoot anyone who came closer to me than I felt comfortable with if that person did not immediately move when I ordered them to do so, keeping in mind I don't speak Arabic." During Lemieux's second tour of Iraq from February to September 2004, his unit was frequently engaged in firefights in the Anbar province. The ROE for that deployment deteriorated from a justified killing being defined as shooting anyone "displaying hostile intent and committing a hostile act" to "everyone wearing a black dishdasha and a red headscarf" to "everyone on the streets was considered an enemy combatant" and could be justifiably shot. Following the firefights, Lemieux said, Marines were told they no longer needed to identify a hostile action; they could use deadly force if they identified hostile intent. "The rules also explicitly stated that carrying a shovel, standing on a rooftop while speaking on a cell phone or holding binoculars, or being out after curfew were automatically considered hostile intent and we were authorized to use deadly force," he said. "I can only guess how many innocent people died during my tour because of those orders." See video excerpts of Jason's testimony at http://www.youtube.com/watch?v=nXJXmQdTg8o&feature=youtu.be.

48. Jonathan Steele, "The War Logs: Samarra: Blow by Blow, the Biggest US Operation since the Invasion," *The Guardian* (London), October 25, 2010, p. 9.

49. Kim Sengupta, "Civilians Bear Brunt as Samarra Pacified," *The Independent* (London), October 4, 2004, p. 23.

50. Ibid.

51. Islam generally considers the embalming fluid's formaldehyde, methanol, ethanol, and other solvents to be impure substances.

52. Thomas S. Mulligan and Edmund Sanders, "U.S. Forces in Iraq Regain Control of Rebel Hot Spot," *Los Angeles Times*, October 4, 2004, p. 1.

53. Sengupta, "Civilians Bear Brunt as Samarra Pacified," p. 23.

54. Rick Lyman and Dexter Filkins, "After 3-Day Fight, U.S. and Iraqi Forces Retake Samarra," *New York Times*, October 4, 2004, p. 10.

55. Logan's full testimony, delivered March 21, 2010, two months after returning from our trip to Rutba, is available at http://conscienceinwar.org/2010/07/24/logan-mehl-laituri-testimony-video/.

56. Logan's testimony at "Winter Soldier Iraq and Afghanistan: Eyewitness Accounts of the Occupations," March 2008. To be fair to the unnamed sniper in this anecdote that Logan told at the Winter Soldier testimonies, the sniper was looking at the target through a rifle scope. Logan was not. In other talks and interviews where he has told this same story of an unarmed Iraqi civilian being gunned down by a U.S. sniper he qualified it with the fact that the sniper had a better view of the pedestrian than he did.

57. John DeRosa, "Operation Baton Rouge: Perspectives from an Iraqi Security Forces Adviser," *Armor* magazine, November 1, 2006, p. 34.

58. Ibid. Also, Batiste and Daniels, "The Fight for Samarra," p. 13.

59. Batiste was a two-star general and a thirty-one-year veteran of the Army when he retired November 1, 2005. He was also a lifelong Republican who voluntarily left

the Army because of disagreements with Defense Secretary Donald Rumsfeld's management of the war. In testimony before Congress on September 25, 2006, the blunt-speaking Batiste fixed Rumsfeld in his sights:

> Secretary Rumsfeld's dismal strategic decisions resulted in the unnecessary deaths of American servicemen and women, our allies, and the good people of Iraq. He was responsible for America and her allies going to war with the wrong plan and a strategy that did not address the realities of fighting an insurgency. He violated fundamental principles of war, dismissed deliberate military planning, ignored the hard work to build the peace after the fall of Saddam Hussein, set the conditions for Abu Ghraib and other atrocities that further ignited the insurgency, disbanded Iraqi security force institutions when we needed them the most, constrained our commanders with an overly restrictive de-Ba'athification policy, and failed to seriously resource the training and equipping of the Iraqi security forces as our main effort. He does not comprehend the human dimension of warfare. The mission in Iraq is all about breaking the cycle of violence and the hard work to change attitudes and give the Iraqi people alternatives to the insurgency. You cannot do this with precision bombs from thirty thousand feet.

60. Within forty-eight hours of the bombing more than two hundred Iraqis died in sectarian clashes stemming from the attack on Al Askari mosque.

61. Federal News Service transcript of President Bush's speech to the American Legion in Washington, DC, February 24, 2006. Read the entire transcript at https://acrobat.com/app.html#d=-EMd9tJq2s6UPWFBFLG4Pg.

62. This presumes that the world's faithful were not offended by American bombings of Iraq, for example, the 38,358 sorties and 29,199 bombs (guided and unguided) delivered by air by the Pentagon in just the first month of the invasion. See T. Michael Moseley, "Operation Iraqi Freedom: By the Numbers," April 30, 2003, CENTAF Assessment and Analysis Division, Prince Sultan Air Base, Saudi Arabia (https://acrobat.com/app.html#d=mzYyIKQO9*FwmY6w2Vtn-w).

By 2006 (and much earlier) you'd think Bush's rah-rah speeches about the War on Terrorism and the war in Iraq would be received in Washington the same way they had long been received in the Middle East—like works of parody, eliciting laughter, perhaps, as in a "Saturday Night Live" skit. But applause?

63. The soldiers died August 22, 2007, when their UH-60 Black Hawk helicopter crashed from what the Army said were mechanical problems. The soldiers were returning from a night mission that included two UH-60 Black Hawk and two OH-58D Kiowa helicopters that picked up two "small kill teams" of soldiers that had been dropped off the night before in Multaka, near the northern city of Kirkuk. A 224-page Army investigation of the crash, obtained by the *Honolulu Advertiser* through the Freedom of Information Act, discovered a gouged and cut tail-rotor shaft and an "unknown foreign object" in the tail-rotor housing. Families of the dead soldiers sued U.S. defense contractor L-3 Communications Corporation and its subsidiary, Vertex Aerospace, which was under contract with the Army to provide helicopter mainte-

nance at Camp Taji, twenty miles north of Baghdad. The lawsuit alleged that a small spool of wire or other foreign object left in the tail-rotor housing caused the Black Hawk to crash. With the helicopter's rapid, tumbling descent the soldiers suffered blunt-force injuries in an impact of 150 Gs, or 150 times the force of gravity (a fighter pilot coming out of a dive can experience up to nine Gs), the *Advertiser* reported.

The deceased soldiers from the Twenty-fifth Infantry Division at Schofield Barracks were identified as Captain Derek A. Dobogai, 26, of Fond du Lac, WI; Staff Sergeant Jason L. Paton, 25, of Poway, CA; Sergeant Garrett I. McLead, 23, of Rockport, TX; Corporal Jeremy P. Bouffard, 21, of Middlefield, MA; Corporal Phillip J. Brodnick, 25, of New Lenox, IL; Corporal Joshua S. Harmon, 20, of Mentor, OH; Corporal Nathan C. Hubbard, 21, of Clovis, CA; Specialist Michael A. Hook, 25, of Altoona, PA; Specialist Jessy G. Pollard, 22, of Springfield, MO; Specialist Tyler R. Seideman, 20, of Lincoln, AK. The Black Hawk's four crew members from the Fourth Squadron, 6th U.S. Air Cavalry Regiment, Fort Lewis, WA, were also killed. They were identified as Captain Corry P. Tyler, 29, of Woodbine, GA; Chief Warrant Officer Paul J. Flynn, 28, of Whitsett, NC; Sergeant Matthew L. Tallman, 30, of Groveland, CA; Specialist Rickey L. Bell, 21, of Caruthersville, MO.

64. 2 Timothy 4 (KJV).

65. Romans 13:10 (KJV): "Love worketh no ill to his neighbour: therefore love is the fulfilling of the law."

66. Ar-Razzaq Islamic Center, on the corner of Carroll and West Chapel Hill streets in Durham, is a nonprofit charity and mosque founded in the early 1970s as Mosque #34 by the Nation of Islam. When Nation of Islam leader Elijah Muhammad died February 25, 1975, his son, imam W. D. Muhammad, broke with the Nation of Islam's black-separatist leanings and attempted to align the group with a more inclusive and mainstream strain of Islam. Today, Ar-Razzaq, led by imam Greg Rashad, is part of imam W. D. Muhammad's group rather than the Nation of Islam movement led by Louis Farrakhan. Rashad explained to readers on the front page of Durham's *The Herald-Sun* newspaper on November 22, 2011: "You can't be a separatist today and expect to get anything done. We have to link to one another in order to become contributors to humanity."

Chapter 7
Face to Face with the Enemy

1. This quote is from a column by Chris Hedges titled "Death and After in Iraq," posted March 21, 2011, on Truthdig.com (http://www.truthdig.com/report/item/the_body_baggers_of_iraq_20110321). Or read the column at https://acrobat.com/app.html#d=iXXFrYAbYYhX1V7KGteUuA. Seriously, *read* it. Please. If you're a civilian you probably don't realize the full extent of what this nation asks of its soldiers when it sends them to war. It's barbaric, primitive, and, in many cases, literally maddening. See also Jessica "Jess" Goodell's memoir with author John Hearn, *Shade It Black: Death and After in Iraq* (Havertown, PA: Casemate, 2011). In reading Hedges's column and Goodell's memoir I'm reminded of President Dwight D. Eisenhower's

quote: "I hate war as only a soldier who has lived it can, only as one who has seen its brutality, its futility, its stupidity."

Goodell served in the U.S. military's first officially declared Mortuary Affairs Platoon, based at Al Taqaddum Airbase, forty-six miles west of Baghdad. Her job in 2004 required her to help collect the bodies (and body parts) of dead soldiers, to go through their pockets and personal belongings, and to collect and catalog everything in possession of the dead before shipping their remains back to their loved ones via Dover Air Force Base (the same Dover that is now notorious for its landfill burials). Goodell's account is a powerful book that should make all civilians toss and turn like combat vets.

Of the items found in soldiers' pockets, Goodell recalls on p. 38: "Some items were uncommon, like the sonogram of a fetus. Some were not uncommon enough, like a suicide note."

Of the nightmarish work caused by Improvised Explosive Devices (IED) used by insurgents to blow apart Humvees and soldiers, Goodell says on p. 52: "Some of the remains had to be scooped up by putting our hands together as though we were cupping water. We put the body parts and pieces from the [Humvee] and the surrounding ground into a body bag, then scooped up the liquidy remains and poured them in too. When we finished, the contents—the clumps and chunks and pieces and parts—didn't resemble a human body. Nor did they remain equally distributed within the body bag. If we picked up the body bag at one end, everything moved to the other end. When we lifted it at both ends, it all slid to the middle."

Reading this last description I can sympathize with Dover's lapse of perspective.

2. The supersized importance placed on American sports has never felt so surreally ridiculous to me. I watched parts of the Super Bowl from Washington Dulles International Airport before my flight to the Middle East, but only after searching through the terminal for CNN or some other news channel—something, anything that might give me updates about the approaching war. Every TV at Dulles (just twenty-six miles west of the White House) was tuned to Super Bowl XXXVII on ABC. The storyline of the Tampa Bay Buccaneers coach Jon Gruden versus his nemesis and former team, the Oakland Raiders, proved gold for ABC. Super Bowl ads sold that evening for $2.2 million per thirty-second commercial slot.

Two nights later, Bush's State of the Union address drew the most TV viewers by far of any State of the Union address since President Clinton's first in 1993. Bush in 2003 drew ten million more viewers than his first post-9/11 State of the Union speech in 2002, which had been the largest since Clinton's mea culpa Monica Lewinsky State of the Union in 1998. Storylines sell. Like Gruden versus Raiders' owner Al Davis, Bush versus Saddam made for compelling television. ABC, NBC, CBS, MSNBC, CNN, FOX, and FOX News Channel televised the prewar State of the Union address live to the world on January 28, 2003. It went into more households (41.4 million) than any other State of the Union speech before or since. Still, according to the Nielsen ratings, ABC's broadcast of Gruden's first Super Bowl victory won easily. Gruden: 88.6 million total viewers. Bush: 62 million. (For comparison, Obama drew 42.7 million viewers for his 2011 State of the Union address.)

3. Andrew Marks, "Wall Street Analysts Counting Down to War," *Business Times Singapore*, January 27, 2003.

4. If being a perfect dove means behaving perfectly as a pacifist, count me out. At dinner during our first night in Amman in 2010, before Shane and nonpacifist brethren and filmmaker Jamie Moffett arrived, Cliff, Weldon, Peggy, Logan, and I ate dinner together in the hotel's small diner. I was outnumbered—the only "nonpacifist" at the table. I explained to the group how I am absolutely certain that I would/could/should kill another person if that person were threatening to kill my wife and/or children, and if the attacker were in a position to immediately act on the threat. It's the way I'm wired. I didn't apologize for it. I dared to suggest that it might be the way each of them was wired. How can a pacifist know if he or she is truly a pacifist until put in a wrenching jam like the one I described? Who in their right non-Gandhi mind watches a family member get murdered without using all the force at-hand to stop it? Cliff explained how he had once talked sense into a suicide bomber and saved a roomful of beloved CPT members. He had never felt compelled to attack the man. That proved to him that pacifism could work even in dire situations—that is, dialogue and intelligence trump brute force. Weldon, our perpetually smiling and affable Mennonite preacher, argued adamantly against my just-war theory of using lethality to protect my family. He said the act of killing deeply violated the divinity in humanity. Christ forbids the taking of another person's life. Period. There is no asterisk or footnote, no courtroom wiggle room allowing for self-defense. If ever I find myself in that situation I should dissuade, subdue, and/or disarm the attacker, Weldon explained, but never, ever kill. To kill with intent cuts against the grain of evolution. So, I'm left looking for my ideal bumper sticker: "Don't mess with my honor roll kids. I have not evolved."

5. See transcript of President Bush's 2003 State-of-the-Union address at https://acrobat.com/app.html#d=pvrcerZWgh-sAU25wWHloA.

6. Named after Iraq-born poet Abu at-Tayyib Ahmad ibn al-Husayn al-Mutanabbi.

7. Since 1980, the Iraqi economy had endured Saddam's eight-year war with Iran, his gassing of Iraqi Kurds in the north, his invasion of Kuwait, his swift defeat in the first Gulf War, his brutal quashing of an Iraqi Shiite revolt in the south and Kurdish revolt in the north. Combine all of that with UN economic sanctions, and an economy that was once robust goes bust. By the time I arrived in 2003 the relative wealth and well-being of everyday Iraqis had been completely sapped. A sophisticated population that had once been the envy of the Middle East was attempting to survive on government food rations and a currency deflated by some 6,000 percent.

8. A move I seriously considered after the 2004 U.S. presidential election.

9. As if one justified the other. But, for the record, like the rest of the news media, I documented Saddam's sick transgressions against Shia and Kurds. Those stories had to wait until I arrived back in Amman and Washington.

10. For example, from *The Idaho Statesman* Letters-to-the-Editor page, dated February 28, 2003: "In regard to Gannett reporter Greg Barrett's article printed in The Statesman on February 4, I say 'stay in Iraq.' I am saddened to see The Statesman chose to print this garbage, especially with Boise being home to the Idaho Air National Guard. Tell the families here who have loved ones over there protecting Mr. Barrett's

right to freedom of speech. Mr. Barrett stated he would rather lie about his nationality than to say he was an American. Mr. Barrett also stated all the things his country has done to the Iraqi people. I say Mr. Barrett tell them also of all the horrific things their leader has done to them and not only them, to us too, your country. If I read another article published in The Statesman by Mr. Barrett, you can cancel my subscription immediately. Pamela Nelson, Boise."

To be fair to the good people of Idaho, it's not like all readers of the *Statesman* were insulted by stories that were critical of Washington's preemptive war. For example, this letter-to-the-editor was published the same day as Pamela Nelson's:

"War with Iraq may mean death to thousands and thousands of civilians. Forty-two percent of the population in Iraq are children. They have been decimated by war and years of sanctions. Their military and economy are weak. With the presence of U.N. inspectors, Saddam Hussein is contained. The people who will suffer from war have already been victimized. I fear that war with Iraq will fuel Islamic anger and exponentially increase terrorism to Americans. The United States is the richest, most powerful country on earth. We should be a model of diplomacy in solving problems. We would not want other countries such as Pakistan and India or China and Taiwan to settle their problems with force. Speak out against violence as a solution. Beverly Ferrell, Weiser (Idaho)."

11. In January 2003, when I first met Kathy, her group was known primarily as Voices in the Wilderness—a voice for Iraqis suffering from the UN economic sanctions. But as Voices in the Wilderness narrowed its focus to the Iraq invasion and occupation, and often teamed its efforts with CPT, it became known as the Iraq Peace Team. Later, as it broadened its focus to include the West Bank, Gaza, Pakistan, and Afghanistan, it changed its name to Voices for Creative Nonviolence (http://vcnv .org/).

12. Beginning in December 1988, Kelly served nine months in a maximum security federal prison in Lexington, KY, for repeatedly trespassing on a Missouri nuclear missile silo to plant corn. The trespasses were part of an organized nonviolent protest called Missouri Peace Planting. In 2004, she served three months at Illinois' medium-security Pekin Prison for trespassing on Fort Benning's Army base during a peace vigil at the Western Hemisphere Institute for Security Cooperation, better known by its former name, the School of the Americas or SOA, derided by peacemakers as School of Assassins. The SOA is notorious for its alumni, for example, former Bolivian dictator General Hugo Banzer; former Panamanian military dictator Manuel Noriega; Salvadoran military strongman Roberto d'Aubuisson, suspected in the 1980 death-squad killing of San Salvador archbishop Oscar Romero, one of South America's most prominent Catholic priests.

13. One month earlier, in December 2002, Kathy had been in Iraq when she told me by phone that she didn't know who at that moment was living in her apartment in Chicago's gritty Uptown area, a neighborhood more reminiscent of Archie Bunker's Queens borough in New York than of Jimmie Walker's *Good Times* Chicago housing project. During the previous six years, Kathy's nonviolent activist group, then called Voices in the Wilderness, had sent some five dozen groups of activists into Iraq in defi-

ance of the UN embargo. As I write this in July 2011, Kathy is on the *Audacity of Hope* in Greece with the activists who are attempting to break an Israeli embargo/siege of Gaza by taking humanitarian supplies to the Palestinians there. Update: The *Audacity of Hope* was eventually stopped from making the trip to Gaza and detained by Greece and impounded in a port outside of Athens.

14. Speaking to a reporter in 2009 for a story about the three-day-long Gandhi-King Conference on Peacemaking held at Christian Brothers University in Memphis, Tennessee, Kathy was especially blunt in explaining her refusal to pay Uncle Sam. "There is no way, no how I would give my money to the Mafia, much less the IRS," she told Ryan Poe of Memphis' *The Commercial Appeal* newspaper. "We face a serious question about whether or not to continue to pour resources and productivity into military projects while we cannot meet human needs." She was in Memphis as a panelist for a discussion titled "The Power of the Purse: Women and War Tax Resistance."

15. The National War Tax Resistance Coordinating Committee (NWTRCC), based in Brooklyn, New York, is a coalition of local, regional, and national groups that support war-tax resistance. The difference between war-tax resisters and the garden-variety tax evader is this: pacifists and peacemakers refuse to pay federal taxes because of the violence that could be committed on their dime, and they often *want* the IRS to know that they are not filing a Form 1040. For example, soon after the War Resisters League partnered with the Center on Law and Pacifism in 1981 to form the NWTRCC, freelance writer April Moore from Washington, DC, felt a tug of conscience. She could no longer in good conscience pay a percentage of her income, knowing full well that it was going to buy weapons for wars in Central America and elsewhere. But instead of hiding from the IRS, she wrote "a long, from-the-heart letter" to Uncle Sam explaining her reasons for no longer supporting the Pentagon and Washington. See Colman McCarthy, "Private Lives: The 'War Tax' Resisters," *Washington Post,* March 26, 1981, Style, p. D5.

16. Kathy Kelly, *Other Lands Have Dreams* (Oakland, CA: CounterPunch and AK Press, 2005), p. 18.

17. Richard Mertens, "A Radical Takes Root," *University of Chicago Magazine,* April 2001 (http://magazine.uchicago.edu/0104/features/).

18. Ibid. Discussing his time in the minimum-security federal prison in Sandstone, Minnesota, Mertens quotes Meyer saying, "Nine months in prison was a more valuable educational experience than nine months at the University of Chicago, because of what it told me about the human condition and about our society. It was an education in trying to see the world the way it is—like Socrates—not to see the shadows, but the reality."

19. There has long been a campaign afoot to have Dorothy Day canonized. Although not beatified alongside Blessed Pope John Paul II in May 2011, as some Catholics thought she would be, it is believed by many theologians and Catholic scholars that Dorothy Day is on the fast track to sainthood. For her part, Day considered such talk frivolous. She thought it was a way for mainstream Christians and others to dismiss their own involvement in peacemaking and leave for others the heavy lifting of social justice.

20. The nine-minute-long *Duck and Cover* video was made by Archer Productions for the Federal Civil Defense Administration. It is widely available today in the public domain. See http://www.youtube.com/watch?v=IKqXu-5jw60.

21. The Manhattan Project, leading to the 1945 bombings of Hiroshima and Nagasaki, began the threat with its initial research in 1939. Bert the Turtle skipped that bit of history.

22. The following U.S. bombing survey conducted for President Truman and dated June 19, 1946 (nearly one year after the atomic bombings of Hiroshima and Nagasaki), was not undertaken for humanitarian concerns. Rather, the study's purpose was to evaluate the potency of U.S. air power "as an instrument of military strategy, for planning the future development of the United States armed forces, and for determining future economic policies with respect to the national defense." Judged solely by the subsequent expansion of the defense budget and military industry, the Pentagon and Washington were wildly encouraged by the lethality of atomic bombs "Little Boy" and "Fat Man."

The "U.S. Strategic Bombing Survey," established on November 3, 1944, in response to a presidential directive, was intended to provide an expert and impartial study of the effects and significance of U.S. aerial attacks on Germany and Japan. In evaluating the damage that two atomic bombs inflicted on the populations and infrastructures of Hiroshima and Nagasaki, the report read in part: "The most striking result of the atomic bombs was the great number of casualties. The exact number of dead and injured will never be known because of the confusion after the explosions. Persons unaccounted for might have been burned beyond recognition in the falling buildings, disposed of in one of the mass cremations of the first week of recovery, or driven out of the city to die or recover without any record remaining. . . . In this uncertain situation, estimates of casualties have generally ranged between 100,000 and 180,000 for Hiroshima, and between 50,000 and 100,000 for Nagasaki. The Survey believes the dead at Hiroshima to have been between 70,000 and 80,000, with an equal number injured; at Nagasaki over 35,000 dead and somewhat more than that injured seem the most plausible [estimates]."

The survey goes on to say that all known cases of pregnant women who were within 3,000 feet of the bombs' targets had miscarriages. "Even up to 6,500 feet they have had miscarriages or premature infants who died shortly after birth."

Of the damage to infrastructure and buildings, it concluded: "The entire heart [of Hiroshima], the main administrative and commercial as well as residential section, was gone. In this area only about fifty buildings, all of reinforced concrete, remained standing. All of these suffered blast damage and all save about a dozen were almost completely gutted by fire; only five could be used without major repairs."

As for Nagasaki, it began, "Because the most intense destruction was confined to the Urakami Valley, the impact of the bomb on the city as a whole was less shattering than at Hiroshima. . . . [However] over 80 percent of the city's hospital beds and the Medical College were located within 3,000 feet of the center of the explosion, and were completely destroyed. Reinforced concrete buildings within this range, though standing, were completely gutted by fire; buildings of wooden construction were destroyed by fire and blast. The mortality rate in this group of buildings was between 75 and

80 percent. Exact casualty figures for medical personnel are unknown, but the city seems to have fared better than Hiroshima: 120 doctors were at work on 1 November, about one-half of the pre-raid roster. Casualties were undoubtedly high: 600 out of 850 medical students at the Nagasaki Medical [College] were killed and most of the others injured; and of the 20 faculty members 12 were killed and four others injured."

The entire survey is archived at the Harry S. Truman Library & Museum, "U.S. Strategic Bombing Survey: The Effects of the Atomic Bombings on Hiroshima and Nagasaki," June 19, 1946. President's Secretary's File, Truman Papers. Available at http://www.trumanlibrary.org/whistlestop/study_collections/bomb/large/documents/index.php?pagenumber=2&documentid=65&documentdate=1946-06-19&studycollectionid=abomb&groupid=.

23. Kathy Kelly, "Epilogue: The Pilgrim," in *Hope Dies Last*, ed. Studs Terkel (New York: New Press, 2003), p. 319.

24. Richard Mertens, "A Radical Takes Root," *University of Chicago Magazine*, April 2001 (http://magazine.uchicago.edu/0104/features/).

25. Ibid.

26. Certainly neither Dorothy Day nor Christianity in general is alone in this gospel. Many religious texts discuss the profound connection between each person's thoughts, words, and actions and humanity's collective well-being. Just one example, the *Bhagavad Gita* (or just *Gita*), a sacred text of Hindu. In its seven hundred verses the *Bhagavad Gita* places human destiny entirely in human hands, as explained by Eknath Easwaran, translator of a modern English version of the scripture and the book (*The Bhagavad Gita* [Tomales, CA: Nilgiri Press of the Blue Mountain Center of Meditation, 2007]). As Easwaran explains, the *Gita*'s "world is not deterministic, but neither is it an expression of blind chance: we shape ourselves and [the] world by what we believe and think and act on, whether for good or for ill." In *The Bhagavad Gita*, Easwaran discusses the *Gita*'s three *gunas,* or strands, which he translates roughly into inertia (*tamas*), activity (*rajas*) and harmony (*sattva*). "In the Gita the gunas are described as the very fabric of existence, the veil that hides unity in a covering of diversity. Tamas is maya's power of concealment, the darkness or ignorance that hides unitive reality; rajas distracts and scatters awareness, turning it away from reality toward the diversity of the outside world. Thus the gunas are essentially born of the mind. When the mind's activity is stilled, we see life as it is." Which is to say, connected, that is, each individual decision is a falling domino with infinite consequences good and bad, seen and unseen.

27. The Sermon on the Mount contains the central tenets of the Christian faith as revealed by Jesus Christ in Galilee, just north of Nazareth. Christian peacemakers frequently refer to its teachings. For example, Matthew 5:5 ("Blessed are the meek, for they shall inherit the earth"); Matthew 5:7 ("Blessed are the merciful, for they shall obtain mercy"); Matthew 5:9 ("Blessed are the peacemakers, for they shall be called the children of God"); Matthew 5:10 ("Blessed are they which are persecuted for righteousness' sake, for theirs is the kingdom of heaven"); Matthew 5:21 ("You have heard that it was said of them of old time, You shall not kill; and whosoever shall kill shall be in danger of the judgment"); Matthew 5:38-39 ("You have heard that it has been said, An eye for an eye, and a tooth for a tooth. But I say unto you, that you resist not evil, but whosoever shall smite you on your right cheek, turn to him the other also"); Matthew

5:43-44 ("You have heard that it has been said, You shall love your neighbor, and hate your enemy. But I say unto you, Love your enemies, bless them that curse you, do good to them that hate you, and pray for those who despitefully use you, and persecute you"). Eight months before Sen. Barack Obama announced his presidential candidacy in February 2007 the freshman senator from Illinois delivered the keynote address at the annual Call to Renewal Conference in the historic National City Christian Church in Washington, DC, a Disciples of Christ congregation located exactly one mile from 1600 Pennsylvania Avenue. In his speech he referred to the various interpretations of Christian teachings and the unambiguous lessons of nonviolence found in the Sermon on the Mount. Its message, he said, "is so radical that it's doubtful that our own Defense Department would survive its application . . . So before we get carried away, let's read our Bibles. Folks haven't been reading their Bibles." Then, after being elected the 44th president of the United States, he increased the size of the U.S. military in Afghanistan; maintained the fattened Pentagon budget at Bush-era levels; and in 2011 proposed a record-high base budget ($553 billion) for the Pentagon in fiscal 2012 with another $118 billion for the wars in Iraq, Afghanistan, and Pakistan; escalated U.S. airstrikes in Yemen with unmanned drones; approved the building of a CIA base in Yemen to serve as a hub of future military operations; and sent U.S. troops to war in Libya without the approval of Congress. He also won the 2009 Nobel Peace Prize.

28. See Peter Grier, "Tracking the Military Industrial Complex," *Christian Science Monitor*, January 17, 1986, National, p. 3. General Andrew Goodpaster, a key aide to President Eisenhower, tells Grier that the first drafts of Eisenhower's farewell address told the nation to guard against the acquisition of the unwarranted influence from the "military-congressional-industrial complex" rather than the "military-industrial complex"—the description Eisenhower ultimately used. Goodpaster explained that the speech's final draft was changed because Eisenhower didn't want his farewell address to be seen as a partisan slap.

29. Kelly, *Other Lands Have Dreams*, p. 17.

30. Evidently Washington keeps a close eye on prominent peacemakers. In *The Irresistible Revolution*, Shane describes how he arrived back in the United States from a church conference in the Bahamas, not long after he had been in Iraq, and was greeted at the airport by two officers from the Department of Homeland Security. As they questioned him about his activities at Nassau's New Providence Community Church, they sifted through some documents. "I hesitate to say it since it seems uncannily like Hollywood," Shane writes, "but I kid you not, they opened up a thick file with my name on it. I could see pictures and articles and pieces of the Simple Way website."

31. Richard Mertens, "A Radical Takes Root," *University of Chicago Magazine*, April 2001.

32. Ibid.

33. By most measures the socialist Sandinista National Liberation Front improved Nicaragua's economy and education. Initially at least. From 1979 (when the Sandinistas overthrew the forty-three-year rule of the Somoza family) until 1983 (when Washington ratcheted up its support of the Contras), Nicaragua's GDP per capita grew 7 percent while the GDP of neighboring Central American countries declined by as much as 14 percent. The Sandinistas opened nearly 800 new schools and, within

the first month of the overthrow, it appointed Father Fernando Cardenal to lead a national literacy program. The Sandinista Literacy Campaign of 1980 would eventually include some 80,000 volunteers spread throughout the country's urban and rural areas. It won the 1980 United Nations Educational, Scientific and Cultural Organization literacy award. According to UNESCO, whereas the Somoza dictatorship had shown contempt for adult literacy and education, the Sandinistas saw an opportunity "to encourage an integration and understanding between Nicaraguans of different classes and backgrounds; to increase political awareness; to nurture attitudes and skills related to creativity, production, co-operation, discipline, and analytical thinking; to support national cohesion and consensus; and to strengthen the channels for economic and political participation." For Somocism, literacy was "unnecessary, inappropriate and impossible," read a 2005 UNESCO background paper about the Sandinistas literacy program (http://unesdoc.unesco.org/images/0014/001460/146007e.pdf). The new government leaders saw literacy as an integral part of national development. UNESCO highlights two primary reasons for the Sandinistas motivation to educate the public: "Firstly, justice and a moral obligation of the revolution towards the population; and secondly, literacy was seen as a part of the preparation of the whole population to manage the big task of national reconstruction."

34. International Court of Justice Pleadings, Oral Arguments, Documents Case Concerning Military and Paramilitary Activities in and against Nicaragua (*Nicaragua v. United States of America*), volume V, "Evidence of Father Loison," p. 85. To download the case's testimony go to https://acrobat.com/#d=pNILuZqat920A4SF3fyjug.

35. Following various news media and UN reports of how the Contras were terrorizing Nicaraguan towns on the back of CIA training and some $80 million in American funds, U.S. lawmakers passed a bill in October 1984 prohibiting further "military" aid given to the Contras. Eight months later, the money would begin to flow again, same direct route to the Contras, same murderous results. All that changed was the terminology. The $27 million approved by Congress in June 1985 was now called "humanitarian assistance." Although Reagan described the aid as humanitarian, in a letter to Congress he described the purpose of the money as funds to "support . . . the military efforts of the resistance." In a secret report that accompanied his initial request for military aid in April, President Ronald Reagan said his goal was to enable the contras to expand from 16,000 men to as many as 35,000, to "levels sufficient to create real pressures on the government of Nicaragua." See Doyle McManus, "House Approves Votes for Contras; Officials Say Vote Will Escalate War, Embolden Allies," *Los Angeles Times*, June 13, 1985, p. 1. Also, see Milt Freudenheim, Richard Levine and Henry Giniger, "The Rebels Are Back in the Money in Nicaragua," *New York Times*, August 11, 1985.

36. Don Shannon and William R. Long, "U.S. Warns Nicaragua on Regional Terrorism," *Los Angeles Times*, July 19, 1985.

37. From the manual's English-translated version: "CIA Psychological Operations in Guerrilla Warfare: A Tactical Manual for the Revolutionary," preface. Download or view the manual at https://acrobat.com/#d=VOqVpuO6tTSVCVun*PDQKQ.

38. Ira R. Allen, "Reagan Hits Liberals and Sandinistas," United Press International, March 1, 1985. No doubt Reagan felt safe in this embellishment of Contra

heroics. He was speaking to an adoring crowd during the annual and highly partisan Conservative Political Action Conference (CPAC) in Washington, DC. This is the fuller context of his quote: "They are our brothers, these freedom fighters, and we owe them our help. I've spoken recently of the freedom fighters of Nicaragua. You know the truth about them. You know who they're fighting and why. They are the moral equal of our founding fathers and the brave men and women of the French resistance. We cannot turn away from them. For the struggle here is not right versus left but right versus wrong." Reagan also said that "perhaps the greatest triumph of modern conservatism has been to stop allowing the left to put the average American on the moral defensive." Liberal Democrats are "bankrupt of ideas," he added, and their past victories at the polls have led to "chaos, weakness, and drift." However, he concluded gleefully, "Their failures yielded one great thing: us guys." See transcript of Reagan's speech at http:// www.conservative.org/cpac/archives/cpac-1985-ronald-reagan/. Curiously, archival footage of that 24-minute speech has been scrubbed of Reagan's gung-ho references to the "Freedom Fighters" of Nicaragua, his equating of the Contras to John Adams, Benjamin Franklin, Alexander Hamilton, John Jay, Thomas Jefferson, James Madison, and George Washington. Missing also is Reagan's subsequent appeal to the 1,700 conservatives in attendance to endorse Washington's backing of the Contras for the sake of freedom, democracy, and keeping communism at bay. At the 18:05 mark of a video uploaded to Youtube on February 12, 2010 (see http://www.youtube.com/ watch?v=du_dA7wP688), by The Ronald Reagan Presidential Foundation those 233 words of Reagan's 2,909-word speech have been edited out.

39. CIA, "Psychological Operations in Guerrilla Warfare," p. 60 (http://www .whale.to/b/CIA%27s%20Psychological%20Operations%20in%20Guerrilla%20 Warfare.pdf).

40. Consider, for example, Secretary of Defense Donald Rumsfeld speaking to the 88th annual American Legion National Convention on August 29, 2006. This was more than three years after the invasion of Iraq, and the Pentagon had failed to find Iraq's alleged weapons of mass destruction. Rumsfeld was under especially heavy criticism from the news media. Midway into his rah-rah patriotic convention speech Rumsfeld juxtaposed Hitler and World War II with Iraq and the U.S. War on Terror. He then posed four rhetorical questions, one after another: "With the growing lethality and the increasing availability of weapons, can we truly afford to believe that somehow, some way, vicious extremists can be appeased? Can folks really continue to think that free countries can negotiate a separate peace with terrorists? Can we afford the luxury of pretending that the threats today are simply law enforcement problems, like robbing a bank or stealing a car; rather than threats of a fundamentally different nature requiring fundamentally different approaches? And can we really afford to return to the destructive view that America, not the enemy, but America, is the source of the world's troubles?" With the invasion of Iraq justified and the War on Terror ideally framed, Rumsfeld then attacked his attackers. "It's a strange time when a database search of America's leading newspapers turns up literally ten times as many mentions of one of the soldiers who has been punished for misconduct—ten times more!—than the mentions of Sergeant First Class Paul Ray Smith, the first recipient of the Medal of Honor in the Global War on Terror. Or when a senior editor at *Newsweek* dispar-

agingly refers to the brave volunteers in our armed forces—the Army, the Navy, the Air Force, the Marines, the Coast Guard—as a 'mercenary army.' [Or] when the former head of CNN accuses the American military of deliberately targeting journalists; and the once-CNN Baghdad bureau chief finally admits that as bureau chief in Baghdad, he concealed reports of Saddam Hussein's crimes when he was in charge there so that CNN could keep on reporting selective news. And it's a sad time when Amnesty International refers to the military facility at Guantanamo Bay—which holds terrorists who have vowed to kill Americans and which is arguably the best run and most scrutinized detention facility in the history of warfare—'the gulag of our times.' It's inexcusable!" Applause interrupted Rumsfeld's speech, but he wasn't finished. As any Central American revolutionary (or author of CIA manuals on psychological warfare) knows, the prolepsis is soon followed with an exhortation toward action. "Those who know the truth need to speak out against these kinds of myths and distortions that are being told about our troops and about our country," Rumsfeld exclaimed. "America is not what's wrong with the world!" Cue the rousing applause.

41. In the *Republic of Nicaragua v. the United States of America* case heard by the International Court of Justice in 1985, the Court rendered sixteen final decisions. In No. 9, the Court stated that the United States had encouraged human rights violations by the Contras with its manual titled *Psychological Operations in Guerrilla Warfare*. However, the Court added, this did not make such acts attributable to the United States. In other words, no acts of terror committed by the Contras could be directly linked to Washington.

42. An earlier and perhaps more honest request for $21 million in supplemental funds to support the Contras had been rejected by Congress. That request had stated candidly that the money was needed "to continue certain activities of the Central Intelligence Agency which the President has determined are important to the national security of the United States." See "Case concerning Military and Paramilitary Activities in and against Nicaragua," International Court of Justice, June 27, 1986, General List No. 70, p. 41 (http://www.ilsa.org/jessup/jessup08/basicmats/icjnicaragua.pdf).

43. Paul Laverty, "British Shame in Backing US Overkill in Nicaragua," *Manchester Guardian Weekly*, Letters to the Editor, July 7, 1985.

44. In November 1984, five years after the overthrow of dictator Anastasio Somoza, the Nicaraguan junta held open elections and Sandinista National Liberation Front leader Daniel Ortega was elected president with more than 60 percent of the votes. In Nicaragua's ninety-six-member National Constituent Assembly, the Sandinistas held sixty-one seats. The remaining thirty-five were divided among six other political parties. The Reagan administration called the Sandinistas' victory a "farce" because there was "no meaningful opposition," according to the Associated Press and various other news reports. Ortega's standing with Washington would not be helped two months later when a surprise guest showed up at his January 10, 1985, inauguration in Nicaragua's capital, Managua: Cuba's Fidel Castro.

45. "Economic Sanctions against Nicaragua," transcript, Department of State Bulletin, July 1, 1985.

46. Michael T. Klare and David Andersen, *A Scourge of Guns: The Diffusion of Small Arms and Light Weapons in Latin America* (Washington, DC: Federation of

American Scientists, 1996), p. 81. In their book, Klare and Andersen use the National Security Archives to illustrate how bloated the U.S.-to-Contra arms-supply line was even as Reagan lobbied Congress for $100 million in military aid: "Although the full extent of covert arms aid to the contras has never been established, the available documentation suggests that it was substantial. In one memo sent to CIA Director William Casey in July 1986, retired Major General John Singlaub (a key figure in the covert supply operation) discussed a pending delivery of 10,000 Kalashnikov AKM assault rifles, 200 RPG-7 rocket launchers, 200 60 mm mortars, 50 82 mm mortars, 60 12.7 mm machine guns, 50 SA-7 portable surface-to-air missiles, and related ammunition. Other evidence of large arms shipments comes from the transcripts of radio communications between the contras and their contacts at the CIA. On April 12, 1986, for instance, a rebel field commander radioed a CIA official to acknowledge that his forces had just received an airdrop of 20,000 pounds of military equipment, including German-type G3 assault rifles, rifle magazines and ammunition, RPG-7 rockets, grenades, and grenade launchers. Because supply operations of this type were conducted on a regular basis for several years, it is clear that substantial quantities of small arms and other light weapons were given to the contras during this period."

47. Joel Brinkley, "Reagan Plans to Seek New Military Aid to Contras," *New York Times*, February 14, 1986, p. A-10.

48. Ibid.

49. Norman D. Sandler, United Press International, March 10, 1986.

50. Participating in the briefing were representatives of Citizens for America, Renaissance Women, the Eagle Forum, the American Security Council, Citizens for Reagan, the Baltic American Freedom League, the Federation of Hungarian Americans, the Polish American Congress, the Veterans of Foreign Wars, and the American Legion.

51. "Aid to the Contras," Public Papers of the Presidents, March 10, 1986. A transcript of his speech is available at https://acrobat.com/app.html#d=T2Oz Vo9*yHEwF3ym5QRUgw.

52. Susanne M. Schafer, "Reagan Says House Vote Gives Contra Chance for Victory," Associated Press, June 26, 1986.

53. The fourteenth annual conference was titled "The Reality of Islam in a Changing World." A consensus among speakers was that in the heightened fears generated by 9/11 Islam was increasingly being misunderstood, especially in the West. Therefore, it was critically important for followers to demonstrate that Islam is not a violent religion and to patiently explain the teachings of the Prophet Muhammad, for example, that killing innocent civilians or committing acts of terrorism against them is forbidden.

54. According to the PanAfrican News Agency (PANA) Daily Newswire, May 21, 2002, conference attendees included imams, religious scholars, muftis (interpreters of Islamic law), mosque officials, and Islamic academics from eighteen Arab, thirteen African, thirteen Asian, ten European, and four North American countries, and a delegate from Australia.

55. That same week in the same hotel, Egyptian playwright Ali Salem cringed at the virulent language being used in the wake of 9/11. Both sides had been playing aggressive with their word choices—Muslims and non-Muslims, the Arab world

and the West. In a thick Egyptian accent and baritone as deep and rich as James Earl Jones's, Salem said to me, "Words are real. Words are things. Words are actions. *Good* things start with words. *Bad* things start with words. So when you talk, you have to be *responsible* for your words." Salem, age sixty-six at the time and a bear of a man, had bowed his head into his large hands, as if to say he was frustrated by all of the reckless language. In Arabic he recited advice that he said was Egyptian but I recognized as global. *Lau maendaksh haga kuwayessa te'olha, khaleek saket ahssan*, he said before repeating it in English. "If you don't have something nice to say, then shut up." At the Islamic World Conference, the PanAfrican News Agency Daily Newswire reported that Sheik Akrema Sabry, a Jerusalem mufti who led a Palestinian delegation to the Cairo Marriott, urged all Muslims at the conference "to improve communication skills in order to rationally address the international public opinion and [to] use the right and convincing language."

56. PanAfrican News Agency Daily Newswire, May 21, 2002. In his message, Mubarak went on to state that "there are more common denominators between the different religions than points of divergence" and that war was never a solution. Also, he said that the 9/11 attacks had "clearly provoked a negative impact on Islam worldwide, just because the perpetrators were Muslims." Therefore, it was important to support "all genuine efforts aimed at reforming and enlightening the world."

57. *Al-Ahram (Pyramid)* newspaper as quoted by PanAfrican News Agency, May 23, 2002. Seif Nisrawi, "Mubarak Calls for Islamic Moderation," United Press International, May 23, 2002.

58. Nisrawi, "Mubarak Calls for Islamic Moderation."

59. George W. Bush, "Remarks to a Special Session of the German Bundestag," May 23, 2002. See http://georgewbush-whitehouse.archives.gov/newsreleases/2002/05/20020523-2.html.

60. When the Reichstag parliament building burned on Monday, February 27, 1933, six days before Germany's parliamentary elections were scheduled to be held, Adolf Hitler was the country's newly appointed Chancellor of Germany, the equivalent of a prime minister. In *Hitler* (New York: Harcourt, 1974), the late German historian Joachim C. Fest describes how the Nazi Party used the fire to incite public fear about an alleged Communist Party of Germany (or KPD) plan to terrorize all of Germany. Immediately after the Reichstag arson the German government released an official but falsified account of the terror plot. In *Hitler*, Fest quotes from it: "Large scale pillaging in Berlin was planned for as early as four o'clock in the morning on Tuesday (February 28). It has been determined that starting today throughout Germany acts of terrorism were to begin against prominent individuals, against private property, against the lives and safety of the peaceful population, and general civil war was to be unleashed." On February 28, 1933, Hitler convinced German president Paul von Hindenburg to sign an emergency decree. Fest writes that the Decree of the Reich of the President for the Protection of People and State "utilized the pretext of the fire in truly comprehensive fashion, annulling all important fundamental rights of citizens ... providing the Reich government with numerous levers against the states." Within a month the parliament passed a second decree, the Enabling Act of 1933, which gave the German chancellor plenary (or absolute) power in certain circumstances. When Hindenburg died eigh-

teen months later at age 86, Hitler declared the office of president vacant and moved in. The rest is messy history. Critics of the Uniting and Strengthening America by Providing Appropriate Tools Required to Intercept and Obstruct Terrorism Act of 2001 (aka the Patriot Act), signed into law by Bush on October 26, 2001, frequently point out the similarities between the evaporation of civil liberties in the aftermath of the Reichstag fire and the watered-down civil liberties that followed 9/11.

61. Consider the context and setting of this statement. Bush is speaking from a parliamentary building that burned under suspicious circumstances and proved to be the springboard for Adolf Hitler, Nazi Germany, and the Holocaust. *Moral* heritage?

62. Bush, "Remarks to a Special Session of the German Bundestag."

63. Dana Milbank, "Bush Links 'Totalitarian' Terror, Nazism but Germany Balks at Idea of Attacking Iraq," *Washington Post*, May 24, 2002.

64. Bush, "Remarks to a Special Session of the German Bundestag."

65. David E. Sanger, "In Reichstag, Bush Condemns Terror as New Despotism," *New York Times*, May 24, 2002.

66. Bush, "Remarks to a Special Session of the German Bundestag."

67. When asked about Iraq at a news conference in Berlin, Bush responded: "I have no war plans *on my desk*" [*emphasis added*]. To me and every other reporter who heard or read Bush's quote, it seemed as evasive and misleading as President Clinton's "I did not have *sex* [*emphasis added*] with that woman." We all knew the war plans for Iraq were on the desk of U.S. defense secretary Donald Rumsfeld.

68. As of this writing Thorne is an assistant professor for the Mayborn School of Journalism at the University of North Texas in Denton, Texas, about forty-five miles north of the Dallas–Fort Worth metropolis.

69. Edward F. Murphy, *Vietnam Medal of Honor Heroes* (New York: Presidio Press, 2005), p. 171.

70. Ibid.

71. After a second tour of Vietnam in 1970, Liteky resigned his military commission, gave up the priesthood, and married his sweetheart, Judy. "When I got back over there, I really got turned off by the war," he told Edward F. Murphy, author of *Vietnam Medal of Honor Heroes*. "I thought we should get out of there with all possible speed. I really got disgusted with things I saw. The insensitivity toward life; the emphasis on body counts—a mania."

72. Murphy, *Vietnam Medal of Honor Heroes*, p. 172.

73. "Medal of Honor Winner Renounces over Contra Support," Associated Press, July 29, 1986. Also, Matt Soergel, "Hometown Hero, Medal of Honor, Peace Activist," *Florida Times-Union* (Jacksonville), April 19, 2009, p. A-1.

74. Ibid.

Chapter 8
Braveheart

1. C. S. Lewis, *Mere Christianity* (San Francisco: HarperSanFrancisco, 2001), p. 208. The fuller context of that quote is from a chapter titled "New People or New

Men," and it follows a chapter in which Lewis asserted that the command from Jesus as quoted in Matthew 5:48, "Be ye perfect," is not idealistic gas. The transformation is a long and sometimes painful process, Lewis explained:

> The change will not be completed in this life, for death is an important part of the treatment. How far the change will have gone before death in any particular Christian is uncertain. I think this is the right moment to consider a question which is often asked: If Christianity is true why are not all Christians obviously nicer than all non-Christians? What lies behind that question is partly something very reasonable and partly something that is not reasonable at all. The reasonable part is this. If conversion to Christianity makes no improvement in a man's outward actions—if he continues to be just as snobbish or spiteful or envious or ambitious as he was before—then I think we must suspect that his "conversion" was largely imaginary; and after one's original conversion, every time one thinks one has made an advance, that is the test to apply. Fine feelings, new insights, greater interest in "religion" mean nothing unless they make our actual behavior better; just as in an illness "feeling better" is not much good if the thermometer shows that your temperature is still going up. In that sense the outer world is quite right to judge Christianity by its results. Christ told us to judge by results. . . . *When we Christians behave badly, or fail to behave well, we are making Christianity unbelievable to the outside world.* The war-time posters told us that Careless Talk costs Lives. It is equally true that Careless Lives cost Talk. Our careless lives set the outer world talking; and we give them grounds for talking in a way that throws doubt on the truth of Christianity itself.

2. For the first several years of Akhenaten's seventeen-year reign he was known as Amenhotep IV. He became one of the most controversial leaders of ancient Egypt's Eighteenth Dynasty (c. 1550 - c. 1292 B.C.E.) after he attempted to replace polytheism with his brand of monotheism. He insisted on worshiping only one god, the solar deity named Aten. Amenhotep IV changed his name to Akhenaten, which meant "living spirit of Aten." His queen, for whom the hotel is named, was Nefertiti. In part because of her famous bust on display in Berlin's Neues Museum, Nefertiti is better known today than her ruler husband. Akhenaten probably would have been fine with that. Counter to his era's culture, Akhenaten deferred to his first wife on many things, and historians believe Nefertiti was afforded as much power as the pharaoh.

3. Full-time workers for the CPT receive a monthly "subsistence stipend" intended to cover only basic needs. In it there isn't a cushion for things such as savings accounts, stock options, 401K plans, paid vacations, sick leave, maternity/paternity leave, annual pay raises—all things I took for granted when on the payroll of corporate media. None of the committed peacemakers or CPT employees I've met are likely to, say, consider the merits of satellite dish versus cable (I'm guilty of it) or to lapse into consumer comas at Best Buy, Costco, Home Depot (guilty, guilty, guilty) or while perusing exotic vacation destinations online (guilty). The CPT website (http://www.cpt.org/about/faq#7) explains the organization's pay grade like this: "CPT full-timers don't make

any money, but they don't lose money either. . . . We estimate it costs U.S.$15,000 each year to support one full-time field worker. While this may seem *high* [emphasis added by author], we note that the US, Canada and the UN spend roughly U.S.$150,000 or Cdn.$220,000 per soldier per year to maintain a war-fighting or 'peace-keeping' capability. . . . We are able to keep costs down because CPTers choose to live simply and stipends are based on what will cover their needs, rather than on what would support a middle-class lifestyle."

4. According to the Labor Department's most recent study on the working poor (see http://www.bls.gov/cps/cpswp2009.pdf), dated March 2011 but pulled from 2009 census data, "The working poor are persons who spent at least 27 weeks in the labor force (that is, working or looking for work) but whose incomes still fell below the official poverty level."

5. For example, after spending ten days at the Nefertiti in Amman and Rutba General Hospital in Iraq, Shane and I made a trip to the Palestinian territories and Israel. We were meeting a group of people at a very nice, moderately priced hotel in Bethlehem's Manger Square, the Casa Nova. There were no guest laundry facilities, but you could drop your clothes off at the front desk and pay for hotel staff to launder them. I don't remember the exact price, but compared to hotels in North America I recall thinking it was a great deal. At the Nefertiti and Rutba General we had not been able to do laundry, so I handed a duffel bag full of clothes to the front desk. I returned to our room to find Shane bent over like a question mark at the bathroom sink. He was washing his clothes by hand; socks, skivvies, T-shirts, the works, and hanging them neatly on the shower rod, sink, closets, wherever. A bestselling author, a CNN.com columnist, one of *Esquire* magazine's Best & Brightest of 2009, a popular speaker booked for events around the world, Shane, with his vow of poverty, couldn't stomach the idea (or maybe the expense) of using a "service" to wash and dry his clothes. I felt about as soft and spoiled as that millionaire on Gilligan's Island, Thurston Howell III.

6. That's a reluctant confession, nothing I'm proud of.

7. Ever wonder what "turn the other cheek" looks like in practice rather than theory? Well, here's another anecdote from Shane's Kensington neighborhood: A few years after Shane suffered his broken jaw, he and a friend named Kasim were jumped on the street by a gang of teenagers. The teens were eager for a fight so they taunted Shane and Kasim, a middle-school kid. They threw stuff at them. But Shane and Kasim kept walking and attempted to ignore them. Suddenly Shane stops walking and says to Kasim, "Let's not run from them. Let's go back." So they do. Shane returns to the gang and says, "My name is Shane. This is Kasim." The teens looked dumbfounded. "They totally didn't know what to do with that," Shane recalled a couple of weeks later for Krista Tippett on her American Public Media radio show. When Shane and Kasim turned to walk again, one of the teens hits Kasim with a club on his head. Shane says something inside him snapped. He turned around and shouted, "You guys are created in the image of God and you're made for something better than this!" The teens stopped fighting and, as Shane tells Tippett, "disintegrated into every different direction, you know? And Kasim looks at me and he goes, 'What was that?' And I'm like 'I don't know what it was,' you know?"

Kasim wasn't injured, and after he and Shane returned to the Simple Way house he said to Shane, "You know, we get to go to bed tonight, thinking that we acted like Jesus. And those kids have to go to bed thinking about how they acted." Later that night Shane explained to Kasim that he wasn't sure how Jesus would have responded in that same situation. However, he added, "I know . . . he would not have run from those kids, and he would not have hit those kids." He explained to Tippett, "To me, the idea that we can look in the face of evil and say that you are better than the worst things that you do, it's a beautiful, beautiful story." For more on the American Public Media interview, see the transcript at http://being.publicradio.org/programs/newmonastics/transcript.shtml.

In Dorothy Day's *The Duty of Delight: The Diaries of Dorothy Day* (Maryknoll, NY: Orbis Books, 2008), p. 30, Day writes on August 7, 1937: "Toothaches, bruised faces even, received in street fighting are ugly and grotesque. It is hard to heroically receive blows in the face from a policeman, for instance, and take it like a Christian, in the spirit of non-resistance. A spirit of hatred and a fierce desire for retaliation seems more manly, more human. Moral force, being hard to see, is a thousand times harder than physical force. Strength of spirit is not so often felt to be apparent as strength of body. And we in our vanity wish this strength to be apparent. Human respect again. And yet moral force is always felt."

8. Four days later in Iraq some of us were criticizing radio talking head, Rush Limbaugh, for discouraging his listeners from responding to President Obama's plea for donations to Haiti relief efforts. Limbaugh argued that contributions would only help Obama's credibility. "Besides," he added, "we've already donated to Haiti. It's called the U.S. income tax." As a few of us railed against Limbaugh for being an insensitive gas bag and, quite possibly, the devil incarnate, Cliff's calm, nonjudgmental voice interjected its usual wisdom. "He's just never met them, that's all," he said of Haitians whom he had worked alongside. "If he had a chance to know them he wouldn't talk like that." In other words, Limbaugh's response to Haitians wasn't the expression of a darkened soul; it was simply the voice of inexperience. Limbaugh needed to spend more time in the world's sketchy neighborhoods.

9. *We don't hate Americans, just your government.* I've heard that from Iraqis, Palestinians, and Egyptians from Cairo to Bangkok to Basra and the West Bank. It's as if they don't blame the American electorate, like we're not responsible for the people we put in office. Considering their own sordid histories with "elected" leaders, I guess they see our political process as a system that favors well-heeled individuals and powerbroker corporations. I can't imagine why they would think that [*sarcasm inserted by author*].

10. Today, Bethany Theological Seminary is located in Richmond, Indiana.

11. Tad Walch, "Utahn Recalls Terror of Iraq Kidnapping," *Deseret Morning News* (Salt Lake City), February 16, 2007, p. A-1 (http://www.deseretnews.com/article/660196185/Utahn-recalls-terror-of-Iraq-kidnapping.html?pg=1); and Jim Phillips, "Athens-based Activist Spends Two Days as Captive in Northern Iraq," *Athens News* (Ohio), February 22, 2007. Also, author interview with Peggy Gish on November 23, 2011.

12. Tom Fox served as a Marine during the Vietnam War, but he opposed war and never served in combat. He played clarinet in the U.S. Marine Band.

13. Walch, "Utahn Recalls Terror of Iraq Kidnapping," p. A-1 (http://www.deseret news.com/article/660196185/Utahn-recalls-terror-of-Iraq-kidnapping.html?pg=1); and Phillips, "Athens-based Activist Spends Two Days as Captive in Northern Iraq . . ." Also, author interview with Peggy Gish on November 23, 2011.

14. Author interview with Gish on November 23, 2011.

15. Nasser Shiyoukhi, "Israeli Troops Demolish Market Stalls, Close Palestinian Police and TV Stations," Associated Press, January 30, 2003.

16. Author interview with Peggy Gish on November 23, 2011.

17. Ibid. Art Gish died tragically on July 28, 2010 when his tractor flipped and rolled on top of him as he worked on his and Peggy's organic farm in Athens County, Ohio. He was seventy years old. The accident occurred about six months after Peggy had returned to Rutba with us. At the time of Art's death Peggy was back at work with CPT in Iraqi Kurdistan. See Jim Phillips, "Prominent Local Activist Dies in Farming Accident," *Athens News* (Ohio), July 28, 2010 (http://www.athensnews.com/ohio/article-31680-prominent-local-activist-dies-in-farming-accident.html).

18. Ibid.

19. Walch, "Utahn Recalls Terror of Iraq Kidnapping" , p. A-1; http://www.deseret news.com/article/660196185/Utahn-recalls-terror-of-Iraq-kidnapping.html?pg=1.

20. According to Washington's Brookings Institution, more than 300 foreign nationals were kidnapped in Iraq between May 2003 and June 2010. Of these, 149 were released, 60 murdered, four escaped, six were rescued (like three CPT members kidnapped at the same time as Tom Fox). As of June 30, 2010, the status of 94 of these kidnappings remains unknown.

21. Sami used to work in Iraq with Tom Fox, and he recalls asking him, "What makes you come here and do this phenomenal work in a violent environment?" Sami had recently moved home to Najaf from Minneapolis, Minnesota, to help his family and countrymen, but the willingness of foreign peacemakers to work amid the threats and harsh conditions of post-invasion Iraq astounded him. "I was born here," Sami told Fox. "I'm like a salmon. The salmon will go upstream to die at home. I've traveled upstream. But you are not Iraqi. You do not have family in Iraq. Why do it?" Tom answered, "Sami, you must remember that our great father, Abraham, was born here. We are related." Sami says at that moment he felt a need "to break this barrier that [says] I am a Christian, you are a Muslim; I am an Iraqi, you are an American."

22. Peggy asked CPT to sponsor the trip for her but officials declined. They told her our plans go into Al Anbar unprotected with a large group of Americans prior to volatile provincial elections was unwise (read: foolish). They believed we were putting ourselves and the Rutba locals who hosted us in a dangerous situation. They advised Peggy not to go.

23. Yes, in some cases *mercilessly*. Recall Linda Robinson's account about Major Gavrilis and the Special Forces bombing the Rutba area on March 21, 2003, eight days before Shane, Cliff, and Weldon were rescued: "The immediate goal was to put enough ordnance onto the ground to shock the Iraqis into halting their advance, so *no effort was made to match bomb to target* [emphasis added by author]. The planes dropped whatever they had, laser-guided JDAMS or dumb bombs, 500-, 1,000-, or

2,000-pounders. . . . The air force passed the team sortie after sortie of aircraft. At one point four planes were stacked up waiting to make bombing runs." See Linda Robinson, *Masters of Chaos: The Secret History of the Special Forces* (New York: PublicAffairs, 2004), p. 203 (Kindle edition).

24. Various author interviews with Jamie Moffett, the last occurring by phone on August 25, 2011.

25. The Donuts Factory attempt to mimic Dunkin' Donuts, right down to its signature pink and orange, is so dead-on that Shane said it *"has* to be" a franchise within the Dunkin' Donuts chain. It's not. The nearest Dunkin' Donuts franchise store is 737 miles away in Kuwait. A couple of weeks later in the occupied Palestinian territory of Ramallah in the West Bank, roughly six miles north of Jerusalem, Shane and I would see similar knockoffs, for example, a Star & Bucks Café decorated in Starbucks green and a Kentucky Fried Chicken restaurant, if only in name. See http://goo.gl/CZQLb.

26. Several years ago Amman's much-ballyhooed Planet Hollywood became one of fifty-five international Planet Hollywood restaurants to close long after the Florida-based company filed for Chapter 11 bankruptcy protection.

27. By law Amman's buildings all have limestone facades. Travel writers frequently refer to it as "the White City," but in reality the buildings are a mix of white, beige, and gray.

28. "Greater Middle East" is an artificial political term coined in 2004 by the Bush administration to capture a few select (read: suspect) North African and Asian countries (e.g., Egypt, Afghanistan, Turkey, and Iran) in the geographic designation that Westerners associate with us (read: United States and Israel; Jews and Christians) vs. them (rogue Arab states and Islam).

29. McDonalds Arabia might plant a dozen franchises in Amman but nothing on the menus are supersized; and the most popular sandwich is not one you are likely to find stateside: the McArabia Kofta is made from two *halal* (animals slaughtered according to Islamic law, e.g., sharp knife to the jugular for a swift, and ideally more humane death) beef patties, American cheese, tomatoes, lettuce, onions, and salsa on Arabic flat bread.

30. According to reports from United Press International, organizers of the protests wanted to march to the fortress-like U.S. Embassy in Amman's affluent Abdoun district, but Amman officials would issue permits only for demonstrations that stayed within a specified area of the Shmeisani district.

31. Including a broad coalition of Islamist and political groups working together under the umbrella of Jordan's Higher Coordinating Committee of Opposition Parties. This includes the Islamic Action Front, the political arm of Jordan's Muslim Brotherhood. The group's leaders had issued a statement prior to the march in Shmeisani on February 15, 2003, that called for an emergency Arab summit and asked that all Arab governments ban the U.S.-UK militaries from using Arab soil or airspace for their invasion of Iraq. They also called on Arab leaders to activate their joint defense treaty and to send troops in support of Iraqis in their fight with the "U.S.-Zionist enemy." At a protest the previous week in Shmeisani, Islamic Action Front Secretary General Hamzeh Mansour told the *Jordan Times*, "Our message to the American

administration and Zionist enemy is that your war will not only be with Palestine and Iraq but the entire [Arab world]. If you are capable of starting this war, you will be caught in a huge swamp from which you will not be able to emerge." See Alis Shukri Hamzeh, "More than 3,000 Protest against Plans to Attack Iraq," *Jordan Times*, February 2, 2003; and Alia Shukri Hamzeh, "Jordanians Protest US War Plans," *Jordan Times*, February 16, 2003.

32. Islam considers Ibrahim a prophet and a patriarch, and it reveres him as a model of the perfect Muslim. The Qur'an credits Ibrahim and his firstborn child, Ishmael, with raising the foundation for the construction of the Kaaba in Mecca, Saudi Arabia, the most sacred site in Islam.

33. The Baqa'a camp began with 26,000 refugees forced from homes in the West Bank and Gaza Strip. Today it is Jordan's largest Palestinian refugee camp with more than 104,000 residents, according to the UN Relief and Works Agency. See http://www.unrwa.org/etemplate.php?id=123.

34. Ignoring a decree that allows only portraits of Jordan's king to be displayed in public, protestors held large portraits of Saddam that showed him looking regal with a cigar; another with him brandishing an AK-47.

35. Ironically, that same day (February 15, 2003) in Tel Aviv some 3,000 peace advocates—Jewish and Arab—were demonstrating together against the war. It marked the first large demonstration in the Jewish state that opposed Washington's intention to invade Iraq and remove Saddam Hussein. See "Arabs Take to Streets in Protest against US War on Iraq," Agence France-Presse, February 15, 2003.

36. Sebastian Rotella, "Showdown with Iraq: Antiwar Rallies Draw Millions around the World," *Los Angeles Times*, February 15, 2003, p. 1.

37. Hamzeh, "Jordanians Protest US Iraq War Plans."

38. Ibid.

39. "Antiwar Protesters Surge in Arab Capitals," United Press International, February 15, 2003.

40. Ibid.

41. Ibid.

42. "Thousands Demonstrate for Iraq in Middle East," Agence France-Presse, February 14, 2003.

43. Rehim's song was so popular in the Middle East, I suspect, because the lyrics to *The Attack on Iraq* echoed exactly the conversation many Arabs were having among themselves. For example, Rehim sang, "Leave Iraq in peace; you inspected it; it has no arms of mass destruction, but they are still bombing it. Go inspect Israel instead; there are lots of arms of mass destruction there." See Mark MacKinnon, "Arabs Rock to Anti-U.S. Song, Lyrics," *Toronto Globe & Mail*, March 15, 2003.

44. Rotella, "Showdown with Iraq," p. 1.

45. Just as likely, I suspect, the applications were lost or destroyed. Twenty days after I delivered them to the Iraqi consulate office in Washington, DC, the Iraqi national government in Baghdad was under heavy attack for the third time in five months. In coordinated bombings of government, education and banking facilities, insurgents attempted to disrupt the government's ability to function after nationwide elections

were planned for January 2010. In August 2009 two suicide car bombs hit the offices of Iraq's Finance and Foreign Ministries, killing more than 122 people. Two months later, on October 25, 2009, suicide bombs destroyed three Iraqi government agency offices in Baghdad, killing more than 150 people. On December 9, 2009, after it was announced that national elections would be postponed until March 2010, five bombs exploded through a Baghdad courthouse, two colleges, a mosque, and a bank where workers from the Finance Ministry had relocated after the August bombings. The *New York Times* reported that the December bombings (three by suicide attackers) killed at least 121 people and wounded more than four hundred. If the bureaucratic process moves slowly under normal circumstances, imagine how well it works while offices and workers are under attack.

46. Saad Al-Hayani remained the Iraqi Ambassador to Jordan through 2010. As of this writing, January 2012, he is the Iraqi Ambassador to Tunisia. Some news reports about the arrest warrant issued for Al-Hayani in September 2009 said the ambassador was charged with harboring a fugitive diplomat implicated in the 1994 assassination of Sheikh al-Tamimi, a prominent Iraqi exile who opposed Saddam and was allegedly planning a coup from his home in Beirut. Other reports quoted a Supreme Criminal Court judge saying that Al-Hayani was charged according to Supreme Criminal Court Law Number 10, Article 12, which would mean "crimes of mass annihilation" were involved in the charges. In an *Al Jazeera* political talk show that aired September 10, 2009, noted Iraqi lawyer and legal expert Tariq Harb, and the other panelists, said the charges against Al-Hayani were suspect and that the arrest warrant was a sloppy and politically motivated move by a Shia-dominated Supreme Court. With Iraqi national elections planned for March 2010, the panelists thought appointed officials were attempting to look strong by going after prominent former Ba'athists.

47. Built near present-day Al Hillah in the Babil province of Iraq.

48. *Eight Cups of Tea*—that was going to be the title of this chapter before the Greg Mortenson scandal.

49. Sami and the ambassador spoke the entire time in Arabic, but Sami recounted the conversation for us after we left the embassy and regrouped at Amman's Coffee Station cafe.

50. Because he was breaking with protocol and, perhaps, because he was already on the bad side of the new Iraqi government, the ambassador asked us to stay out of Baghdad with the "special visas." He preferred that we travel no farther than to Rutba and back.

51. The cab ferrying Shane, Jamie, Logan, and myself had four bald tires, two with plugged punctures, and periodically accelerated on Jordan's straightaways at speeds exceeding ninety miles per hour. Lordy. And we were told Iraq would be dangerous.

52. A lot of this insight and information about Captain Foster is a result of my follow-up emails and phone calls with him several months after we met in No Man's Land. Same with Major Nedal, who asked me not to use his full name. For example, Foster told me that he could have prevented us from entering Iraq if he had wanted. After all, it was a war zone, and he was with the military. But during the conversation with us he had become more comfortable with the idea of us entering Iraq unarmed

because Sami is a native Iraqi who had friends hosting us in Rutba. Like the peacemakers, many soldiers, such as Captain Foster and Major Gavrilis, understand this characteristic about Iraqi culture: If Iraqis welcome you as a guest into their homes they will do everything in their power to protect you. Still, Foster told me, he wasn't crazy about us going into Iraq unarmed, and he would have preferred that we had turned around in No Man's Land and driven back to Amman.

Here is a funny anecdote he told me over the phone in March 2010. One month after he met us in No Man's Land, an American carpenter showed up at the border unannounced. He was a civilian, mid-fifties and from a small town somewhere on the U.S. east coast. He had a U.S. passport, his luggage, and his carpenter tools, but he didn't have a visa permit, a ride, an interpreter, or even the promise of a job. He planned to go to Baghdad and knock on some doors until he found work. "He shows up in No Man's Land and asks us to give him a lift to Baghdad," Foster said, laughing, talking to me long-distance from his next job in Iraqi Kurdistan. "I have no idea how he even made it that far. Anyhow, I told him we didn't provide *rides* to Baghdad, but it didn't much matter because he wasn't going to Iraq."

53. Literally, Foster builds churches (as opposed to being a church planter–builder of congregations). The last one he constructed was the 30,000-square-foot Hope Christ Church near Waterloo, Illinois.

Chapter 9
Pro Choice

1. In preparation for his peacemaking trip to Iraq in March 2003, Shane found himself on a flight to Chicago seated next to two strangers. As Shane tells it in his book, *The Irresistible Revolution*, his seat mates struck up a conversation and discovered they had things in common, for example, they were proud of the country's military might; they supported Bush's decision to invade Iraq; they enjoyed making fun of liberals. (At this point I'm thinking they must also share chronically poor eyesight because the tall man scrunched up in the seat next to them wears his hair in dreads and makes his own pants out of burlap. He probably doesn't want to hear their jokes.) Shane resisted the urge to engage the conversation, preferring instead to fly quietly to Chicago. However, unable to sleep or tune them out, he offered them some of the homemade cookies he'd carried onto the flight. When the seat mates resumed their talk they compared notes on all the places they had traveled. They asked Shane where he was traveling to next. He knew that telling the truth would jeopardize any chance of quiet time. Still, he put it out there: "Actually, next week I plan to go to Iraq." He writes, "Their jaws dropped." He explained the deal with the Iraq Peace Team and Christian Peacemaker Teams and how they were going to Baghdad to reside with the war's victims as witnesses to the use of military might and as diplomats for humanity and Christianity. "I was amazed that they did not start arguing with me. They were intrigued that I believed in something so much that I would risk my life for it," Shane wrote. "We actually had a nice talk. And I will never forget what they said as we parted. These two people, whom I had just met, told me with great drama how they would be glued to the TV as they worried about me, wondering if I would make it back safely. I stood in awe, knowing that this is

the great tragedy: we have not put a face on the war. Degrees of separation allow us to destroy human beings we do not know except as the enemy."

It's true not only in cases of war. Take Rush Limbaugh's callous statements about not giving aid to Haiti after the devastating 2010 earthquake. When Cliff says to us, "He's just never met them, that's all. If he had a chance to know them he wouldn't talk like that." Same is true for the divide between rich and poor. It's hard to see from one side to the other, especially if you don't want to look. In *The Irresistible Revolution* Shane recounts a scene in Michael Moore's documentary *The Big One* where Nike founder Philip Knight is invited by Moore to fly to Indonesia and walk through Nike factories that pay slave wages to the indigent poor. Moore offers Knight a first-class ticket to go see his own factories. "Phil busts out laughing and shakes his head, 'No, no, not a chance,'" Shane writes. "Moore tells him that he just wants to walk through and check out the operation, and then asks, 'Have you ever been to see your factories where your shoes are made? Have you ever been to Indonesia?' Knight says, 'No, and I am not going to go.' These are the layers of separation that allow injustice to happen."

2. He was among the drivers phoned by Ba'athist officials in Baghdad and told to drive the peacemakers out of Iraq. None of the passengers recalled his name, and no one in Rutba knew him because he was from Baghdad, some 280 miles away. The last the peacemakers saw of the driver, he was distraught over the loss of his taxi. In sanctions-decimated Iraq that car the size of a Kia and the color of a banana was probably his sole livelihood and accounted for most, if not all, of his life savings.

3. Bae Sang-hyun, who had been in Baghdad since March 14, 2003, as part of a Korean peace effort, stayed at Hotel Al Fanar with the Iraq Peace Team. He returned to Seoul, South Korea, from Amman in early April and immediately began campaigning against South Korea President Roh Moo-hyun's plan to send noncombat troops to Iraq. Roh (now deceased) was attempting to build a better relationship with Washington and said he supported the war's effort because it was necessary "to get rid of weapons of mass destruction." On April 3, 2003, the same day Roh appealed to the National Assembly for approval to send seven hundred noncombat troops (engineers and medical workers) to Iraq, Bae landed at Seoul's Incheon International Airport and held a press conference. He threatened to relinquish his citizenship and seek asylum in another country if Roh sent troops to Iraq. "Americans are bombarding Baghdad days and nights, maiming and tearing little children into pieces. I saw it with my own eyes," Bae told reporters. "I feel I am a sinner as one of [the] Koreans who [will] send their troops to help murderous Americans." (See Hee-Jae Park, "Human Shield Bae Says He Feels Shamed of Being Korean," *Korea Times*, April 3, 2003.)

Two days later, after the National Assembly approved of Roh's plan to send troops to Iraq, Bae backed off his threat. "I got a little carried away when I conveyed my intention to give up my Korean citizenship," he said of the April 3 news conference. "I still love my country."

4. Author interviews with Shane Claiborne in Philadelphia, Pennsylvania, August 2008.

5. In 2010, when Cliff recounted the out-of-body experience for Jassim and Tarik, the men who had sewn his head back together, Jassim smiled approvingly. "I am

impressed that you believe in this, and this is part of our belief, too," he said in Arabic, with Sami interpreting.

6. Kevin Kilbane, "North Manchester, Ind., Resident Remains in Iraq as Peace Activist," the *News-Sentinel* (Fort Wayne), March 18, 2003.

7. Crystal, MI; New Haven, MI; Chippewa, OH, and Lake Breeze, OH.

8. See BBC footage and commentary of Eisenhower's warning at http://www .flickr.com/photos/universaleducation/6825135591/in/photostream.

9. At the end of each year, the Brethren church Reverend Kindy was pastoring would take his leftover salary and let the congregation decide where to donate the money. Cliff recalls that it became a much-anticipated annual event and an inspiration for the congregations.

10. I learned of this vicarious and delayed gratification method of politics from reading the daily planners of a Redemptorist Catholic slum priest named Father Joe Maier, the subject of my last book, *The Gospel of Father Joe: Revolutions & Revelations in the Slums of Bangkok*. This Sitting Bull quote was cut out from a magazine or book and taped into one of Father Joe's planners, which doubled as personal journals: "Let us put our heads together and see what life we will make for our children." In Father Joe's case, a slum abbot, a slum imam, and the slum Catholic priest had put their religious differences aside and put their heads together in creating Father Joe's Mercy Centre charity. The result was more than three dozen slum schools, four orphanages, two AIDS hospices, slum recreation leagues, slum music and dance programs, and more, all in the forgotten decrepit port area of Bangkok, Thailand.

11. On December 1, 1969, the first U.S. military draft lottery in twenty-seven years was held at Selective Service Headquarters in Washington, DC. The next day, in one of those feel-good policies that Congress occasionally adopts to fool their own conscience and/or the electorate, the House approved by a 334 to 55 margin a resolution endorsing Nixon's efforts to achieve "peace with justice."

12. A rare patriotic hit song during the controversial Vietnam War, the "Ballad of the Green Berets" was the no. 1 hit song in the United States for five weeks in 1966. It finished the decade at no. 21 for the 1960s.

13. Not lost on Christian peace activists are the words of Christian pacifist and anarchist Leo Tolstoy from his 1900 book *Thou Shalt Not Kill*: "If only each king, emperor, and president understood that his work of directing armies is not an honorable and important duty, as his flatterers persuade him it is, but a bad and shameful act of preparation for murder—and if each private individual understood that the payment of taxes wherewith to hire and equip soldiers, and, above all, army-service itself, are not matters of indifference, but are bad and shameful actions by which he not only permits but participates in murder—then this power of emperors, kings, and presidents, which now arouses our indignation, and which causes them to be murdered, would disappear of itself. . . . If men are not yet doing so, this is due only to the hypnosis in which the governments carefully keep them from a feeling of self-preservation."

14. A 2008 Congressional Research Service comparison of war costs estimated the Vietnam War at $686 billion. At that time, the CRS estimated that Washington had spent almost $860 billion in war costs since the terrorist attacks of 9/11. This included

military operations in Afghanistan, Iraq, and elsewhere around the world. The estimates, adjusted for inflation, were based only on the costs of military operations and did not include the ongoing expenses related to war and other peripheral costs, for example, veterans benefits, interest on war-related debts, assistance to war allies, etc. None of this counts the loss of or injury to life: for example, in Vietnam 58,212 American soldiers were killed; 153,452 wounded; 1,678 are still missing in action as of December 15, 2011. Nor does it count children who lost parents; wives, husbands, and lovers who lost significant others; combat veterans who lost their sanity. Additionally, the Vietnamese government in 1995 estimated that 1.1 million North Vietnamese and Viet Cong troops and two million civilians lost their lives in the war. The government said it had no way of estimating the number of dead from the former South Vietnamese army. See Philip Shenon, "20 Years after Victory, Vietnamese Communists Ponder How to Celebrate," *New York Times*, April 23, 1995, p. A-12.

15. Even when Cliff didn't have a home phone and he would use pay phones, he'd refuse to pay the tax. For example, if the operator told him to insert another fifty cents to continue the long-distance call, he'd subtract the 10 percent for the federal excise tax, and then he would tell the operator that he was inserting only forty-five cents. "I'm sorry, but I cannot in good conscience support war," he'd say. This frequently led to lengthy discourses with phone operators who didn't know what in Jim Crow he was talking about.

16. Author interviews with Cliff Kindy in January 2012.

17. Of the 210,000 U.S. men accused of dodging the military draft during the Vietnam War by refusing to register, burning their draft cards or, in rare cases like Cliff's, returning their draft card to voice their disapproval with war, about 30,000 escaped to Canada. The rest took their chances that sheer numbers would overwhelm any attempt by Selective Services to find and prosecute them. For more see Lawrence M. Basker and William A. Strauss, *Chance and Circumstance: The Draft, the War and the Vietnam Generation* (New York: Knopf, 1978).

18. A good friend of Cliff's, Bob Gross, a BVS alum and the person whose family shares the seven-acre farm with Cliff and Arlene in North Manchester, registered for the draft as a conscientious objector at the same time as Cliff. He also returned his draft card to Selective Services at the same time as Cliff, but he gave his card to officials in Maryland. When Cliff returned his card in coastal Mississippi there was a camaraderie among everyone living and working there in an effort to rebuild after the devastation of Hurricane Camille. Officials there accepted Cliff's card gracefully, thanked him for the work of BVS, and they wished him well in life. They never pursued him. Bob's case was handled very differently. Maryland officials prosecuted him for draft evasion, and he was sentenced to three years (serving eighteen months) in a youth detention facility in Ashland, KY.

19. A month or so earlier I had been in a slum of Basra with Kathy Kelly and others, and a mother there offered us a Kool-Aid-like orange drink mixed with tap water. We did like Shane, that is, graciously accepted but never drank. But we weren't the only ones. Even the three Iraqi minders traveling with us held their glasses and never drank.

20. Jonathan Wilson-Hartgrove, *To Baghdad and Beyond: How I Got Born Again in Babylon* (Eugene, OR: Cascade, 2005), p. 82.

21. Ibid., p. 83.

22. Author interview with Shane Claiborne in Philadelphia, Pennsylvania, August 2008.

Chapter 10
Common Ground

1. Cliff Kindy made this comment in 2004 to Lieutenant Colonel Nathan Sassaman in Balad, Iraq, a rugged town sixty miles northwest of Baghdad. Cliff had gone to the U.S. military base there to ask for information about local Iraqi men being held without criminal charges, but as military detainees. At the time, Sassaman, better known then for his college quarterbacking days at West Point, was attempting to tame the volatile Sunni Triangle area of Iraq. (Today, he is also known for lying about the drowning of an Iraqi man to cover up a crime by two of his soldiers.) Sassaman was returning to the base in Balad when he saw Cliff standing outside the entrance. He was familiar with Cliff and other CPT workers living and working in the area. Cliff recalled that Sassaman parked his Bradley Fighting Vehicle, climbed down, and began lecturing him about the danger of going around Iraq unarmed. At one point, Sassaman even removed his armored vest and gave it to Cliff, told him to try it on, wear it, keep it. Cliff politely declined. He explained to Sassaman that he believed he was far safer in Iraq without guns, grenades, and tanks because he resided in Iraq as a guest and a friend of the locals. Cliff recalls that Sassaman was skeptical, but he seemed to be weighing the logic. By the end of the conversation, Cliff was trying to recruit Sassaman for CPT. "If you come with us, you'll see a side of Iraq you've never seen before," Cliff told him.

2. There are variations to the *Tashahhud* depending on the branch of faith (e.g., Sunni, Shia, etc.), but the general expression remains one of devout obedience to Allah (God) and reverence for Muhammad's divinely inspired message.

3. As in Islam, there are variations of the doxology depending on the branch of Christian faith. In my childhood congregation, First Baptist Church Bristol, which straddles the Virginia-Tennessee state line, the doxology went like this:

Praise God, from Whom all blessings flow.
Praise Him, all creatures here below.
Praise Him above, ye heavenly host.
Praise Father, Son, and Holy Ghost.

4. Contrary to first impressions, both men were super friendly. As soon as they found out we were Americans they began speaking a little bit of English and explained that they had been trained by the U.S. military. The man with brass knuckles had a SWAT patch above the Iraqi flag on his right shoulder and said he was trained by U.S. Special Forces. He was clean shaven, which is unusual for an Iraqi man; more typical of an American soldier.

5. You can see and hear that 24-second reading of the Magic Sheet v2.0 at http://vimeo.com/36928410.

6. At the time I didn't realize most of these details. I recorded the three-minute drive with a Flip video camera pointed discretely out a window of the Opel. Aided by subsequent interviews in Rutba and Washington, I now recognize some of the landmarks from the drive, for example, the elementary school, the fruit and vegetable market, etc. As for the Arabic spray painting, which includes a drawing of a child holding a sign aloft with Arabic script on it, I didn't even notice it during the drive. Seeing it later on video, I captured the frame and asked Sami for its translation.

You can go on the three-minute ride into downtown Rutba at http://vimeo.com/36942982.

7. Inexplicable at least to me. I later asked him about the Nike swoosh that he wore on his wrist like a keepsake, but I think he misunderstood me. My southern accent is as thick as his Arabic accent. So when I asked him where he got the bracelet, he just smiled and held it up for me to get a better view of it.

8. Sami and I have sought meetings with Dr. Farouq Al-Dulaimi in Ramadi several times since 2009. We offered to travel to Ramadi in 2010, and we have emailed and phoned him. He confirmed the specific events of March 29, 2003, to Sami in the summer of 2011, but he declined for the second time to be interviewed for the book. He feared reprisals.

9. With the help of Mayor Al-Mar'ai and Sami, Jonathan, Leah, and Logan put together a sister-city proposal for SisterCities of Durham (http://www.sistercities-durham.org/), a nonprofit organization affiliated with Durham City Hall and Durham's other sister-city projects: Durham, UK (paired in 1975), Kostroma, Russia (1989), Toyama, Japan (1989), and Arusha, Tanzania (1991). As of this writing (February 2012) the Durham-Rutba proposal is making its way through various reviews, and Jonathan reports that a sister-city delegation from Durham hopes to one day visit Rutba. He expects the relationship to be formalized within the year. The motto of SisterCities of Durham (that's correct, no space between Sister and Cities) is "World Peace: One Friendship and One Community at a Time."

10. Michael R. Gordon and Alissa J. Rubin, "Sunnis Say Baghdad Hampers Anbar Gains," *New York Times*, November 3, 2007, p. A8. The *Times* story reported five suicide bombers, but Al-Mar'ai said the number was actually only two. Of course, two too many.

11. Notes from follow-up interviews with Al-Mar'ai conducted by Sami Rasouli, June 2011.

12. The influence of insurgent fighters in Rutba was so powerful at one point that the entire ninety-man Defense Force of Rutba—equipped and outfitted by the U.S. military—was disbanded by the U.S. military after Rutba soldiers refused to participate in an American military course in Baghdad. The soldiers said they feared attendance would result in their deaths when they returned to Rutba. "The people here would believe that we were cooperating with U.S. forces and that is a reason for anyone to be killed," said Taha Allawi, a former member of the Rutba defense force. In response, the U.S. military confiscated the force's weapons, uniforms, and identification tags. See "Iraqi Troops Refuse to Attend U.S. Army Training," Reuters, June 4, 2005.

13. Dr. Yaseen did not have a family member killed in the war, as I had suspected in our first meeting. However, he said, he had been handcuffed by American soldiers

on several occasions and for no clear reason. Sometime in 2006 or 2007, he said American soldiers stormed the hospital, blowing open its gate and any locked door. He said he offered them the keys, but they preferred to use explosives. A favorite tool used in U.S. military searches is the C4 plastic explosive, a kind of dynamite putty shaped and pressed into holes, cracks and seams, and onto doorjambs, gates and window frames. It's effective—and deafening. Dr. Yaseen said he was handcuffed once despite telling the soldiers in English, "Please, I am a doctor. This is my hospital," and then watching as they pressed the C4 explosive onto a door. He saw them motion to their Iraqi interpreter to cover his ears, but Dr. Yaseen's hands were bound behind his back. The blast rang in his ears for the remaining three hours that he was handcuffed and through the night.

14. Marc or Marcus was the name U.S. marines gave him when he trained with the military in Mosul. Two other guards who trained with the American military referred to themselves as Pedro. Evidently, the nicknames were easier to remember.

15. I discovered later that one of the guys in the room that morning was on the hospital's cleaning staff, not an officer with the Ministry of Interior. He was in cotton sweats and did not have a gun. Turns out that when Shane, Logan, and I were assigned a room in the living quarters, he was left to sleep on the couches in the downstairs living area. With Lieutenant Marcus interpreting, I apologized to him for taking his sleeping quarters. He smiled and responded in Arabic, "No problem, really. We are like cousins." (Later, he flirted constantly with Peggy, who was two or three times his age, asking her to take him to the United States.)

16. As a kid, even as a preteen, he said the Ba'ath Party was always putting him in jail for something. For example, he was ten years old when police in Rutba came to question his uncle about an infraction. When he said he didn't know where his uncle was or when he'd return, they threw Amar in jail instead. He believes they did it to lure his uncle to the prison to defend his nephew. When that didn't happen, Amar says the police began to beat him, hoping that would lure the uncle. When no uncle showed up, they released him three days later without ever charging him with a crime.

17. He actually describes the one who was murdered as a boy "six months old." But listening to the interview again, and watching a video clip of it, I am pretty sure he confused his English, that is, he meant "years." He was referring to a boy, not a baby. You can decide for yourself in a thirty-second clip of that interview at http://vimeo .com/36920295.

This interview took place in the predawn dark of January 18, 2010, two days after our first meeting. We were in Rutba General's living quarters, and, as usual, the lights had gone out. But instead of wearing his miner's headlamp, he used a penlight and flashlight.

18. For a video of Lieutenant Marcus Amar telling this story verbatim inside the dark of Rutba General, see http://vimeo.com/36941959.

19. Little has changed there since 2003. When we walked through on Saturday, January 16, 2010, there were no lights on, not much furniture or medical equipment, and the hallways were narrow and creepy dark. All in all it feels to me like someplace you'd drag someone to interrogate and/or torture; not bandage and stitch up.

20. You can watch one minute of their performance at http://vimeo.com/36973747. Turn down your audio.

21. Keith Crane, Martin C. Libicki, Audra K. Grant, James B. Bruce, Omar Al-Shahery, Alireza Nader, Suzanne Perry (RAND Corporation, National Defense Research Institute), "Living conditions in Anbar Province in June 2008," 2009, p. 35. See the full report at http://www.rand.org/pubs/technical_reports/2009/RAND_TR715.pdf.

22. Ibid.

23. Ibid., p. 11.

24. Between 1973 and sometime before the first Gulf War, the conversion rate of one Iraqi dinar fluctuated between $3.80 and $3.22. Even after the war and the start of UN economic sanctions the Iraqi dinar traded at first no worse than 10 or 12 dinar to one U.S. dollar. From 1993 to 2003, the devaluation went into a tailspin, and before the war the Iraqi dinar was valued at 3,000 to one U.S. dollar. See Michael Hedges, "Baghdad's Big Board Lives, but No Stock Sold on First Day," *Washington Times*, March 25, 1992, p. A9; also, see Tony Wheeler, *West Asia on a Shoestring* (Melbourne: Lonely Planet, 1990).

25. Sami interviewed Sadiq Majed Mubarak, the head of Rutba's Department of Electricity, twice in early November 2011.

26. Ibid.

27. So, what's next? Occupy Rutba?

Chapter 11
Home of the Brave?

1. In his book *American Sniper: The Autobiography of the Most Lethal Sniper in U.S. Military History* (New York: William Morrow, 2012), Navy SEAL Chris Kyle says he killed Iraqis without remorse because the "savages" trying to kill Americans were blinded by evil." "People ask me all the time, 'How many people have you killed?' My standard response is, 'Does the answer make me less, or more, of a man?' The number is not important to me. I only wish I had killed more." Always the charmer, Kyle says he was never motivated by the heroic narrative manufactured by Washington after Saddam's alleged WMD failed to materialize, that is, the United States was fighting for freedom and democracy. "I didn't risk my life to bring democracy to Iraq. I risked my life for my buddies, to protect my friends and fellow countrymen. . . . I never once fought for the Iraqis. I could give a flying fuck about them." As of this writing, February 2012, *American Sniper* is a *New York Times* bestseller.

2. Jonathan Wilson-Hartgrove, *To Baghdad and Beyond: How I Got Born Again in Babylon* (Eugene, OR: Cascade, 2005), p. 85.

3. Shane Claiborne, *The Irresistible Revolution: Living as an Ordinary Radical* (Grand Rapids, MI: Zondervan, 2006). p. 212.

4. Wilson-Hartgrove, *To Baghdad and Beyond*, p. 88.

5. Claiborne, *The Irresistible Revolution*, p. 213.

6. Ibid.

7. Ibid.

8. When Cliff retold this story to Jassim and Tarik at Rutba General on Sunday, January 17, 2010, Jassim responded matter-of-factly: "You are a kind person, so God sends you kind people. Our creator said, What you plant, you harvest."

9. From Weldon's personal journals, dated 11:40 a.m., Tuesday, April 1, 2003.

INDEX